A HISTORY
OF THE ENGLISH
LANGUAGE
IN 100 PLACES

A HISTORY OF THE ENGLISH LANGUAGE IN 100 PLACES

BILL LUCAS AND CHRISTOPHER MULVEY

ROBERT HALE • LONDON

© Bill Lucas and Christopher Mulvey 2013
First published in Great Britain 2013

ISBN 978-0-7090-9570-5

Robert Hale Limited
Clerkenwell House
Clerkenwell Green
London EC1R 0HT

www.halebooks.com

The right of Bill Lucas and Christopher Mulvey to be identified as
authors of this work has been asserted by them
in accordance with the Copyright, Designs and
Patents Act 1988

A catalogue record for this book is available from the British Library

2 4 6 8 10 9 7 5 3 1

Designed by Eurodesign
Printed in China

CONTENTS

FOREWORD BY DAVID CRYSTAL

Language is people. And people live in places. So if we want to find out about a language, we need to encounter the people and the places that helped make it what it is. That's the premise of this book, compiled by two members of the English Project.

It's an especially appropriate perspective for English, which has connections with more places than any other language. Its global reach has no parallel. And one of the best ways of developing a sense of this reach is to explore some of the places where it is to be found.

To study them all would be impossible, with over 2 billion people speaking English around the world, coming from every country and territory. But when we look at the phenomenon historically, certain places do stand out, either because they are where the language grew up, or because they are where it has achieved a particularly significant contemporary presence.

One of the major themes in the study of global English is to explain the two major forces that have shaped – and continue to shape – the language. Much of the emphasis has been on the notion of a Standard English, a variety that guarantees mutual intelligibility among those who use the language, whichever part of the world they come from. At the same time, a great deal of attention has been paid to the varieties of English that express the local identity of its speakers, viewed both within nations and internationally. Place is a fruitful way of bringing together these two forces, intelligibility and identity.

Some places are included in this book because the people – in some cases the person – who lived there played an important role in the development of the standard language. Others are included because they identify the political and social factors that fostered the spread of the language within the British Isles and around the world. Others are here because they represent the way their communities evolved a linguistic individuality that forms part of the kaleidoscopic mix of varieties we conveniently refer to as 'English'.

It is an exercise in linguistic gazetteering, and one thing that strikes me about it is its highly personal character. It's impossible to say everything relevant about a place –100 things must have happened in London or New York that could be said to bear on the development of English. And 100 other places might compete as candidates for a particular theme. Selectivity is inevitable when creating a language's geobiography. No two people's selection for *A History of the English Language in 100 Places* would ever be the same. The fascination lies in the choices made, and the reasons for them.

It is not surprising to see such an anthology emerge from the English Project, for this is an enterprise intimately connected with the notion of place. Its long-term vision is to provide the English language with a permanent space, within which its history, structure and use can be presented with the same kind of visual appeal that we confidently associate with visits to art galleries, science museums and heritage sites. The chosen place for this enterprise is Winchester, whose crucial role in the history of English is rightly acknowledged in this book.

The places selected for inclusion well illustrate the scope of the English Project. I can easily imagine many of the chapters providing, in a developed form, the content for exhibits in such a gallery. It's easy to do this for the written language, where inscriptions, manuscripts and books readily provide a concrete, visual treat. The spoken language is more of a problem. It is such an evanescent thing that it is difficult to see how it could be turned into a space that visitors might actually walk around and find interesting. One of the solutions is to focus on place. Whether it is Stratford or Singapore, New Orleans or New Delhi, seeing the people in their setting, while we listen to them interact, provides speech with an illuminating reality.

A second thing that strikes me about the places included in this book is the variation in scale that they represent. We read about places as small as Bletchley Park or Hampton Court and as large as Cape Town or San Francisco. The larger locations often receive acknowledgement in textbooks on English. Places such as Boston or Sydney are familiar to the English language enthusiast because historically they are well-known points of entry into a new territory. Smaller places, unless they are very famous, tend to be passed over in silence, if only because there are so many of them.

And yet every small community plays its part in forming the rich tapestry of English. Henry Higgins became famous in *Pygmalion* for his ability to pinpoint accents down to a few miles or even a few streets. He isn't alone. Everyone has a sense of dialect variation operating at the level of the individual town, village and suburb. We all value our local linguistic identity, while recognizing that we are part of a huge global English-speaking community. Both dimensions are there in *A History of the English Language in 100 Places*.

ACKNOWLEDGEMENTS

We would like to thank the English Project's Emma Dovener, Craig Lansdell and Catherine Pinner, all students at the University of Winchester, for their meticulous work in researching images. We also gratefully acknowledge the support of the English Project and all those who support it, especially Evelyn Thurlby and Nick Lodge. Our special thanks to Issy Millett whose initial research for us while she was a school student set us on our way with the book.

1 INTRODUCTION

A History of the English Language in 100 Places is a joyous ride through time, where readers can criss-cross the British Isles and the world at large to land in 100 contrasting places and light on 100 wonderful topics that bring the extraordinary story of the English language alive.

Any selection of places is inevitably personal. Nevertheless, a number of criteria have directed the selection process in this book. Some places represent historic firsts, some are tied to significant people, and some have seen events that have shaped the future of English. Each one takes the reader on an unmissable journey into the rich past of the English tongue.

What began as the language of the Angles, Saxons and Jutes on a small island has become a global property owned and shaped by almost 2 billion English speakers across the world. English has borrowed words from more than 350 languages, and many more languages have borrowed words from English. *A History of the English Language in 100 Places* is a history of the language of the global village.

Today, exciting things are happening to the language of William Shakespeare. 'What seems to me to be happening,' says Salman Rushdie in *Imaginary Homelands*, 'is that those people who were once colonized by the language are now rapidly remaking it, domesticating it, becoming more and more relaxed about the way they use it – assisted by the English language's enormous flexibility and size, they are carving out large territories for themselves within its frontiers.' Words fly round the world in greater numbers and with greater speed than the jet planes that serve the global village.

A History of the English Language in 100 Places tells the unfolding story of global English. Also telling that story is an educational charity called the English Project, with the mission 'to explore and explain the English language in order to educate and entertain the English speaker' (see pages 228–9). Already, the English Project has a new date in the annual calendar of events – English Language Day, 13 October. You can find out why 13 October is important in the story of English by turning to page 39.

The theme of English Language Day 2010 was the language of place. It attracted huge interest and demonstrated just how potent the connection between language and place is. Location Lingo, a partnership with British cartographers Ordnance Survey, sought to find nicknames for familiar places. It led to extensive media coverage and harvested some 3,000 invented names. The Location Lingo project also brought home the potency of place and place names in people's lives and led to the researching and writing of this book.

On the next two pages, you can see maps of the places we have chosen from across the world outside the British Isles. A map of the places in London appears on pages 40–41 and a map of the places elsewhere in the British Isles can be found on page 59.

A History of the English Language in 100 Places should have been a history of the English language in 1,000 places, but then it would have made a book ten times larger than the publisher would allow. None the less, readers will have their own lists of 100 places, and it would be a good thing to hear what those might be.

If you have a place and topic that you think should be covered, send it to the English Project at www.englishproject.org. (See page 227 to find out more.)

All being well, it might make the '101+ Places' on the English Project website.

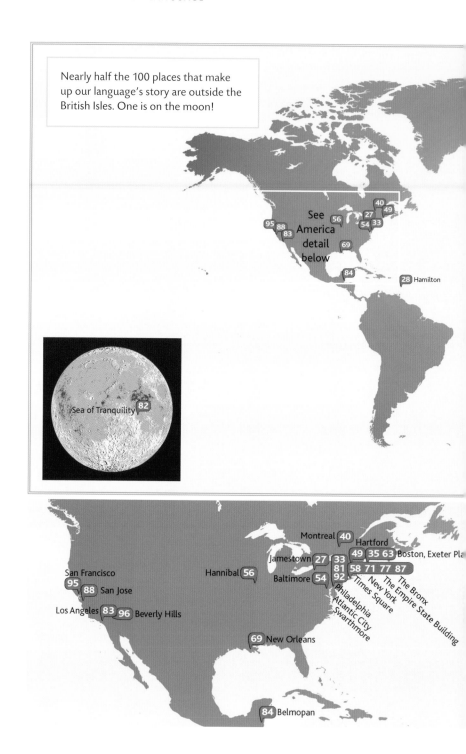

Nearly half the 100 places that make up our language's story are outside the British Isles. One is on the moon!

See America detail below

95 88 83

56

27 54 33

40 49

69

84

28 Hamilton

Sea of Tranquility 82

Montreal 40

Hartford

Jamestown 27 33

49 35 63 Boston, Exeter Pla

San Francisco

95 88 San Jose

Hannibal 56

Baltimore 54

81 58 71 77 87
92

The Bronx
The Empire State Building
New York
Times Square
Philadelphia
Atlantic City
Swarthmore

Los Angeles 83 96 Beverly Hills

69 New Orleans

84 Belmopan

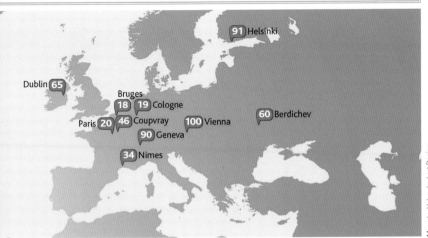

2 THE BEGINNINGS OF ENGLISH

1 UNDLEY COMMON – *the earliest written English* (C.475)

At some point in the second half of the fifth century and in the middle of what is now Suffolk, someone lost a beautiful, round pendant. It was made of wafer-thin gold. It seems that this object was a gift from one warrior to another, a gift so valuable that the warrior bestowing it must have been wealthy and powerful.

'Bracteate' – from the Latin word *bracea*, meaning a leaf or layer of gold – is the formal name for such an object. And as this particular one was found in a field on Undley Common, it is generally referred to as the Undley bracteate. You can see it today in the British Museum. It is a thrilling object, but do not let its size disappoint you. It is quite tiny, just over 2 centimetres in diameter; none the less, it is alive with all the mystery of language.

The maker had modelled the pendant on a Roman coin and engraved an inscription around its edge. While no precise date can be given for the beginning of English, this pendant helps us to place the start of written English because of the inscription it carries. Here are some of the first recorded words of our language. The writing is in runes, an ancient Germanic alphabet, and those runes, most likely, transliterate as 'Gægogæ Mægæ Medu'. 'Gægogæ' seems to be a charm or battle-cry, and 'Mægæ Medu' might mean 'Mead for a Kinsman'. That in turn would mean 'A Reward for a Kinsman'. This writing is so ancient that we cannot be certain that we know what it really does mean, but we can be sure that it is English.

How did the pendant get to Undley? The inscription and the design give some of the answer because they show that it was made in Continental Europe, somewhere in the lands that are now Denmark, Germany and Holland. It came with the peoples who lived in those lands and who began to cross the North Sea to occupy the island that the Romans had abandoned in 410. We can see from the pendant that these Germanics had an advanced culture that included writing and metal skills. And along with the pendant came the English language. The runic inscription tells us that English began well before England.

In fact, English before England was a Continental language called West Germanic, a language from which modern Dutch, modern German

The Undley Bracteate

and modern English have descended. Cousin languages of West Germanic were North Germanic and East Germanic. East Germanic has died out altogether, but North Germanic has become Danish, Swedish, Norwegian and Icelandic. The original of the Germanic languages is called Proto-Germanic, a language presumed to have been spoken by a people who arrived in the Scandinavian peninsula perhaps 3,000 years ago. Proto-Germanic descended from Proto-Indo-European, the language presumed to have been spoken by a people who lived somewhere between Europe and India some 6,000 years ago.

FROM RUNES TO WRITTEN ENGLISH

Although the words on the Undley bracteate are clearly a kind of English, normally referred to as Old English, they are written in a runic alphabet rather than in the Roman one that we now use. 'Runes' originally meant 'secret' or 'hidden', perhaps indicating the magic that early writers felt as they turned the spoken word into written symbols. To understand this sense of mystery today we perhaps have to think of something as extraordinary as the transmission of the first radio signal (see page 159), where words were somehow spoken in one place, sent through the air and arrived intact many miles away. Interestingly, runes are still used by writers and film-makers as a means of suggesting the mysterious or the magical – as the global interest in Tolkien's *Lord of the Rings* trilogy attests.

Though J.R.R. Tolkien was a considerable scholar and fluent in all forms of the ancient Germanic script, his use of runes in his trilogy annoys other scholars. That is partly because he emphasized the mystery of runes and partly because he devised his own runic script for his dwarves of his Middle Earth. Tolkien was however writing novels, not textbooks, a point that a critic like R.I. Page might do well to acknowledge.

Runes would have been hewn by simple tool users, metal on metal, or bone or metal on wood. Consequently each letter is made up of straight lines for ease of creating. But a runic for example is clearly related to the R with which we are familiar. There has been a great deal of argument about the origin of the runic letters. The common theory is that the Germanics adapted Latin script, though some scholars say that runes are an adaptation of Greek script. Either theory could be right, but the latest thinking is that runes are an adaptation of a Northern Italic script. Those were scripts that originated at the same time as the Roman script, but in kingdoms to the north of Rome.

Alphabetic script was invented only the once. It is the great gift of the Phoenicians to the world. All alphabets derive from the Phoenician letters, often by strange routes. The letters evolved on the way, often by revolving and reversing their forms. What happened to the letters depended on whether the writing was up or down, left to right, right to left (or left to right and then right to left), or by chisel, brush or pen.

New letters had to be devised for the different sounds of different languages; old letters would fall away. When the Germanics of Britannia finally adopted Roman script, they had some inventing to do themselves (see pages 19–20).

From the moment English began to be written down, those who could read and write became increasingly powerful – for they possessed the means of recording their assets beyond dispute, or could create stories and record events without the fallibility of oral traditions.

2 CANTERBURY – The adoption of the Roman alphabet (602)

The Jutish kingdom of Kent is the first region of post-Roman Britannia to leave evidence of an organized realm. That is because Kent was the first area to be re-converted to Christianity. Sent by Pope Gregory, Augustine and fellow monks arrived in Canterbury in 597, bringing not only Christianity but also writing in the form of Roman script. In 602, King Ethelbert of Kent had the monks write down the laws of his people in that script.

Those laws, called 'dooms', had been brought to Kent from Continental Europe 150 years before. They are the first surviving example, in any Germanic language, of a legal document. They are the starting point of the Anglo-American common law and tradition. They are also of great importance in the history of the English language.

First, they show that within five years of the arrival of the Roman script, it had been adopted in place of the runic alphabet (see pages 17–19). Second, they provide evidence of Kentish, a dialect of English that was to disappear altogether. Third, they are the beginning of regular and widespread written records in English, as the script of the dooms spread rapidly west and north.

Enough of those records survive from the seventh century to show that there were four distinct dialects of Old English: Northumbrian, Mercian, West Saxon and Kentish. Northumbrian and Mercian were the dialects of the Angles who settled north and south of the River Humber. West Saxon was the dialect of the Saxons who lived to the south and west of the Thames. Kentish was the dialect of the Jutes living in Kent and on the Isle of Wight.

The very names of those peoples, Angles, Saxons and Jutes, come from their first historian, Bede of Monkwearmouth (see pages 22–3). The latest archaeological evidence suggests that Bede's descriptors reflect a dialect sort-out as much as (or more than) a settlement pattern. Bede certainly omitted the Frisians and several other settler groups, but the written evidence does show those four major divisions of English – divisions that have shaped English speech ever since.

However, the influence of Kentish is the weakest of all. Its story begins early, but it ends early too. After the seventh century, few records have survived in Kentish. Remarkably, there is a survival from as late as 1340 – the time of Middle English. At that date, a monk of Canterbury translated a French religious work, and he wrote at the start of it: 'þis boc is dan Michelis of Northgate ywrite an englis of his o ene hand þet hatte Ayenbyte of inwyt' – 'This book is [of] Dom Michael of Northgate, written in English by his own hand. It is called: *Prick of Conscience*.' That is about the last shout of Kentish, though some say that you can still hear traces of it on the Isle of Wight and others state that it survives as Cockney. The first claim is probable; the second is not.

THE POWER OF ALPHABETS

The word 'alphabet' did not enter the English language until 1513. It takes the first two letters of the Greek alphabet, 'alpha' and 'beta', to indicate the whole set of twenty-eight. In fact, what the early missionaries did was to take the twenty-three letters that make up the Latin alphabet and apply them to the English sounds they heard. They added four new letters – 'ash', 'thorn', 'eth' and 'wynn', as well as a form of 'g' called 'yogh'. This early form of the English alphabet had twenty-seven letters (or twenty-eight if you count the alternative form of 'g').

With the adoption of the Roman alphabet, we have the beginning of the means of standardizing the way we render speech and sounds as writing that can be understood even where spoken dialects and accents are difficult to comprehend.

But perhaps most importantly for the history of English, the decision taken by the Christian scribes who landed in Kent, as a result of their shared Roman culture, began the transformation of the old Runic language of the seventh century into the global English of present times. Today, the world depends on the Roman alphabet. Even in those countries where it is not the official script, it is widely used and understood.

 HAMMERWICH – *Mercian English, our ancestor dialect* (*c.*700)

In a Staffordshire field in the parish of Hammerwich in 2009, a man with a metal detector uncovered a collection of 1,500 exquisitely made objects, mostly in gold and silver. The find has been named the Staffordshire Hoard. It has been dated to about the year 700, and it was valued by the British Museum at £3 million. The hoard not only amazed the world, it also thrilled scholars because it called for a re-evaluation of the ancient kingdom of Mercia.

Mercia was in the region that we now call the Midlands, and the valley of the River Trent was its heartland. It was surrounded to the north, east and south by other Angle and Saxon kingdoms. To the west were Welsh kingdoms, so Mercia marked a boundary or a 'march'. From 'march' comes the name Mercia.

The Staffordshire Hoard shows the great wealth of Mercia, but despite that extraordinary evidence of culture, Mercia has left the fewest written records of any Old English kingdom. What we know about Mercia has mainly come from the reports of its enemies, particularly from the kingdoms of Northumbria and Wessex. As a result, the story of Mercia has been vague and distorted. But the landlocked kingdom had its own dialect, Mercian English. And it is Mercian English, not West Saxon nor Northumbrian English, from which Standard Modern English has descended. Mercian is the ancestor of the prose that you are reading at this moment.

Mercia was greatest in the eighth century, and its scholars were sufficiently learned for King Alfred of Wessex to recruit them to embellish his court in the ninth century. It seems that Danish raids destroyed Mercian records as they destroyed the kingdom. When Alfred reached his compromise with the Danes in 880, Mercia was divided in two.

Two forms of Mercian English evolved, described by the great Victorian scholar, Walter W. Skeat, in this way: 'The West Midland does not greatly differ from the East Midland, but it approaches more nearly, in some respects, to the Northumbrian.' The East Midland dialect became the speech of London, Oxford and Cambridge, and for that reason became the dialect of privilege. The West Midland dialect, says Skeat, was superseded by the East Midland dialect.

THE GAWAYN POET

But that was not before it had produced a great poet, the anonymous author of a beautiful Arthurian romance full of dangerous journeys, passionate encounters, chivalric tests and magical events. The poem does not rhyme; it alliterates. In each line, each stressed syllable begins with the same consonant.

The name of the poem is 'Sir Gawayn and the Grene Knyght'. This is how it begins:

> Sithen the sege and the assaut watz sesed at Troye,
> The borgh brittened and brent to brondez and askez,
> The tulk that the trammes of tresoun ther wroght
> Watz tried for his tricherie, the trewest on erthe.

Translated into Modern English, that becomes:

> When the siege and the assault were ended at Troy,
> The city laid waste and burnt into ashes,
> The man who had plotted the treacherous scheme
> Was tried for the wickedest trickery ever.

The poem's alliterative verse is a relic of Old English poetry, none of which rhymed. In the late fourteenth century, when 'Sir Gawayn' was written, alliterative verse was being replaced by rhyming verse, the form already being used by a contemporary of the Gawayn poet, Geoffrey Chaucer.

Both Chaucer and the Gawayn poet spoke descendant dialects of Mercian English, but Chaucer is easier to read because East Midland English is closer than West Midland English to the way we write today. Chaucer wrote poems for the Court of Richard II, and from that time English literature has taken the form of the East Midland dialect of what was once Mercian English (see pages 47–9).

An extract of the Gawayn story from an early manuscript

4 MONKWEARMOUTH – *naming the English language* (731)

Monkwearmouth is at the estuary of the River Wear in Sunderland in Northumbria, and it was once the site of St Peter's Abbey. St Peter's was matched by St Paul's Abbey at Jarrow on the River Tyne. They are 12 miles apart, and today they are linked by a path called Bede's Way. Bede is the man who is the first to speak of the English language, though he did so in Latin, calling it *lingua Anglorum.*

In the eighth century, the twin monasteries were the wealthiest in the kingdom of Northumbria. Furnished with fine libraries, they were among the leading cultural centres of Europe. The monasteries' greatest scholar was Bede, known to history as the Venerable Bede. He may have been born in either Monkwearmouth or in Jarrow (both claim him) in either 672 or 673. He lived out his life in the two monasteries.

Bede's greatest work is his *Historia ecclesiastica gentis anglorum*, his *Ecclesiastical History of the English People.* He finished the book in his fifty-ninth year. That was probably 731. He was the first person to describe the Germanic peoples living in the former Roman province of Britannia as the *gentis Anglorum*, the nation of the

English. Because Bede was an Angle, he used 'Angle' to form a group name. That is why today we talk about the English, and not the Saxish or the Jutish.

Bede began his history with the stories of the Angles, Saxons and Jutes, so why did he go on to treat them as one people and not three? First, those peoples spoke mutually intelligible dialects of what we now call Old English. Second, their royal families regularly intermarried. Third, the Angles, Saxons and Jutes had become Christian by the eighth century, and it was that story of conversion with which Bede was concerned. Gregory the Great, the pope who had sent missionaries from Rome to Canterbury in 595, was Bede's spiritual guide, and the *Ecclesiastical History* took an almost papal view, a view that made light of local divisions.

The opening page of Bede's History

WHAT'S IN A NAME?

English. English-speaking. Anglo-Indian. Anglo-phile. Anglo-phobic. Anglo-Saxon. Anglo-Catholic. Each of these words might not exist today. But each, with a nice irony, can trace its ancestry to Northumberland and to the scholarly Bede's decision to plump for the Latin phrase *lingua Anglorum*.

5 YORK – *the influence of Danish on the English language* (866)

In 866, the Danes overtook the city that the Romans had called Eboracum and the Angles had called Eoforwic. The Danes called it Jorvik, and we call it York. These invaders were Norse-speaking peoples from Scandinavia.

The Danes viewed the sea not as separating the scattered islands of northwest Europe, but as joining them. They are popularly called the Vikings, and the word *vikingr* in Norse means sea traveller and warrior, but in Old English *wicing* came to mean pirate and pillager. The Vikings were, however, doing no more than the Angles, Saxons and Jutes had done before them.

The Danes established settlements on the east coast (and often well inland) from the Thames to the Tweed. A thousand Norse place names can be identified to this day by the suffixes *-by*, *-thorp*, *-beck*, *-dale* and *-thwaite*. In Northern and Scots dialects, there are thousands of Norse words. There are about 900 words of Norse origin in Standard Modern English, and another 900 that linguists cannot be sure whether they come from Norse or were already in Northumbrian and Mercian English. Words like 'egg', 'husband' and 'leg', notable for their commonplaceness, come from Norse. Sometimes the Old Norse and Old English versions of a word for the same thing have survived, with useful to slight to no differences in meaning: *kirk* and *church*, *dike* and *ditch*, *skirt* and *shirt*, *skin* and *hide*, *die* and *starve*, *ill* and *sick*.

Old Norse and Old English may have been mutually intelligible; they were certainly close enough to influence each other in subtle ways. Old Norse even affected that most important of all words – the verb 'to be'. Today, we say 'they are', not 'they be'. Also, Modern English says 'he walks', not 'he walketh' – probably as a result of Norse influence. It is certainly true that English replaced its third person plural pronouns '*hie*, *him*, *hiera*' with the Norse '*they*, *them*, *their*'.

Only French has had such a profound influence on English as the language of the Danes (see pages 29–31).

ENGLAND'S DANISH KING

Most of us know King Canute (Cnut) from the stuff of legend. He sits on his throne in our mind's eye as the tide remorselessly laps about his feet. Too often the story is retold to illustrate the over-reaching ambition of kings. Of course, the episode is historically uncertain. But if it did happen, it is far more likely that Cnut was making a point to his courtiers that, as a Christian ruler, his powers were subservient to God's.

Canute was king of Denmark, Norway and part of Sweden. But most importantly for the story of English, he was king of England between 1016 and 1035. Coins exist with the legend CNUT REX DÆNOR[UM] (Canute king of the Danes) and CNUT REX ANGLORU[M] (Canute king of the English). Some 150 years after

King Canute on a coin of the period

MoneyMuseum Zurich

the Danes took York, the link to Bede's *Historia ecclesiastica gentis Anglorum* is clear to see.

Canute's promotion of himself as an 'English' king was far more than a linguistic gesture. Its lived reality was in the creating of good laws, in the flourishing of commerce and of the arts, in the development of religious harmony, and in the provision of a stable and peaceful, if short-lived, period for the emerging nation of England.

6 WINCHESTER – *West Saxon English and King Alfred* (871)

Winchester was the cathedral city in which the West Saxons crowned their kings from the mid-seventh century. These West Seaxe had settled furthest west during the initial Germanic invasions, and their kingdom came to be called Wessex. The core shires of this kingdom were Hampshire, Wiltshire and Dorset. Winchester was at their centre.

The English of the West Saxons was one of the four dialects of Old English, and most Old English manuscripts were written in West Saxon English, even texts copied far to the north of Winchester. That was because King Alfred, the greatest of the Wessex kings, ordered his monks to translate from Latin a body of work that would guide his subjects. Other monks copied Alfred's monks, and his dialect spread from one manuscript to another and from one monastery to another, so West Saxon became a norm for English texts.

One of the books that Alfred had translated was the greatest work of the Northumbrian monasteries, Bede's *Ecclesiastical History of the English People*, the document mentioned on page 22. Alfred, who had taught himself to read and write, unusual kingly skills, added his own comments to his monks' translations. Alfred, a Saxon, followed Bede, an Angle, in talking about the *gentis Anglorum*, the nation of the Angles, and in talking about the *lingua Anglorum*, the language of the Angles. The Angles, Saxons and Jutes were beginning to call themselves the English, and the language they spoke was coming to be called English.

Alfred died in 899, and Alfred's Court English, at its zenith at his death, held sway for a century and a half. It was replaced as the prestige language by Norman French in 1066. After this date the English of Wessex, and that of Hampshire with it, became a rural dialect. The story of West Saxon is like the story of the d'Urbervilles in Thomas Hardy's novel – once noble, but later peasant. In screen versions, Tess Durbeyfield is always given a broad Westcountry accent, as she should be. However, had Winchester remained the capital of England, Tess's English would now be the Queen's English.

King Alfred as he appears in Winchester today

ALFRED, THE GREAT LINGUIST

From his spiritual base in Winchester, Alfred's influence was immense. His writing is powerful and demonstrates both his linguistic and educational ambitions. Alfred sent a copy of the new translation of Pope Gregory's *Pastoral Care* to Bishop Wærferth of Worcester, saying:

> it seems better to me, if it seems so to you, that we also should translate certain books which are most necessary for all men to know into the language that we can all understand, and also arrange it, as with God's help we very easily can if we have peace, so that all the young freeborn men now among the English people, who have the means to be able to devote themselves to it, may be set to study for as long as they are of no other use, until the time they are able to read English writing well.

Today, the book and the king's letter to the bishop can be found in the Bodleian Library in Oxford.

Alfred bemoans the fact that standards of learning have declined so much in England, and he wonders out loud where the next generation of teachers will come from. He was writing a manifesto for making English a formal language of communication alongside Latin. It is amazing that, at such an early date, he was so concerned with his mother tongue. As a result, English has one of the longest and richest written heritages in all of Europe.

7 CERNE – *Classical Old English* (*c*.1000)

In 987, a young monk left Winchester where he had undergone his education and travelled to the newly founded abbey of Cerne in the southwest of England (now Cerne Abbas in Dorset). The monk was called Aelfric. He is acknowledged as one of the greatest prose writers in English of his time. While at Cerne, he wrote prolifically, both in Latin and in English. In 1005 Aelfric left Cerne for Eynsham where he spent his final years as abbot.

Aelfric's works include two series of homilies (mini-sermons about the events of the church year and the teaching of the Church) and a *Lives of the Saints*. He also wrote three specifically educational texts – the first Latin grammar in English, a glossary of Latin words, and a conversational manual, his *Colloquy*, of which more below.

Aelfric wrote in what used to be called Anglo-Saxon, but is better called Old English. Old English is the form of English found in writings from the fifth century and the middle of the twelfth century. If you were listening to it being spoken now, you might understand a few words and phrases, but the rest of it would probably be unintelligible to you. (A number of websites allow you to do just this if you want to try it out for yourself.)

If listening to Old English presents challenges, reading it is even more difficult for a modern student. The Old English scribes created an alphabet based on the Roman one; most of their letters looked like their modern counterparts, but five of them did not:

æ: called 'ash' was a vowel sound like the 'a' in 'bat'.
Þ: called 'thorn' was a voiced consonant that had the sound of the 'th' in 'thorn'.
ð: called 'eth' was an unvoiced consonant that had the sound of the 'th' in 'thin'.
Þ: called 'wynn' was the forerunner of the letter 'w'.
ȝ: called 'yogh' was a voiced consonant that had the sound of 'ch' in the Scots pronunciation of 'loch'.

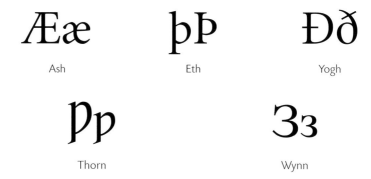

Ash   Eth   Yogh

Thorn   Wynn

There were a number of other ways in which Old English was different from the English we speak, read and write today. A principal difference was that it was an inflected language: the endings of its nouns and adjectives were changed to show their grammatical role. Also, Old English inflexions showed whether words were masculine, feminine or neuter and indicated whether words were singular or plural. Today, we can add an 's' to 'book' to make a plural, 'books', but we have lost the full pattern of Old English inflexions, and we no longer have grammatical gender.

AELFRIC'S INFLUENCE ON ENGLISH

The first great works of literature in the English language were poems, and great poetry often comes before great prose in a language. The significance of the work of Aelfric and others like him was to produce, so early, magnificent prose. It meant that

Old English could serve as a language of general culture and take a place alongside Latin.

One work of Aelfric's is of particular interest, his *Colloquy*. A colloquy is a stylized conversation designed to be educational. In this case it takes place between a master and his pupils. Aelfric's *Colloquy* is especially important because, although it is written in Latin, it also contains an Old English translation that has been written between the lines of Latin. We do not know who undertook the translation, but many suspect that it was done at the beginning of the eleventh century shortly after Aelfric's death.

The master in this case is a monk, and he is talking to his pupils who have an astonishingly broad range of occupations including a ploughman, a shepherd, an oxherd, a hunter, a fisherman, a fowler, a merchant, a leather worker, a salter, a tanner, a cook, a baker and a novice monk.

The monk asks each of them in turn about their work. By way of their answers, Aelfric gives us an extraordinarily vivid picture of medieval life. Towards the end of the colloquy, the monk asks a lawyer to adjudicate as to which of the various trades is the most important. The lawyer argues that those who work on the land matter most as without them we would have no food. That provokes a raucous discussion as each worker argues his case.

Aelfric's *Colloquy* provides a wonderful conversation from the eleventh century – one of the first recorded in post-Roman Europe.

8   HASTINGS – *the influence of French on the English language* (1066)

Hastings was the site in 1066 of an invasion not only of the English kingdom, but of the English language. For the next 300 years, England was ruled in French. French-speaking warriors and administrators arrived in sufficient numbers, with sufficient military power, and they remained dominant for a sufficiently long time to bring about major changes in the grammar of English.

First Norman French, and then Old French, became blended with Old English, and the effects were startling. Grammatical gender was replaced by logical gender; most noun endings were lost; word order was altered. The overall changes were so great that, by 1300, a new form of English had emerged. We call it Middle English.

That English was so different from that of Aelfric the Grammarian – whose English had been the best model in the year 1000 – that he would not at first have recognized it. Once he did, he would have despised it. First, the new English had emerged from the commercial Mercian of the new capital of London rather than the classical West Saxon of the old capital at Winchester. Second, many of the subtleties of grammar conveyed by Old English noun endings were lost. Third,

Part of the Bayeux Tapestry depicting the Battle of Hastings

Aelfric would have been dismayed at the number of French words to be found in daily use.

It is not only in spoken English that Aelfric would have seen French influence. French-trained scribes had trouble with Old English letters, and 'Þ' (wynn), 'ð' (thorn) and 'æ' (ash) had disappeared. At the same time, many Old English spellings had been reshaped to reflect French practice. Aelfric would have found that 'cwen' appeared as 'queen' and 'scip' as 'ship'. Old English had disappeared. To the Modern English reader, it now seems like a foreign language.

The changes did not occur overnight. It took generations of linguistic engagement by way of intermarriage, diplomacy, trade, courtly literature, by preaching in church, and by the legal processes now overseen by the invaders. As well as grammar and vocabulary, pronunciation was affected, but that is difficult to detect, and the greatest changes came after 1400. (See the discussion of the Great Vowel Shift, pages 65–6.)

THE ENGLISH LANGUAGE À LA CARTE

French gradually died out as a working language in England, but not before it had became well and truly embedded in everyday English. The influence of French is especially seen in our vocabulary. English steadily evolved, absorbing some French words, rejecting others, and often keeping its options open by running alternatives for the same object or action. For almost a thousand years, we have been in the habit of taking words from French, a habit that is only just dying out.

Since 1066, French itself has changed a great deal, and the result has been that we have often borrowed a word twice or even three times, each time with a different shade of meaning and in a slightly different form. The Normans (Norse Men) had been Vikings who adopted French as their mother tongue, and the first French words that entered English were from Norman French, the language of Williame FitzRobert de Normandie who had made himself Roi d'Angleterre. From his French, we get words like *carpenter, canon, kennel, catch, cattle, gaol, garden*. The hard 'k' and 'g' sounds (gutturals) are Norman.

In the thirteenth century, English began taking words from Old French, the ancestor language of Modern French. From that French, we took *attorney, bailiff, chase, chatel, chancellor, chalice* and *jail*. The soft 'ch' and 'j' (palatals) show the pronunciation of the Angevin kings who began ruling England in 1154. We continued to borrow from French as it became Middle French, and from that we took words like *crime, evidence, chapel, pavilion, profane, scruple*.

By 1500, English had taken some 10,000 words from French. Since 1500, we have taken another 10,000 words from French. It was only in the twentieth century that the borrowing began to ease up. The older the borrowing the more English the word seems, as the words become anglicized and absorbed into the language. By contrast, with many modern borrowings, the original French survives intact: *au contraire, avant-garde, ballet, cache, chaise longue, charlatan, chauffeur, chic, cliché, communiqué, contretemps, cordon sanitaire, couture, crèche, cul-de-sac*.

 DUNFERMLINE – *the English language in Scotland* (1068)

In 1068 (or perhaps 1069), a Celtic king married a Saxon princess when Malcolm III of Scotland took Margaret of Wessex as his second wife. Malcolm and Margaret made their court at Dunfermline, just north of the River Forth on the opposite bank from the great fort at Edinburgh. Malcolm's father was Duncan, the king killed by Macbeth in a battle at Pitgaveny, not, as Shakespeare staged it, in a bed at Inverness. Macbeth began as thane of Cawdor before becoming king of Scots. 'Thane' is an Elizabethan spelling of the Old English word *þegn*. 'Thegn', originally meaning 'servant', had come to be a title of high rank, second only to earl. It was not by chance that a man with a Scots name called himself by an English title. The Scots nobility were as much Anglo-Saxon as they were Gaelic. Malcolm and Margaret's story shows why.

Before marrying Margaret, Malcolm had been married to Ingibjorg, widow of Thorfinn the Mighty, Earl of Orkney. By his first marriage, Malcolm had made peace with invading Vikings; by his second, he was making alliances against invading Northumbrians. In 1057, King Edward the Confessor had summoned Margaret's father, Edward the Exile, back from Hungary to make him his heir. Unhappy Edward died before Edward the Confessor. Margaret and her brothers fled north. Margaret was then in Dunfermline even before defeated Saxon nobles began to arrive with their retinues following the Norman victory at Hastings. Malcolm's enemies were the Northumbrians, not the Saxons, and he invaded Northumbria again and again. He was killed the fifth time he did so. Malcolm and Margaret had eight children, and three of them became kings of Scots. Through them, a royal line was established for Scotland, and that line continued to intermarry with the noble families of England.

Malcolm, though a Celtic king, spoke English before he ever met Margaret. English was, in fact, his first language because his father had married the daughter of Siward, Earl of Northumbria. The English dialect to be heard in the court of Malcolm and Margaret's descendants was not the West Saxon of Margaret, but the Northumbrian of Malcolm.

THE SCOTS LANGUAGE

The Scots court moved across the Forth from Dunfermline to Edinburgh in the next century when King David I, Margaret's youngest son, made it a royal city and built a chapel there in her honour. As a result of the Norman co-option of the name 'England', the Northumbrian spoken in Edinburgh did not come to be called English; instead, it came to be called Scots. The English of England and the Scots of Scotland are equally descendants of the language brought to the island of Britain by Germanic tribes from the year 400 onwards. We lack a word like 'Scots' to specify the English of England. If the English of England were to be called Anglican, as some American linguists suggest it should be, then we could say that Scots and Anglican are sister languages.

Scots then developed as a language of a court and as a language of a learned class, producing a literature that reached its high point in the reign of James IV (1488–1513). Writers at his court included Robert Henryson, William Dunbar, Walter Kennedy and Gavin Douglas, all 'makars' – Scots for poets. Scots had achieved a classic or standard form under these kings, just as West Saxon had done in the Wessex court and as Westminster English was doing at the court of St James.

The English now to be heard in Edinburgh, sometimes called Scottish Standard English, is a form developed in the eighteenth century following the Act of Union (1707) when the Scottish upper class began to model its speech on London's prestige dialect.

Scots exists today as an endangered dialect, and the number of its speakers is in much dispute. Scots is also called Lowland Scots, and that gives some idea where speakers are to be found. They can also be found in Ulster – everywhere more in the countryside than in the towns. Scots has a lively online existence at *Pittin the Mither Tongue on the Wab*.

3 MIDDLE ENGLISH

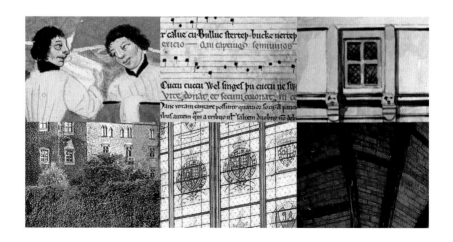

10 PETERBOROUGH – *the Anglo-Saxon Chronicle and the end of Old English* (1155)

Early in the year 1155 in the Abbey of St Peter at Peterborough in Cambridgeshire, a monk made a careful record, in English, of the events of 1154. In itself, that was nothing remarkable. English monks had been making annual records since at least the late ninth century. Such a record is called a chronicle, and seven of them have survived. They are, by and large, copies of each other, copies of what is now called The Anglo-Saxon Chronicle. What was remarkable was the fact that the entry for 1155 was the last that the Anglo-Saxon Chroniclers ever made.

It may have been King Alfred who started the practice of making year-by-year records. Certainly the earliest surviving chronicle comes from Winchester. It begins: 'Sixty winters ere Christ was born.' That first entry provides an account of Julius Caesar's invasion of Britain, an island 'eight hundred miles long, and two hundred miles broad: and here are in the island five [languages]: English, Brito-Welsh, Scottish, Pictish, and Book-Latin'. The Chronicle is partly world history, partly English history, and partly monastic history. The chroniclers often added details about the deeds of their own abbots as well as those of emperors, popes and kings. Even before the Conquest, England was a well-documented land with records of every kind, many of them administrative, enabling efficient taxation and revenue collection. Its consequent wealth made it a target for Danish, Norwegian and finally Norman aggression.

The practice of copying and then updating a chronicle spread from monastery to monastery, and these records provide not only a wonderful historical resource but also a rich linguistic treasury. They are the major depository of Old English prose that has survived. They amount to 234 pages in Benjamin Thorpe's composite edition, published in 1861. The language is mainly West Saxon, and that reflects the role that King Alfred had in making his language the language of Old English scholarship.

THE ENDING OF A LINGUISTIC ERA

The monks of St Peter's Abbey were the last men to maintain a chronicle in Old English. After them, monastery records were made in Norman French or, more commonly, in Latin. The Peterborough additions to the Anglo-Saxon Chronicle begin with the year 1131. Its language marks a transition from Old to Middle English and the beginning of an eclipse of English. After the Peterborough Chronicle, for the next 200 years almost all formal records were made in Latin or French.

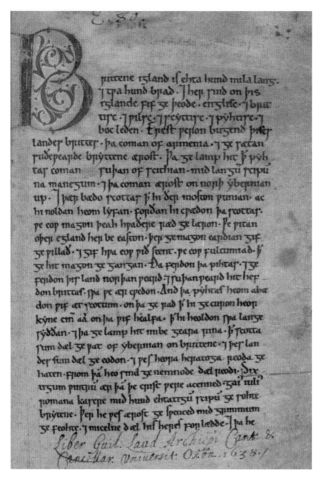

The first page of the Peterborough Chronicle

Here is Benjamin Thorpe's translation of the last entry:

An. MC.LIV [YEAR 1154]. In this year king Stephen died, and was buried where his wife and his son were buried, at Faversham, the monastery which they had founded. When the king was dead the count was beyond sea; but no man durst do other than good, for the great awe of him. When he came to England he was received with great worship, and blessed for king in London on the Sunday before Midwinter day; and there he held a great court. That same day that Martin, abbot of Peterborough, should have gone thither, he sickened and died, on the IVth of the Nones of January [Jan. 2nd]; and the monks within a day chose another for themselves, William de Waltevile, a good clerk and good man, and well loved of the king and of all good men. And all the monks buried the abbot honourably; and soon the abbot elect went, and the monks with him, to the king at Oxford; and the king gave him the abbacy; and soon went to Peterborough.

11 READING – *the English language in popular song* (*c*.1235)

Sometime around the year 1235, in Reading Abbey, a monk working in the scriptorium wrote down the words of a song that has been loved ever since:

Sumer is icumen in,
Lhude sing! cuccu
Groweth sed and bloweth med
And springth the wude nu,
Sing! Cuccu

That is the first English popular song that we know. It was written in West Country Middle English, a dialect that had descended from West Saxon Old English (see pages 25–7). In Modern English, we would sing:

Summer is acoming in,
Loud sing, Cuckoo!
Seeds grow, meadows blow,
And springs the wood anew,
Sing Cuckoo!

Sumer is icumen in from Reading Abbey's Summer Canon

'Sumer is icumen in' was soon after set to music for singing in six parts so that each singer sang a different part, or harmony, repeating different words, or rounds. That was a sophisticated kind of singing, but it is likely that 'Sumer is icumen in' was originally a folk song that the monks wrote down and then elaborated. In fact, the scribe has given us a clue about how the round should be sung. Instructions in Latin after the song suggest that 'four friends can sing this round' and then give advice as to when each starts and how they should pause for the length of one long note to allow each singer to join in the right order.

Medieval Europe was filled with all kind of songs for special occasions and 'Sumer is icumen in' is an example of a reverdie, 'a re-greening'. These were songs written to celebrate spring, the end of winter and the promise of fruit and harvest. The language of the second verse is as lively as the first:

Awe bleteth after lomb,
Lhouth after calve cu.
Bulluc sterteþ, bucke verteþ,
Murie sing cuccu!

In Modern English that becomes:

Eve bleats after lamb,
Lows after calf [the] cow,
Bullock leaps, buck farts
Merrily sing Cuckoo.

Scholars are in dispute about the third line, and some say that the buck leaps as well as the bullock.

THE POWER OF SINGING

Medieval England's canticles, carols, dirges, lays, lyrics, noels, rounds, roundelays and serenades evolved into the ballads, chanties, ditties, glees, jingles and vocals that become evident in the eighteenth century, often because that was when they were first written down.

In 1783, Joseph Ritson published three volumes of *English Songs, With Their Original Airs*. It remained popular into the Regency period. Drinking songs made up a good part of the collection, songs such as 'Better our heads than hearts should ake', 'Some say women are like the seas', and 'She tells me with claret she cannot agree'. In the later nineteenth century, songs for singing round the parlour piano became popular, songs such as 'Any Old Iron', 'Boiled Beef and Carrots', 'Burlington Bertie', 'Daddy Wouldn't Buy Me a Bow Wow', 'I Do Like to Be Beside the Seaside', and many, many more.

In the twentieth century, the popular song in Britain underwent a change as it was increasingly influenced by American popular song. Up until the 1830s, American songs were not noticeably different from British ones, and an eighteenth-century drinking song had provided the tune for both Britain's 'God Save the Queen' and America's 'My country, 'Tis of Thee'.

In the 1840s, Negro Minstrel songs such as 'Massa's in de Cold Ground', 'My Old Kentucky Home', and 'Old Folks at Home' showed the influence of African American music that was to become dominant first in the United States and then in the United Kingdom. Negro minstrel songs were followed by Negro spirituals in the 1880s, and ragtime in the 1910s and 1920s. That resolved into the jazz and blues singing of the 1920s. Those forms were long popular in the black community before they became popular in the white one. In the 1930s and 1940s, African American records were labelled Race Music, later to be called Rhythm and Blues, before turning into the Rock'n'Roll of Bill Haley, Elvis Presley and the Beatles (see pages 187–9).

 WESTMINSTER – *the recovery of the English language* (1362)

On 13 October 1362, the Chancellor of England for the first time opened the Houses of Parliament with a speech in English.

That event took place in the City of Westminster because it was the city of royal power. It was located within walking distance of the City of London, the city of commercial power. At Westminster were to be found the royal palace, the law courts, the chancellery and Parliament. The Anglo-Saxon King Edward the Confessor drew royal attention to Westminster by founding a monastery there to be his burial place. What Edward had begun suited the Norman-French kings. They never liked nor trusted London.

The Normans ruled England in French. The use of English was forbidden in Parliament and in the law courts. English was a despised language of a defeated people. It was not until the fourteenth century that there was any change in its formal status. In 1362, Parliament approved the Pleading in English Act, often referred to as The Statute of Pleading. This Act permitted the use of the English language in Parliament on the grounds that French was 'much unknown' in England.

The Statute of Pleading was primarily aimed at one of the most powerful of institutions, the legal system. It required that 'all Pleas which shall be pleaded in [any] Courts whatsoever, before any of his Justices whatsoever, or in his other Places, or before any of His other Ministers whatsoever, or in the Courts and Places of any other Lords whatsoever within the Realm, shall be pleaded, shewed, defended, answered, debated, and judged in the English Tongue, and that they be entered and inrolled in Latin'. Ironically the law was written in French, but it was nevertheless approved by predominantly French-speaking parliamentarians. And, in January 1363, the first speech in Parliament was at last made in English.

French may have been on the way out as a working language in England, but it was well and truly embedded in the everyday speech of the English. Here, French may be said to have gained a singular victory. There was hardly a human activity that could be discussed without the use of French words. The English had been taking French words wholesale since 1100, and they continued to do so for another 500 years.

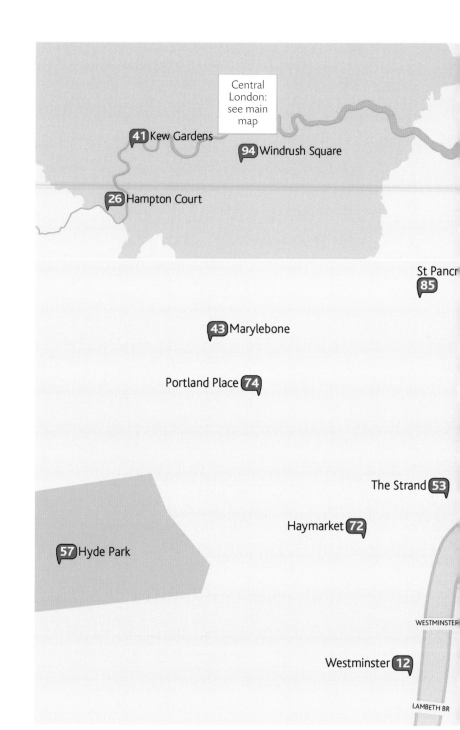

Central London: see main map

41 Kew Gardens

94 Windrush Square

26 Hampton Court

St Pancr
85

43 Marylebone

Portland Place 74

The Strand 53

Haymarket 72

57 Hyde Park

WESTMINSTER

Westminster 12

LAMBETH BR

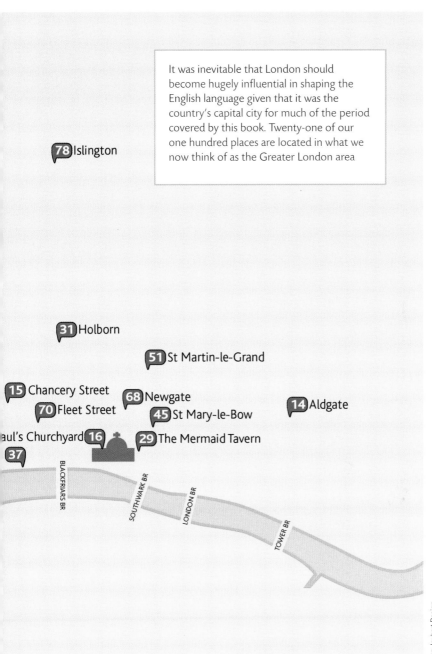

It was inevitable that London should become hugely influential in shaping the English language given that it was the country's capital city for much of the period covered by this book. Twenty-one of our one hundred places are located in what we now think of as the Greater London area

78 Islington

31 Holborn

51 St Martin-le-Grand

15 Chancery Street   68 Newgate   14 Aldgate
70 Fleet Street   45 St Mary-le-Bow

aul's Churchyard 16   29 The Mermaid Tavern
37

BLACKFRIARS BR

SOUTHWARK BR

LONDON BR

TOWER BR

Maps by Helen Joubert Design

The Chapter House of Westminster Abbey where Parliament met during the fourteenth century

Various reasons have been offered to explain the distribution of French words in English. A popular Victorian notion was that in the field the Old English *bull*, *sheep* and *pig* were tended by the lowly Saxon, but at the table the French *beef*, *mutton* and *pork* were eaten by the lordly Norman. The low/high distinction was used to explain *house*/*mansion*, *chair*/*stool* and several other doublets. But that pattern is not consistent. It does not work for *board*/*table*. *House* can be highly dignified as it is in the phrase 'House of Lords'. The adoption of *beef*, *mutton* and *pork* is more likely, says David Crystal, to be a result of English's borrowing of French culinary terminology from the fourteenth century onwards. The relationship between words of Germanic and French origin in Middle English is endlessly and fascinatingly complicated.

ENGLISH BECOMING OFFICIAL

The date 13 October 1362 symbolizes the survival of English and is a landmark in its development as a world language. From 1300, English had begun to recover ground. By the end of the century, great poets like Geoffrey Chaucer, John Gower and William Langland were once again making it their language of choice.

During the fourteenth century, although the Church was still largely using Latin, a group known as the Lollards began to write in English and preached, appealing mainly to the lower classes – which was where their supporter base was – and arguing that not using English was an example of many corrupt religious practices. By 1400, the first complete translation of the Bible into English had appeared. During this period, while Latin remained central to the curriculum, English gradually replaced French as the language of instruction.

In 1362, English had 2 million speakers and was the language of an underclass; today, it has 2 billion speakers and is the language of the world.

In 2010, the English Project adopted 13 October as an annual date to create the first English Language Day. Every year we remember this event in 1362, and take the opportunity to celebrate the English language in all its glory (see page 229).

 KILKENNY – *the English language in Ireland* (1366)

At Kilkenny, in 1366, King Edward III of England called a Parliament to reinforce English rule in Ireland. One outcome was the Statutes of Kilkenny. They ordered, among other matters, 'that every Englishman shall use the English language and be named by an English name, leaving off entirely the manner of naming used by the Irish'. If any Englishman failed to do so, he was to 'be seized into the hands of his immediate lord until he come to one of the places of our lord the King and find sufficient surety to adopt and use the English language'. The Statutes of Kilkenny were written in French, exactly like the Statute of Pleading (see page 39), a law that had been approved by the Parliament of Westminster four years before. That law had granted Englishmen the right to speak English in Parliament; now, the English were attempting to prevent English from dying out in Ireland.

After 1366, there was an increasing use of English in the formal documents of Ireland, but little evidence that many people were speaking it. There was no great change until James, king of Scots, took the English throne in 1603. He encouraged his fellow countrymen to migrate from Scotland to Ulster. Between 1610 and 1640, some 10,000 Scots-speaking Presbyterians took the land of Irish-speaking Catholics. From the language of the Scots settlers has evolved Ulster Scots, a form of English spoken in Northern Ireland today (see pages 32–3). The Scots-Irish began migrating again at the beginning of the eighteenth century. They moved to North America,

Kilkenny Castle at the turn of the nineteenth century

entering by way of the port of Philadelphia. Finding the best land taken, they settled the Appalachia hill country. The Scotch-Irish, as they name themselves today, call their dialect Mountain Talk. Its formal name is Southern Highland English.

THE DEVELOPMENT OF ANGLO-IRISH

South of Ulster, two further kinds of English developed in Ireland. Following the Westminster Parliament's Act of Settlement in 1650, increasing numbers of English landlords built homes in Ireland. These Anglican households lived lives separate from those of their Catholic tenantry. The name the English gave themselves in the eighteenth century was 'the Ascendancy'. Their males were regularly educated in England. The speech of the Ascendancy provided modern Ireland with an Anglo-Irish that is Dublin in vowels and Oxford in grammar.

The tenants of the English landlords remained Gaelic speaking until the middle of the nineteenth century when famines convulsed Irish peasant society. The loss of half the population to starvation and immigration restructured social, family and religious life in such a way that it reinforced Catholicism at the same time as it resulted in increasing numbers speaking English.

Today only 1 per cent of the Irish population can speak Gaelic, but for a long time a bilingual population created an Irish English that is strongly influenced by Gaelic. The grammar of that language is directly reflected in formations such as: 'Ah, it was no good for me to go to England, if I couldn't talk nothing only Irish, was it?';

'But only for the Famine, there wouldn't be a half as many Protestants in Ireland, do you see?'; 'In some building he is working with the couple of weeks'; 'There's no loss on him'. Gaelic stress also accounts for the Irish lilt, much as it does in the Welsh lilt.

 ALDGATE – *the development of Middle English* (1374)

Geoffrey Chaucer lived at a remarkable time for the English language. He was born in 1343 (or thereabouts), and he might well have been taught in English and Latin rather than in French and Latin. That was something new. The long cultural and linguistic dominance of French was nearing its end.

Chaucer's father was a prosperous London wine merchant who gave his son a good education and paid for him to be a page boy at the English court. There, the poet learned the ways of the aristocracy. He also gained noble patronage that secured for him the post of Comptroller of the Customs for the Port of London. An apartment above the Aldgate, the easternmost gate in London Wall, went with the job. It was a fine place in which to write poetry as well as to oversee the collection of duties.

Chaucer is the poet that everyone who reads English and who loves poetry will find themselves reading even though he was born almost 700 years ago. There are two reasons why we read him today. First, he is a glorious, joyous poet. Second, he wrote an English from which Standard Modern English descends directly. The English of the earliest period we call Old English; the English from about 1150 to 1500, we call Middle English. Chaucer is the great poet of Middle English. English poetry goes back some 600 years before Chaucer, but suddenly with him English poetry opens its treasures to us.

Chaucer lived above the Aldgate from 1374 to 1386, and they were prolific years. While there, he wrote *The Parlement of Foules*, *The Legend of Good Women* and *Troilus and Criseyde*. Very probably, he began *The Canterbury Tales* before he left.

Chaucer's English was lively, modern and stylish. The opening of *The Canterbury Tales* gives the flavour of the new English and its new poetry:

Whan that Aprille with his shoures soote
The droghte of Marche hath perced to the roote,
And bathed every veyne in swich licour,
Of which vertu engendred is the flour…

Listening to *The Canterbury Tales* as Chaucer himself would have read them is a special experience. It gives a real sense of just how close and just how distant Middle English is from Modern English. Several renderings of the opening lines are avail-

Aldgate, over which Chaucer lived when he was Comptroller of the Customs

able on YouTube. They are well worth listening to. You can also visit Chaucer's grave in Westminster Abbey. Fittingly, Geoffrey Chaucer is the first occupant of Poets' Corner.

THE FATHER OF ENGLISH LITERATURE

Chaucer has had a pervasive influence on our vocabulary. We can never be sure when words first enter the spoken language, but the *Oxford English Dictionary* (*OED*) gives us the first date at which a word has been found in the written language. Chaucer's name appears against the first instances of very many words, including *accident*, *agree*, *cinnamon*, *desk*, *examination*, *funeral*, *laxative*, *outrageous*, *scissors*, *vacation*, *village*, *vulgar* and *wallet*. Chaucer became, almost at once, a model for written English – and especially for subsequent poets. The Elizabethan poet Edmund Spenser called Chaucer the 'Well of English undefiled' and, until Shakespeare displaced him, Chaucer's language was the most admired.

His chosen form of English showed the shift from the West Saxon dialect of Alfred to the London dialect that was to become the foundation of Standard English. But whether he caused, accelerated or was simply part of this linguistic movement is disputed. London as the centre of power, along with Cambridge and Oxford, was already exerting a strong force.

 CHANCERY STREET – *Chancery English* (c.1419)

Sometime between 1417 and 1420 a letter written by King Henry V while on military campaign in France arrived in the hands of the regent of England, the Duke of Bedford. The letter referred to intelligence the king had gleaned about fears of attack from Scotland, along with advice on the treatment of French prisoners. The king's words would have required immediate action. It would have needed to be consistently communicated to a number of nobles in England. Consequently, it is possible to imagine it being read in the king's command centre for such matters, the Lord Chancellor's office, increasingly known by its shortened form as Chancery. We do not know whether this letter actually passed through the office of Chancery. But we do know that, unlike letters from previous kings written in Latin or French, this one was written, possibly by the king himself, in English.

Chancery was located in Chancery Street off The Strand and close to St Paul's Cathedral. The word 'chancery' first appears in English in the fourteenth century to describe the court over which the Lord Chancellor presided. It is a shortened form of the late Middle English word 'chauncelerie'. But it is what took place under the Chancellor's extensive offices that is important for the story of English.

A fifteenth-century illustration of the Court of Chancery

By the fifteenth century there were some 120 scriveners – clerks and apprentices – whose job was to write and to make copies of other people's writing. Like some gigantic human photocopier, these men ensured that records were made of every-thing that mattered to the king and that messages were intelligible in Ludlow, Lichfield and Leicester, as well as in London.

There were also twenty-four cursitors, a special kind of clerk, whose job was to create new writs (the medieval equivalent of a note or memo or short report). Here in the great offices of Chancery and, down the road, in the Exchequer was an insa-tiable hunger for reliable reports, notes, records and many other forms of writing to ensure that government was effective. What we now think of as a civil service, the machinery of government, was being born.

THE BEGINNINGS OF STANDARD ENGLISH

In his legal and financial dealings, the Lord Chancellor required a certain precision and, under previous kings, his office had become adept at dealing in French and Latin. But from the time of Henry V onwards, Chancery scriveners plied their trade in English. The output of Chancery has become known as Chancery English. It is seen by many as a powerful standardizing influence on the English language.

One of the main areas of potential confusion at this time was the profusion of different spellings, and Chancery scribes certainly played a standardizing role here. But huge variety was to remain a feature of English for a long time to come.

David Crystal suggests a number of more significant features of Chancery English. These include:

-*ed* for past tense verb endings, e.g. *assembled*;
-*yng* for present participle ending, e.g. *dewllyng*;
-*th* for third person singular forms, e.g. *doth*;
shulde rather than *schulde* for *should*.

In many cases it was perhaps inevitable that the forms of English spoken by Londoners (the London and East Midland dialects) tended to win out and be adopted in Chancery English. But there were interesting anomalies such as the northern forms for the pronouns 'they', their' and 'them' rather than the more local 'hi', 'hir' and 'hem'.

16 ST PAUL'S CHURCHYARD – *the English language and the book trade* (1456)

In 1456, John Shirley died after a lifetime of buying and selling manuscripts near St Paul's Cathedral in the City of London. Shirley often made his own translations from Latin texts. His *Dethe of the Kynge of Scotis* has a note on the last page that reads:

> And thus nowe here endethe this moste pitevous Cronicle of th'orribill dethe of the kyng of Scottes translated oute of Latyne into owre moders Englisshe tong bi youre symple subget Iohn Shirley in his laste age after his symple vnderstondyng whiche he recommendethe to your supportacione and correccion as that youre gentilnese vowchethe safe for his excuse &c

It is probable that he did not write out the particular manuscript copy from which this quotation comes. He no doubt left copying to his scriveners, men whose job it was to keep Shirley's shop filled with manuscripts.

The date for *Dethe of the Kynge of Scotis* is about 1449, and Shirley's late Middle English is not far from Early Modern English. It is easy enough to read. Though the spelling appears idiosyncratic to us, it provides a good reflection of his accent so that 'our mother's English tongue' is rendered 'owre moders Englisshe tong'.

Shirley died just twenty years before the printing press began to revolutionize the book trade (see pages 56–7), but though the first presses were set up in Westminster, the centre for book selling remained in the City of London, and booksellers continued to give their address for the next 500 years as Amen Corner or Paternoster-Row, St Paul's Churchyard. The area was destroyed by bombing in December 1940, and the booksellers moved out, but even greater changes were coming for the book trade.

THE CHANGING FACE OF BOOKS

The revolution in the manufacture of books that began to take place in the twenty years after Shirley's death was the greatest change to have taken place since the codex began to give way to the biblio in the two centuries after the death of Christ. The codex was a scroll; the biblio was a bound set of pages. The Christians are said to be the first people to cut up the pages of the scroll and make them into what we now call a book. They did that to make easy the comparison of pages of the New Testament with those of the Old Testament. The Greek name for a book provided the Christians with the name for their combined testaments: the Bible.

Then, in the mid-fifteenth century, Europe saw the first movements from hand-written books to printed books. That transition took 200 years or more and gave rise to the book trade and the various book shops that we still see around us.

The early twenty-first century has witnessed a similar great change to those from scroll to book and from manuscript to print. The appearance of the electronic text at the end of the twentieth century has brought about an equally profound change in the way that we think about the written word. Libraries have been radically transformed, with computers sitting alongside shelves of books. The 1 million titles on Google Books provide a research facility in many people's homes. Amazon.com sells as many books online as people buy from high street shops. And 'to kindle' is fast becoming a verb meaning 'to read an electronic book'.

 PEMBROKE – *the English language in Wales* (1457)

In Pembroke Castle in 1457, Lady Margaret Beaufort, wife of Edmund Tudor, gave birth to a son, named Henry Tudor. The boy lived at Pembroke until he was fourteen. Then he went first to live in Brittany and, after that, in France. At the age of twenty-eight, with French aid, he entered England at the head of an army that defeated and killed Richard III. Henry Tudor became Henry VII of England.

That might have been a great moment for the Welsh language. The Welsh bards declared Henry Tudor to be *y mab darogan*, 'the son of prophecy', and Henry did make some small gestures to his father's Welsh ancestry. He called his eldest son

Pembroke Castle today

Arthur and occasionally flew the red dragon banner of Cadwallader, but the important thing for Henry was his mother's ancestry. In that lay his claim to the throne of England.

Henry's need to seem English meant that the Welsh language did not profit from his being a Welshman. In fact, the need for the Tudor dynasty to make itself English and the demands of the centralized state that the Tudors ruled meant that it was the English language, not the Welsh language, that was advanced. Henry Tudor's son, Henry VIII, had Acts promulgated that made English the language of the Welsh law courts and of public administration.

A STORY OF LANGUAGE IMPERIALISM

Henry VIII's instruction relating to language gives a good flavour of this approach as well as tantalizing insights into the style, spelling and punctuation of Tudor English:

> All other officers and ministers of the lawe shall proclayme and kepe the sessions courtes hundreds letes Shireves and all other courtes in the Englisshe Tonge. [...] And also that frome hensforth no personne or personnes that use the Welsshe speche or langage shall have or enjoy any maner office or fees within the Realme of Englonde Wales [...] onles he or they use and exercise the speche or langage of Englisshe.

In 1847 came what the Welsh call 'the Treachery of the Blue Books' and what London called 'The Report of the Royal Commission on Education in Wales'. For the Commissioners, the Welsh language was 'a manifold barrier to the moral progress and commercial prosperity of the people'. English was made the language of the schools, and children were whipped for speaking Welsh. England's English language laws and policies for Wales were not fully repealed until the Welsh Language Act of 1993.

Though the English language long needed to be promoted by the force of law, it has had a lengthy presence in Wales. The inhabitants of what came to be called the English Boroughs, like that in and around Pembroke Castle, spoke a native English. These communities were granted special privileges from as early as the eleventh century, and their position, reinforced by Edward I's castle building at the end of the thirteenth century, became unassailable after Henry VIII's language laws.

The Welsh resisted the imposition of English, and as late as the 1890s only a third of the population spoke it; none the less, English in Wales developed its own distinct accents, marked by a lilting quality that reflects a Celtic stress pattern falling on Germanic words. Welsh speakers of English developed two distinctive forms. The first was heard in the rural districts of north Wales; it was an English that developed in bilingual communities where the first language was Welsh. The second was heard in the nineteenth-century industrialized towns of south Wales. There, new English-speaking communities arose, formed by those who had had Welsh-speaking parents or grandparents but who had lost or were losing their own ability to speak Welsh.

Today, Welsh is enjoying something of a revival. The Education Act of 1988 made Welsh a compulsory subject in all secondary schools in Wales, and since 1996 Welsh has been compulsory at primary level. This current resurgence has arisen partly through these educational initiatives, but it has also been the result of confidence born of the independent Welsh Assembly's power to legislate, and so control the country's destiny more effectively than when subject to Tudor impositions.

4 THE BEGINNINGS OF MODERNITY

Oledjio for Yay Images

Bruges today showing houses virtually unchanged from the time when William Caxton worked as a printer in the fifteenth century

18 BRUGES – *the English language and the printing press* (1474)

In 1474, Bruges was not only one of the cities where the Duke of Burgundy held court, it was also the site of the printing of the first book in English. A London merchant had settled in Bruges in the late 1440s and had prospered to the point that he became a member of the household of Margaret, Duchess of Burgundy, sister to Kings Edward IV and Richard III of England. The merchant's name was William Caxton and, typically for the time, he was as much at home on the Continent as in England. The English were then as fluent with foreign tongues as the Dutch are today.

Visiting the German states, Caxton became fired up by the latest technological breakthrough – the printing press. In 1454, Johannes Gutenberg had amazed Europe by printing its first book. In the 1470s, Caxton saw presses at work in Cologne and, in 1474 very probably (1473 and 1475 are also cited), he collaborated with Flemish printers to produce the first printed book in English, *The Recuyell of the Historyes of Troye*. Caxton had translated it himself from French. His English word 'recuyell' comes from the French *recueil* and means 'a collection'. Words moved very easily from French into English in the fifteenth century.

Caxton had gone from England to Burgundy to trade. He now returned to England to print. Realizing the potential of the press, he set up shop in the City of Westminster where he printed and published a hundred titles. Caxton courted the court and was nimble in pursuit of royal patronage. Having served Edward IV and Richard III, he was, within a few years of Richard's death, working for Henry VII. Caxton undertook the job of printing Henry's parliamentary statutes. Their printing was in itself an innovation, but as significant was the fact that they were printed in English and not in French.

CAXTON'S LEGACY

The printing press that Caxton brought from Bruges to London transformed the reading world. Romances, prayer books, treatises, ballads and advertisements flooded London. Within a hundred years of printing's introduction, 25 per cent of Londoners had become readers – a remarkable percentage. Reading books and printed material became the pleasure of the common man rather than the preserve of the rich or the religious. When we cast our eye over today's best-selling book lists, we are unwittingly benefiting from Gutenberg's technological revolution. Caxton was not a linguist, but the dilemmas he faced are those faced by any book or internet editor today. What's the best word? How formal should I be? Which spelling do I use?

In his preface to a translation of Virgil's *Aeneid*, Caxton revealed his concerns:

And that comyn Englysshe that is spoken in one shyre varyeth from another. In so moche that in my dayes happened that certayn marchauntes were in a shippe in Tamyse [on the Thames] for to have sayled over the see into Zelande. And for lacke of wynde thai taryed atte forlond and wente to lande for to refreshe them. And one of theym named Sheffelde, a mercer, cam into an hows and axed for mete and specyaily he axyd after eggys. And the goode wyf answerde that she coude speke no Frenshe. And the marchaunt was angry, for he also coude speke no Frenshe, but wolde have hadde egges; and she understode hym not. And thenne at laste another sayd that he wolde have eyren; then the good wyf sayd that she understod hym wel. Loo! what sholde a man in thyse dayes now wryte, egges or eyren? Certaynly it is harde to playse every man bycause of dyversite and chaunge of langage.

The London printers' search for common forms drove the standardization of English. It is this that has ensured that English readers like you, wherever you are in the world, can comprehend this book. (See pages 71 and 97 for more on this.)

View of canal, belfry and houses in Bruges, Belgium

© Shutterstock

19 COLOGNE – *the Bible in English* (1525)

In 1521, William Tyndale was ordained a priest. He began preaching radical outdoor sermons in Cambridge and trying his hand at translating the Bible so that it might be understood, as he was later to say, by the ploughboy as easily as by the priest. Persecuted by local religious leaders, he headed for London. Three years later he fled to the independent city of Hamburg in order to continue the work of translating the Bible into English. That was something that his ecclesiastical superiors had forbidden him to do.

Tyndale was not the first Englishman to undertake a translation of the Bible; John Wycliffe and fellow Oxford scholars had translated Saint Jerome's Latin Bible, completing the great task by 1400. However, the English Bible's spread was hampered everywhere by the hostility of both the civil and ecclesiastical authorities. Possession of a Wycliffe Bible was made a heretical offence, punishable by the owner's burning.

Since 1522, when Martin Luther had translated the New Testament into German, there had been mounting pressure to produce an English version of the Bible. Luther, crucially, decided not to rely for his text on Saint Jerome's Latin Bible, the preferred text of the Catholic Church. Instead, he turned to materials in the original Greek and Hebrew. Luther inspired Tyndale to do for the English language what Luther was doing for the German language.

Having landed in Hamburg, Tyndale worked in various German towns until, in 1525, he began to print his New Testament initially in Cologne and then in Worms. In the next two years, 18,000 copies were printed. Although many of these were seized, sufficient numbers got through to enthusiastic followers in England. Then Tyndale began to work on the Old Testament. His Luther-inspired labours were seen to be a threat not only to the English, but also to the papal authorities, and in 1535 he was arrested and imprisoned. In 1536, he was strangled and burned.

Although Tyndale had not finished his translation, his work was taken up by Myles Coverdale who completed the final books of the Old Testament in a language little different from that of Tyndale himself. It was a language that Tyndale wanted to be as widely accessible as possible.

In 1538, Coverdale published a full English translation of the Bible. It came to be called the Great Bible; it was adopted by Henry VIII, who was by then in full opposition to the Pope, and it was ordered to be placed in every church in England. Then came a third name to join those of Tyndale and Coverdale – that of Thomas Cranmer.

In 1549, Cranmer used the Tyndale-Coverdale translations for The Book of Common Prayer that he created for the Church of England, as it had become. The Book of Common Prayer provided the order for daily and Sunday services through

Dunfermline 9 38 Canongate
93 Nicholson Street

98 Newcastle
4 Monkwearmouth

48 Stockton-on-Tees

5 York

Salford 55
Liverpool 80   59 Manchester

Smock Alley 39
Dublin 65

Llanfair 62 Hammerwich 3

Kilkenny 13

36 Lichfield   10 Peterborough
1 Undley Common
Stratford 24   Carleton 21 32 Trinity College
76 Bletchley Park
Christchurch College 61   Northolt
Pembroke 17   Oxford 75
Reading 11 22 London   Canterbury
79   2
Eton
Salisbury 30 6 Winchester   8 Hastings
Cerne 7   25
Chichester
Poldhu 67

73 Guernsey

Maps by Helen Joubert Design

Cologne Cathedral by night

the Christian year with biblical passages to be read in English for all to hear. For many, that was the way that they came to know the Bible. Cranmer could share Tyndale's and Coverdale's turn of phrase and language, thus making The Book of Common Prayer a seamless whole. At the same time, the Great Bible became the basis for a whole series of translations that culminated in the King James Bible of 1611 (see pages 73–5).

THE EXTRAORDINARY POWER OF TYNDALE'S TRANSLATION

The modern notion that all Christians should own a copy of the Bible became at least technically possible after 1450, when Johannes Guttenberg invented printing (see pages 56–7). Even so, in the face of considerable opposition from the Catholic Church, the invention of the printing press did not immediately lead to mass-produced vernacular versions of the Bible in England as it did in other parts of Europe. That had to wait until the seventeenth century.

But if Tyndale's Bibles were produced in relatively small numbers, the influence that his prose has exerted is enormous. It is shot through with phrases that are still widely used today. Examples include:

'Lead us not into temptation but deliver us from evil';
'fell flat on his face';
'the powers that be';
'signs of the times';
'sour grapes'.

cxiv.

The Gospell off
Sancte Jhon.
The fyrst Chapter.

I̅n the begynnynge was that worde/ a̅d that worde was with god: and god was thatt worde. The same was in the begynnynge wyth god. All thyngf were made by it/ and with out it/ was made noo thige/ that made was. In it was lyfe/ And lyfe was the light of me̅/ And the light shyneth i darck nes/ a̅d darck nes co̅prehe̅ded it not.

There was a ma̅ sent from god/ whose name was Jhon. The same ca̅ as a witnes/ to beare witnes of the light/ that all men through hi mygbt beleve. He was nott that light: but to beare witnes of the light. That was a true light/ whi ch lighteneth all men that come ito the worlde. He was in the worlde/ a̅d the worlde by hi was made: and the worlde knewe hym not.

He ca̅ ito his awne/ a̅d his received hi not. vnto as meny as received hi/ gave he power to be the so̅nes of god: i that they beleved o̅ his name: which were borne not of bloude no2 of the will of the flesshe/ no2 yet of the will of men: but of god.

And that worde was made flesshe/ and dwelt amonge vs/ and we sawe the glory off yt/ as the glory off the only begotten sonne off the father.

The first page of St John's Gospel in the Tyndale Bible

Lovers of Tyndale's language have included George Herbert, John Milton, John Bunyan, Isaac Watts, Alexander Pope, Charles Wesley, William Blake, Samuel Coleridge, Percy Shelley, Thomas Macaulay, Emily Dickinson, Thomas Hardy, D.H. Lawrence and T.S. Eliot. Talking of her childhood in Mississippi, Eudora Welty said that Tyndale's cadences 'entered our ears and our memories for good'. Tyndale's language is immediate, elliptical, pithy. It means more than it says. That is the Tyndale effect. Arguably, it is that effect that has been progressively lost since the Victorians began the process of modern translation.

 PARIS – *the beginnings of punctuation in the English language* (1530)

In 1530, Geoffroy Tory became official printer to King Francis I of France, and in 1532 he was made a librarian at the University of Paris in the Ile de France. With these appointments, he was in a position to do what he wanted to do with the French language. What he wanted was to make it fit for printing. The French people of the sixteenth century felt about French exactly as the English of the same century felt about English: the printing press was driving glorious, universal Latin out in place of an inferior, local tongue.

Geoffroy Tory was particularly concerned about French words that had lost their Latin spelling and had become, in his view, corrupted. He felt that the best thing to do was to indicate in various ways what the original forms had been. To that end, he introduced the apostrophe, accents, the comma and the cedilla to France. The cedilla he took from the Spanish. The comma he took from the Venetians. Accents in the form of diacritical marks had been used by the Ancient Greeks. Tory himself may have invented the apostrophe.

In fact, Classical Latin had used no punctuation at all. Writers, whether with the pen or the chisel, wrote in an unbroken flow of letters, thus: THEYWROTEINA- NUNBROKENFLOWOFLETTERS. Medieval scribes had introduced spaces between words, capital letters at the beginning of sentences, and small letters for the remainder. Stops and dashes were used fitfully, if at all.

THE POWER OF THE APOSTROPHE

English scholars shared Geoffroy Tory's concerns about the corruption of the Latin language, and they attempted some reforms such as rewriting the Middle English *dette* as 'debt' to remind users that the words came from the Latin *debitum*. That programme did not go very far, but English scholars were highly impressed by Tory's apostrophe.

Tory had used the apostrophe to indicate missing Latin letters; English scholars used it to indicate missing English letters – in particular in the possessive and the

Carolus

The chateau at Fontainebleau where King Francis held his court

plural forms of nouns. Once 'book's' had been spelled (and sounded) *bookis* and 'books' had been spelled (and sounded) *bookes*. Tory's apostrophe could be used to indicate the missing letters. In the eighteenth century, reformers refined this pattern. They banned the apostrophe for the plurals of nouns except in the possessive case, moving the apostrophe to the end of the noun so that 'books'' would mean 'of the books'. Tory's apostrophe was a poor solution for a problem that did not exist, and its use in the English language has been in a tangle ever since. Though the English also took the comma (see page 83), they left the accents and the cedilla to the French.

Shakespeare's pedant, Holofernes, advises that the 'apostrophas' be noted closely. And pedants today still delight in reminding us how inconsistently the apostrophe is used. The use of something like the simple apostrophe 'incorrectly' can provoke outbursts of anger. It can also be greeted with indifference. In 2003 Lynne Truss became something of a linguistic celebrity with her book *Eats, Shoots & Leaves* (the title dramatically changes its meaning according to whether there is a comma in it or not!). Her book's sub-title is indicative of its contents: 'The Zero Tolerance Approach to Punctuation'. She rails against examples where the singular possessive is used instead of the plural as in *Adult Learner's Week*, where plural is adopted instead of singular possessive *Bobs' Motors'*, or, hilariously, a host of occasions where it is either missed out – as in *Dicks in tray* – or extraneous to requirements – with perhaps the most ubiquitous of contemporary uses being examples such as *Cyclist's only*.

Truss, like Holofernes, is a pedant, albeit an amusing one. But she is by no means alone in her concern to punctuate righteously as if the English language is governed by laws, not conventions. Many others sit with eager eyes, waiting to rise up when their pet solecism is discovered in someone else's writing. (Yes, that last apostrophe is called for!)

21 CARLETON - *the influence of Latin on the English language* (1531)

Latin has been influencing English for well over 1,500 years; in fact, the original Germanic settlers of fifth-century Britannia brought with them a hundred or so Latin words that they had picked up from Roman soldiers on the northern frontier of the Roman Empire. These words included *butter*, *chalk*, *cheese*, *dish*, *mile*, *pepper*, *pound*, *sack*, *street* and *wine*.

The arrival of Christianity brought yet more words to seventh-century English, and then in the period from 1066 to 1500 thousands of words flowed from Latin into English, many by way of French. Therefore English was already used to taking words from Latin when there began the great infusion of Latin vocabulary that marks the English Renaissance.

In 1531, Sir Thomas Elyot of Carleton in Cambridgeshire published *The Boke Named the Governour*. He dedicated it to his king, Henry VIII, and told its reader that it 'explores the kind of moral principles which those intended for high office might need'. It was a best-seller in its day. Both Oxford and Cambridge claim Elyot as a student, though there is no clear evidence that he was at either university. For his part, he said that he had no tutor other than himself after the age of twelve.

The Governour established Elyot's reputation as someone who was passionate about classical thought and values. John Colet and Thomas More were also of this group. They were men with a deep knowledge of languages, and they based their own use of Latin not on church Latin, but on classical Latin – above all, that of Cicero. His complex, rich and rhetorical style was the model for their own.

It is significant that Elyot wrote *The Governour* in English for, although the Latin of his day was being refined and elevated, Latin was also coming to the end of its long period of domination. All across Europe, writers of learned works were beginning to use their own languages – Italian, French, Spanish, German, English. However, to find the vocabulary needed to give expression to all the arts, disciplines, letters and sciences, scholars took words wholesale from Latin, giving that ancient language a pale afterlife in the vernacular tongues.

That was a straightforward enough matter for Italian, French and Spanish, all of them descendants of Latin, all of them members of the Italic language family. Things were different for German and English, members of the Germanic family. German writers often decided that Italic words would look awkward in a German setting and so they tended to reconstruct Latin words as German words by translating the Latin elements. Latin had a word *d bilit re*. The Germans made it *entkräften*. However, the English made it 'debilitate', and they made no attempt to anglicize the new words. The fact that English had been taking words from French since 1066 meant that Italic or Latinate words did not upset the English eye and ear.

A TORRENT OF LATIN WORDS

The *Oxford English Dictionary* tells us that Sir Thomas Elyot was the first person to use the words 'abbreviate', 'abdicate', 'abhor', 'abide', 'abode', 'abolition', 'abortion', and 1,950 further words. Not all of Sir Thomas's new words came from Latin, but the majority did. Following the example set by the humanists, English writers imported some 20,000 words from Latin in the next three centuries. Words continued to be imported from French, and since most of those come ultimately from Latin, the English of the well-read person has today some 40,000 of Italic origin. It has only about 10,000 of Germanic origin.

Not everyone was as keen as Elyot on the changes that the humanists were bringing about. The new Latinate words were denounced as 'inkhorn' terms. An inkhorn was an inkwell made of horn and much used by scholars. When used as a term of criticism it meant 'pedantic', 'over-scholarly' or 'fussy'. Elyot described his coinings as 'necessary augmentations of our language'. In fact, some of his new words had a musty quality, among them 'deambulation', 'misentreating' and 'zelator'. Those and several others have not survived, but many of his imports have become familiar to us all.

Latin had a further influence on the English language when the humanists of the seventeenth century took a long look at English grammar and decided that it should be made to conform to Latin grammar. (That painful story is told on pages 97–9.)

22 NORTHOLT - *English spelling and the Great Vowel Shift* (1551)

In 1551, John Hart wrote *The Opening of the Unreasonable Writing of our Inglish Toung*. It was never published in his lifetime, but it was about English spelling, and it is thought to be the first systematic study of the subject. Hart suggested that, to bring order into English spelling, it was necessary for spelling to be phonologically based, arising directly from the way words were pronounced. To make this possible he introduced six new phonetic symbols for consonant sounds. He also developed a system of dots below and above vowels to indicate whether they were long or short forms.

Little is known about the man John Hart. Swedish scholars think he was born at Northolt in Middlesex, but English scholars are not so sure. What is definitely known is that he was dismayed by a phenomenon that English readers of today recognize only too well – that there is a misfit between the way English is spoken and the way it is spelled. No one had commented on this before the appearance of Early Modern English, and for an eminently sensible reason. There was a good fit between Old English speech and spelling and a pretty good fit between Middle English speech and spelling.

The good fit means that you can read *The Canterbury Tales* aloud as Chaucer spells it, and the bad fit means that you cannot read *Love's Labour's Lost* aloud as Shakespeare spells it. Something happened to English pronunciation between the death of Chaucer (1400) and the birth of Shakespeare (1564). What happened is called the Great Vowel Shift.

Chaucer's long vowel sounds, close in value to those of Modern Italian, were moved up and forwards in the mouth to give Shakespeare's long vowels new values, close to those of Modern English. No one knows why this vowel shift took place. It had the greatest effect in Midland English, especially East Midland English, the dialect of London.

The shift took place within 150 years, the fastest change in the history of the English language for a phenomenon on such a scale. It may have been the result of people changing from one dialect to another. Some say that the Black Death was the trigger because, having killed a third of the English population between 1348 and 1349, it then caused a population shift from the north of England to the southeast to fill a labour gap.

FIXING ENGLISH SPELLING

A prime reason for the distress of John Hart in 1551 and of continuing generations of schoolchildren is that the spelling of English got its fix in the last quarter of the fifteenth century. That was a time when London's pronunciation was in greatest flux, but it was also when the printing press arrived (see pages 56–7). William Caxton got to work in Westminster in 1476 and soon published a hundred books. Unfortunately, he and fellow printers were using a spelling system that was already out of date.

John Hart tried to reform things in the 1550s, but it was too late. Matters only got worse as English took words in not only from French, Latin and Greek, but from increasing numbers of foreign languages. To some extent, the French try to naturalize foreign words, but the English have never done that, and English spelling is in a parlous state today.

Early nineteenth-century America achieved a partial reform with the work of Noah Webster, but he only dealt with about 500 words and his spellings are only to be found in American English. The joke, attributed to George Bernard Shaw, is that 'ghoti' spells 'fish' if you take the 'gh' from 'enough', the 'o' from 'women', and the 'ti' from 'dictionary'. Shaw probably did not say this, but he did leave a substantial sum in his will for the reform of English spelling. Nothing came of it.

If we were now to attempt to reform English spelling, the first question would have to be: on whose accent should we base the new spellings?

23 ARCHANGEL – *business English* (1553)

In 1553, English seamen navigated a new trade route by way of the Barents and White Seas. They were looking for a northeast passage to China. What they found was the city of Arkhangelsk or, as they called it, Archangel in Muscovy. They met with Tsar Ivan IV, and they returned to London with a letter from him expressing a desire to trade. Encouraged, 240 London merchants banded together to create an entity that they called the Muscovy Company by which they would share both the expenses and profits to be made through exploiting the new trading opportunity. Their venture was given a charter by Queen Mary of England and special privileges by Tsar Ivan of the Rus. The world's first joint-stock company had been created.

The joint-stock company shared the risk of a venture among a number of merchants, but offered great prospects in proportion to the stock in the company that the individual purchased. The Muscovy Company was followed by many others, among them the East India Company, the Virginia Company, and the Plymouth Company. By the end of the seventeenth century, London had registered over a hundred companies, and a lively trade developed that focused not merely on the commodities that the companies traded, but also on the stock in the companies themselves.

By 1700, the modern business world had emerged and, with it, new meanings to the words 'auditor', 'bond', 'call', 'demand', 'equity', 'fixture', 'gross', 'hedge', 'index', 'junk', 'liability', 'margin', 'market', 'net', 'offer', 'pit', 'reserve', 'share', 'tick', 'underwriter', 'volume', and 'yield'.

Arms of the East India Company in St Matthias Church, Poplar, showing three ships in full sail

THE DEVELOPMENT OF BUSINESS ENGLISH

All trades and professions have their own vocabularies or 'jargons' and the business world is not unusual in that respect. However, there is worldwide idiom called Business English, and that is more than a special vocabulary. It is an English made up of the conventions that have developed in the last 300 years to guide business correspondence.

By the nineteenth century, there were available numerous guides containing model letters to cover every business eventuality, and they were filled with abbreviated forms, often based on Latin phrases such as *inst.*, *prox.*, *ult.* They meant 'this month', 'next month', 'last month'. *Inst.* is an abbreviation of *instante mense*, and a letter might begin: 'Thank you for yours of the 2 inst', meaning: 'Thank you for your letter of the 2nd of this month'. The formulas and abbreviations speeded things up, especially when everything was being written by hand.

Early twentieth-century business letters in the United States were already moving towards a less crabbed style, demonstrated in this model letter of 1911:

> Mesdames :
>
> Will you kindly furnish us with information respecting Messrs. Brown Brothers, of Columbus, Ohio? These gentlemen have given your name as reference, saying that you would probably recommend that a credit of $50,000 (fifty thousand) be given them. This is a large sum to grant under the circumstances, so we should be greatly indebted to you for your opinion as to their trustworthiness. As the matter is urgent you may 'phone us on 'Change here at our expense. We shall hold ourselves at your disposal at any time for a corresponding service here in the East.
>
> Respectfully yours,

Today, there are hundreds of books available to teach Business English. The language has become less formal, but still relies on formulas so that business can be transacted with the minimum of friction. In addition to the standard model letters, twenty-first-century guides provide both models for the new forms of communication and warnings against using them improperly:

> Do NOT send or receive personal e-mail at work. (Don't surf the Web or shop online.) Besides the fact that using your company's computer for personal tasks is inappropriate and unprofessional, it can also cost you your job. Remember, E-MAIL IS NOT PRIVATE. It can be monitored. It is stored. And it can be used against you at any time.

The e-mail is probably the most used business format, accounting for millions of messages daily, the majority of them in English (see pages 195–6). It is just one of many electronic formats that have made English the dominant language of the internet, and Business English the language of world business.

© Shakespeare Birthplace Trust

Anne Hathaway's cottage, where Shakespeare courted his wife

24 STRATFORD – *the development of Early Modern English* (1564)

William Shakespeare was born in a place that has become a shrine to the English language, but the English celebrated at Stratford-upon-Avon today is not the English spoken in the Stratford-upon-Avon of 1564. Stratford is in Warwickshire where the local speech derived from Mercian. Mercian had been the Old English dialect once heard from the Wash to the Welsh Hills and from the Humber to the Thames (see pages 20–22).

In this great midland region of England, the counties of the east coast were very much more influenced by invading Norse speakers than the counties to the west. Those counties were beyond the Danelaw with its western boundary of Watling Street. Either side of it, Mercian gave rise to two Middle English dialects, East Midland English, the dialect of *The Canterbury Tales*, and West Midland English, the dialect of 'Sir Gawayn and the Grene Knyght'.

Midland English is what Shakespeare spoke as a boy. It had its own accent, vocabulary and grammar. These features, what the Victorians called Warwickshireisms, can be detected in his plays. Words and personal names provide the greatest number, but perhaps the most significant feature is a grammatical one. West Midlanders said 'he walks', not 'he walketh'.

'Walks' and 'walketh' alternate in Shakespeare's plays, and when he went to London in the 1580s, he would have found a linguistic contest going on between the two forms. People came to London speaking every kind of English, but, primarily, London's English was East Midland English. That was the dialect closest to Shakespeare's own, and, at the West End of London, East Midland English was turning itself into a prestige dialect. The equality of dialects that was characteristic of Middle English was going. At the same time, English was turning itself into a learned language so that it could be a vehicle for every kind of knowledge. To do that, written English was regularizing its spelling and grammar and expanding its vocabulary. Between 1500 and 1700, it took some 20,000 words from Latin.

London, as always, was the place to be, but perhaps never more so than when Shakespeare arrived. London English was a focal point of every kind of linguistic pressure and excitement, and Londoners more than others must have been exposed to unfamiliar voices. Shakespeare made fun of characters who speak with rural, Welsh, Irish or Scots accents. All the playwrights of his day enjoyed doing this. At the same time, playwrights mocked people who filled their language with fine-sounding, foreign-sounding words. In *Love's Labours Lost*, one of his earliest plays, Shakespeare laughed at the Latinate language of Holofernes the scholar as much as he did the country talk of Costard the clown.

THE INFLUENCE OF SHAKESPEARE ON THE ENGLISH LANGUAGE
With his plays and poems, Shakespeare made East Midland English an immortal language, and his works have become the possession of the world. English has now become a global language, and Stratford-upon-Avon has become a place of pilgrimage, but, when there, language lovers may like to keep half an ear open for Warwickshireisms.

Shakespeare influenced English vocabulary on so many different levels – through coining new words, by using existing words in different ways, and by creating idioms and sayings that are still used today. The *Oxford English Dictionary* lists Shakespeare as the first person to give written evidence of some thousand words. Like Chaucer (see pages 45–7), Shakespeare's use of these words led others to use them so that they have regularly entered the general vocabulary. Shakespeare's contributions include: *auspicious, barefaced, chimney-top, dog-weary, enmesh, featureless, generous, honey-tongued, ill-tempered, jaded, kitchen-wench, lacklustre, marketable, neverending, olympian, priceless, quarrelsome, retirement, sanctimonious, tardiness, uneducated, varied, well-read, yelping* and *zany*.

His idioms and sayings still resonate. Here are a few of them:

'The course of true love never did run smooth' (*Midsummer Night's Dream*);
'Truth will out' and 'All that glitters is not gold' (*Merchant of Venice*);
'Short shrift' (*Richard III*);
'Method in my madness' and 'More in sorrow than in anger' (*Hamlet*);
'Set your teeth on edge' and 'Send him packing' (*Henry IV Part I*);
'Wild goose chase' and 'A rose by any other name' (*Romeo and Juliet*);
'Too much of a good thing' (*As You Like It*);
'All's well that ends well' (*All's Well That Ends Well*).

William Shakespeare's English put the language on a footing equal to that of Homer, Virgil and Dante.

25 CHICHESTER – *English grammar* (1586)

In 1586, a Chichester schoolmaster published *William Bullokarz pamphlet for grammar: Or rather too be saied hiz abbreuiation of hiz grammar for English, extracted out-of hiz grammar at-larg.* More generally known as *Pamphlet for Grammar* by William Bullokar, it was the first grammar of the English language. (Its title reflected one of many failed plans to reform English spelling – see pages 65–6.)

Pamphlet for Grammar was a classroom book that Bullokar wrote to teach his children to read and write the English language. In the sixteenth century, those skills were usually expected to be a side effect of learning to read and write Latin.

Although Bullokar was taking a radical step, his English grammar was modelled on a Latin one, Lily's *Royal Grammar*, which had been compiled by William Lily and ordered by Henry VIII to be used in all the grammar schools of England. The *Royal Grammar* set a pattern that led teachers to believe that English should follow Latin, and, over the course of the next two centuries, new rules were created for English grammar. Children were told that sentences should not end with a preposition; double negatives should not be used; double comparatives should not be used; infinitives should not be split.

As a result of a bias towards a foreign grammar, written English was set against the grain of spoken English. English writers had to be constantly on guard. When grammarians turned to the great writers to find good models, it was an unhappy fact that not a single one of them could be relied upon to write according to the new idea of correctness. Shakespeare, Milton, Dryden, Addison and Pope were all found to have broken some of the rules at some time in some of their works. Grammarians delighted in pointing that out. In his *Grammar of the English Language*, William

Cobbett had a section entitled 'Specimens of False Grammar, Taken from the Writings of Dr. Johnson'.

STANDARDIZING ENGLISH GRAMMAR

Cobbett picked on Johnson because, with the publication in 1755 of Samuel Johnson's *Dictionary of the English Language*, it may be said that the rules for a Standard English Grammar had been established. Johnson's Preface to the *Dictionary* is one of the best statements of those rules; the *Dictionary* itself, of course, fixed some 40,000 English spellings (see pages 97–9).

At the end of the eighteenth century, what is probably the most influential of all English grammars was published. It was the work of an American called Lindley Murray. It appeared in its first edition in 1795 with the title *The English Grammar Adapted to the Different Classes of Learner*. It was in use, along with the cane, in every public school in nineteenth-century England. So many children had suffered at the hands of Murray's *Grammar* that Charles Dickens only had to mention it to make his readers roar with laughter. It has never been out of print.

The term 'an English grammar' popularly means a book that gives people the rules for correct English. Such a book is a prescriptive grammar. Linguists prefer descriptive grammars, books that describe how a language works – not ones that prescribe the rules for a language.

What, then, is grammar? An answer is provided by the linguist Daniel Everett. He points out that humans use words – as animals do – but humans also use sentences. Humans 'organize their sounds into patterns and then organize these sound patterns into grammatical patterns of words and sentences. This layered organization of human speech is what enables us to communicate so much more than any other species.' By way of changing word order and changing word endings, grammar provides that second level of patterning.

Grammar enables humans to go beyond the codes of animals and to express complex meanings. Children have an innate understanding of the grammar of the languages they learn naturally. However, some educationalists argue that children should be given an explicit understanding of grammar. Such an understanding is unnecessary for most of English grammar, but it is useful for understanding those Latinate rules imported into English in the sixteenth and seventeenth centuries.

26 HAMPTON COURT – *the English Language and the King James Bible* (1604)

In 1604, James, king of England and king of Scots, convened a Conference at Hampton Court to order a new translation into English of the Bible. James was a man of religious conviction, and that might not have boded well for the venture on which he launched his scholars. Previous translations had generated theological acrimony and religious rivalry, but when, in 1611, the job was done, the King James Bible began its progress to become one of the most loved books in the English language.

Martin Luther's German translation of the New Testament that appeared in 1522 prompted William Tyndale and Miles Coverdale to start on English translations (see pages 58–62). Many followed their lead, and fifty different English versions of all or parts of the Bible were published between 1526 and 1611. The part translations were commonly of the Psalms or of a Gospel, but many full translations appeared, notably the Great Bible of 1538 that Henry VIII ordered for his English Church, the Geneva Bible of 1560 that the Puritans ordered for the Calvinist Church, the Bishops Bible of 1568 that the Anglicans ordered for the Church of England, and the Douay Bible of 1610 that the Catholics ordered for the Church of Rome.

The major difference between those Bibles were their notes; theological commentaries that were, in James's opinion, often 'partiall, untrue, seditious, and savouring, too much, of dangerous, and traiterous conceipts'. The king wanted a Bible that could be the common property of the Puritan and Anglican parties in the Church of England, and in 1611 his Bible appeared without notes. It offered such a sound translation that for the next 250 years few English scholars felt that any significant changes needed to be made. The English had their Bible.

THE INFLUENCE OF THE KING JAMES BIBLE

The King James Bible began a steady advance into the consciousness and then into the language of English speakers, the majority of whom were hearing readings from it every Sunday in their churches. Its influence has probably been more upon the written language than the spoken language, but the latter is formidable, and it is recognized mainly via the Bible's provision of everyday sayings. In *The Stories of English*, David Crystal lists the ones we have taken from the King James's version of St Matthew's Gospel:

man shall not live by bread alone; the salt of the earth; the light of the world; an eye for an eye and a tooth for a tooth; our daily bread; treasures in heaven; no man can serve two masters; pearls before swine; [a wolf] in sheep's clothing; weeping and gnashing of teeth; new wine [in] old bottles; lost sheep; the blind leading the blind; the signs of the times.

The title page of the first edition of the King James Bible

English speakers have taken a thousand more sayings from the King James Bible, and these are used today by people who have neither read nor heard the version. The sayings cover a multitude of everyday situations, and the phrases wait, ready coined, to be used as good currency in everyday speech. Even those few sayings above from Matthew give the feel of the King James language. We sense that there is so much more being meant than is actually being said. Those sayings also give a good sense of the remarkable vocabulary of that language.

There are some 800,000 words in the King James Bible, but a vocabulary count shows that it uses no more than 8,000 root-words. Plain, simple language accumulates great force.

5 THE BEGINNINGS OF WORLD ENGLISH

JAMESTOWN – 1607

HAMILTON – 1609

THE MERMAID TAVERN – 1623

SALISBURY – 1631

HOLBORN – 1660

TRINITY COLLEGE – 1670

PHILADELPHIA – 1682

NÎMES – 1695

BOSTON – 1704

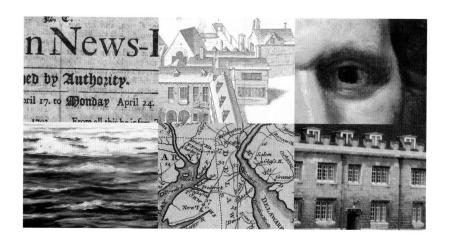

Map of Virginia as described by the expedition leader, Captain John Smith

27 JAMESTOWN – *the English language in the Americas* (1607)

In 1607, after a difficult Atlantic voyage and much hardship, 105 people established the first permanent English settlement in the Americas. They sailed up a river they called the James, and they set up home in a place they named Jamestown after their king, James I of England.

If the first settlers in a country come in large enough numbers, they can set continuing language patterns. That is the case with the Jamestown settlement. The James flows into Chesapeake Bay, and by 1700 over 250,000 men and women had migrated to the region. The majority of them came from the English West Country by way of Bristol. The speech of those people provided the starting point of Southern English, a dialect heard today in the seaboard states south from Delaware through to Georgia and then west as far as Texas.

Southern English is not a single thing, and it had already begun to develop three forms in Virginia by 1700. Jamestown initially had more deaths than births, and it was only sustained by new arrivals from England until the settlers discovered ways of growing tobacco. A single ship-load landed in London could set a man up for life. The best tobacco land was the lowland between the coast and the foothills; the settlers called it the Tidewater. The second best was the higher land, the foothills of the Appalachians; they called that the Piedmont.

In the Tidewater, the first plantations were established and the first fortunes made. Although the main body of migrants came from the English West Country, a large number of Londoners got land in the Tidewater. An accent resulted that mixed elements of London English with West Country English. The London English was one much influenced by an upper class. Tidewater English then became a mark of prestige. Tidewater is the aristocratic drawl to be heard in the voices of the wealthy planter and his lady in films showing the Old South. That has made a Southern drawl an admired characteristic of a number of American accents. In Britain, by contrast, the drawl is seen as characteristic of rural dialects, like that of the West Country. Whether or not a particular speech feature is attractive is a matter of social tuning, not linguistic fact.

Tidewater and Piedmont English (now called Southern Coastal English and Southern English) are both different from a third English that developed from the original West Country English of Virginia. Those who learnt this third form of English were the Africans who were enslaved to work on the tobacco plantations. Their dialect, called today African American English, is a variant of American Southern English, but it has evolved very differently in the 300 years of its existence. That story is told on pages 164–5.

THE DIVERSITY OF AMERICAN ENGLISHES

Reaching from the Arctic to the Rio Grande and from the Atlantic to the Pacific, North American English has a number of dialects, but far less than in the British Isles. Dialects develop through time and in isolation. English has been in the Americas for just over 400 years, and first the railroad – and then the automobile – have kept English speakers well mixed. None the less, North American English shows distinct dialectal differences, and the majority of linguists trace the origins of these to the different starting points of seventeenth-century settlers.

Westcountry people, Londoners and Africans are among the founder groups for North American English. Other accounts, though, need to be told about the English-speaking groups entering America by way of Philadelphia and Boston to get the fuller pattern of North American English. But it is interesting to note that the majority of linguists do not attribute much more than vocabulary to the vast numbers of immigrants who did not speak English. They are not thought to have made any great impact on North American accents or grammar.

All of this diversity can trace its origins back to a small band of Jamestown pioneers. And today the 335 million people of the North American English-speaking community have become the largest group of native English speakers in the world.

28 HAMILTON – *the English language in the West Indies* (1609)

Two years after the party of merchant adventurers had founded Jamestown, in Virginia, another London party, attempting to join them, was shipwrecked on an island that the Spanish had named Bermuda. The year was 1609. The voyagers rebuilt their ship and finally reached Jamestown in 1610. Their adventure became so well known that William Shakespeare alluded to it in *The Tempest*, a play about a storm, a shipwreck and an island. Meanwhile, the English decided to keep hold of Bermuda. By 1629, there were around 2,000 people on Bermuda at a time when New England had no more than 500 or so. In 1793, Bermuda was given a capital city called Hamilton.

Bermuda is not geographically in the West Indies, but it is linguistically part of them. The English language spread from Bermuda as the English spread, occupying one island after another – the Bahamas, Jamaica, the Caymans, Antigua, Montserrat,

Christopher M. Grimes

Wreck of the *Sea Venture* off Bermuda on 28 July 1609, as depicted in a contemporary oil painting by Christopher M. Grimes

the Virgin Islands, Barbados, St Kitts, the Turks and Caicos Islands, Dominica, Grenada, St Lucia, St Vincent, Trinidad and Tobago. Beyond Trinidad, the mainland of South America can be seen, and the English even made a settlement there called Guiana (now Guyana). Today, in all these countries, a British English has become the prestige dialect. At the same time, English is not the only post-colonial language in the West Indies. Spanish, French, Dutch and Danish are all to be heard on the Caribbean islands.

AN ACCIDENT OF WAR

The story of the English language in the West Indies might have been part of the story of the English language in North America. Bermuda was, indeed, initially incorporated into the colony of Virginia. In 1775, there would have been little difference in the speech of the British (as the English were now calling themselves) in Bridgetown, Barbados and Boston. The break came in 1776 when the British in the West Indies sided with Great Britain, and not with the newly declared United States.

In the event, the story of the English language in the West Indies is like that of the English language in West Africa. On the bigger islands – Jamaica, Barbados and Trinidad – the evolution of English has paralleled the evolution of English in countries like Ghana and Nigeria. Formal, patois and creole versions of English work side by side. Many people are fluent in all three. A difference between the West Indies and West Africa is that the indigenous languages of the West Indians have disappeared, along with the people who spoke them. The original Caribs and Arawaks were exterminated. They were replaced by enslaved Africans. Millions of slaves passed through the West Indies en route to the Americas, but many went no further than the deadly Caribbean sugar plantations. Their descendants make up the majority of the island populations today.

West Indians can usually tell at once from which of any of a dozen islands a speaker comes. The larger islands have developed English creoles – complex, natural languages that have emerged from simple contact languages. Visitors to the islands are addressed in easily understood West Indian English, but if islanders are talking among themselves in Jamaican Labrish, Barbadian Bajan or Trinidadian Patois, that may be too fast for the visitor to understand.

The Jamaican poet Louise Bennett provides a chance for us to hear Labrish:

An wen we try fe warn you Lize,
Yuh always chat we out,
Yuh chat an chat till govament
Come income-tax yuh mout!
Start a-talk yuh neighbor busines
Form a labrish committee!

[And when we tried to warn you, Liz,
You always talk us down,
You talk and talk until the government
Will income-tax your mouth!
Start a talk-about-your-neighbours business,
Form a gossip committee!]

29 THE MERMAID TAVERN – *the refining of English punctuation* (1623)

Portrait of Ben Jonson by Abraham van Blyenberch

When he was not writing, Ben Jonson was likely to have been found in the Mermaid Tavern in Cheapside where he spent much time drinking, listening and talking. While Jonson is well known for his plays and poetry, especially the former, he is much less remembered for his contribution to English punctuation. In 1623 a fire in Jonson's library destroyed a book he had been labouring at for some time. It was the first draft of his *English Grammar*. In 1640, three years after his death, this little-known book was published.

Jonson's grammar was not the first in English: that honour goes to William Bullokar some thirty-seven years earlier. But Jonson's version really broke free of the domination of Latin that was evident in Bullokar's work (see pages 71–2). The full title, *The English Grammar, made by Ben Jonson, for the benefit of all strangers, out of the observation of the English language, now spoken and in use*, also points to an important new interest in the spoken as well as the written word.

Jonson has one of the most extraordinary handwritten signatures – Ben:Jonson. By separating his two names with a double *punctus* ('double pricks' as he termed it) or, as we would say, a colon, Jonson was consciously distinguishing himself from others. For while important ecclesiastical figures sometimes inserted a colon between their names when they used a Latinized signature on official documents, no one else used the colon like Jonson did. It has been suggested that Jonson is deliberately using the colon to separate his first and last name, his private and public personas, just as a colon might be used to separate, yet connect, two clauses within a sentence. Or maybe it just shows his fascination with punctuation marks.

THE DEVELOPMENT OF PUNCTUATION MARKS

At the dawn of printing in England in the fifteenth century, William Caxton used three punctuation marks. Strokes (/) marked groups of words, colons suggested pauses in syntax, and full stops showed the end of sentences. In 1530, as we read on page 62, Geoffroy Tory was influential in introducing the apostrophe. In 1566, a precocious young Italian printer, Aldus Manutius the Younger, attempted to write a standard guide to punctuation.

But in the first part of the seventeenth century there was still huge variation among printers as to the way punctuation was to be used in English. In his *English Grammar*, Jonson seeks to bring some order to the use of punctuation marks which, for him, seem to have served not only to make sense of the rhythm of any text, just as an actor and playwright of his talents might well have done, but also to suggest its syntax more clearly.

Apostrophe (apostrophus) = the 'rejecting of a vowel from the beginning or ending of a word';

Comma = 'a mean breathing, when the word serveth indifferently, both to the parts of the sentence going before and following after';

Semicolon = 'a distinction of an imperfect sentence, wherein with somewhat a longer breath, the sentence following is included';

Colon (pause) = 'a distinction of a sentence, though perfect in itself, yet joined to another, being marked with two pricks';

Full stop (period) = 'is the distinction of a sentence, in all respects perfect';

Question mark = 'if a sentence be with an interrogation';

Exclamation mark = 'if it be pronounced with admiration'.

Jonson even describes parentheses as 'wherein two comma's include a sentence'. Interestingly, the smart-eyed among you will have spotted a strange use of the apostrophe before the letter 's' in 'comma's'. The rules for the apostrophe varied from one writer to another and from one expert to another. They remain filled with contradictions to this day.

English punctuation has never been settled, and the rules have changed every century. Today, texters, tweeters, bloggers and e-mailers often dispense with punctuation altogether. It is instructive to realize what little difference it makes.

30 SALISBURY – *the English language and the language of the law* (1631)

In his diary, Samuel Pepys recorded 'a good story of a prisoner's being condemned at Salisbury for a small matter'. In January 1631, the prisoner, while waiting to hear his sentence, took the opportunity to throw a stone at the judge, Chief Justice Richardson. The stone missed. However, Richardson, who was considering handing out a reduced sentence, immediately ordered the man's hand be cut off and nailed to the gibbet. After that, the man was hanged.

Pepys's account was short and pithy, but the legal record of the incident was not. Supplied in a footnote to a nineteenth-century edition of the diary, it read as follows:

Richardson, ch. Just. de C. Banc al Assises at Salisbury in Summer 1631. fuit assault per prisoner la condemne pur felony que puis son condemnation ject un Brickbat a le dit Justice que narrowly mist, & pur ceo immediately fuit Indictment drawn per Noy envers le Prisoner, & son dexter manus ampute & fix al Gibbet, sur que luy mesme immediatement hange in presence de Court.

That report was written in a combination of Law French, Law Latin and Law English. The French was Anglo-Norman, the Latin was medieval, and the English was a four-teenth-century add-in. Translation is needed:

> Richardson, Chief Justice of Common Bench at the Assizes at Salisbury in Summer 1631. There was an assault by a prisoner there condemned for felony; who, following his condemnation, threw a brickbat at the said Justice, which narrowly missed. And for this, an indictment was immediately drawn by Noy against the prisoner, and his right hand was cut off and fastened to the gibbet, on which he himself was immediately hanged in the presence of the Court.

The legal language of the seventeenth century represented an extreme form of linguistic and professional conservatism. It was a final refuge of the use of French in England, and it had become so grotesque that lawyers were finally obliged to abandon it.

THE LEGACY OF LEGAL ENGLISH

None the less, lawyers have kept a great number of Latin and French words and phrases as special terms. The normal thing is for words to change their meanings, either by a sudden shift or by a slow drift. Lawyers resist that linguistic tendency, attempting to give a legal and restricted meaning to the words that they use. Latin and French fossils, impervious to meaning change, serve them well.

As a result, Law Latin is still used in court. Examples are *ad hoc, ad hominem, ad infinitum, bona fides, de facto, de jure, et cetera, habeas corpus, Magna Carta, magnum opus, non sequitur, nota bene, per se, post mortem, quantum, veto, vice versa.*

Law French still gives us *attorney, bailiff, culprit, defendant, escheat, allodial, estoppel, force majeure, mortgage, plaintiff, profit a prendre, recovery, remainder, replevin, torts, voir dire.*

It is worth noting that Law English can be as difficult as Law Latin and French. Law English uses words that are common enough in everyday conversation, but in the courts and in legal documents they have unexpected meanings. Among them are words like *alienation, bar, best, brief, consideration, count, dock, hearing, infant, leave, lodging, presentment, satisfaction, stay, title.*

Why do lawyers hold on to old meanings? One reason is that old words and phrases have been tested in court time and time again. Lawyers need to be accurate, and they need to be sure that they are not going to get things wrong by allowing some misunderstanding to creep in. If lawyers stick to the language they learn in law school, they are less likely to go wrong, and, if they do go wrong, they are less likely to be blamed.

A good conversation is a kind of dancing, but what goes on in court is a kind of wrestling. And verbal wrestling is what we see in legal documents. It is the outcome of using language when the users cannot trust one another. The wiliness of legal language reflects the wiliness of human beings rather well.

31 HOLBORN – *making English the language of science* (1660)

With the Restoration of King Charles II to the throne of England in 1660, a group of learned men elected to meet regularly at Gresham College in Holborn, London, 'for the Improving of Natural Knowledge'. In 1662, the king was pleased to show his favour to these philosophers and scholars by allowing them to call themselves the Royal Society.

In place of the painstaking study of ancient authorities, the Society required that intuitions about the nature of things should be tested by experiments that were to be judged valid by a process of publication and replication. If the learned world could replicate the original experimenter's results and they were judged to be important, those results would be admitted to the sum of new knowledge.

Publication was crucial to the new method, and the Fellows believed that their

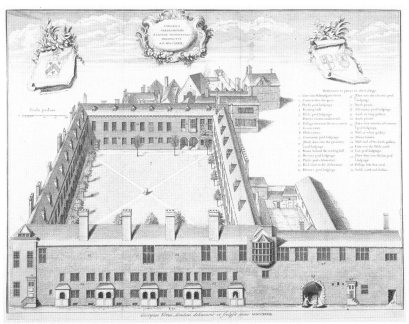

An eighteenth-century engraving of Gresham College by John Vertue

Courtesy of Gresham College

new learning required a new kind of writing. Their first historian, Thomas Sprat, feared that the scientific enterprise was endangered by men's love of rhetoric, the ancient art of public speaking. What he wanted was plain speaking; he wanted evidence-based argument, not emotion-based argument. For Sprat, rhetoric was 'in Open defiance against Reason; professing, not to hold much correspondence with that; but with its Slaves, the Passions: they give the mind a motion too changeable, and bewitching, to consist with right practice. Who can behold, without Indignation, how many mists and uncertainties, these specious Tropes and Figures have brought on our Knowledge?'

Sprat wanted the language of scientific publication to be English, not Latin, but, to rival Latin, English had to be brought to the level of Latin. Latin had been Western Europe's learned language for a thousand years; none the less, Latin was being replaced by new learned languages. The lead had been taken by the Italians and the French. The Accademia della Crusca had been founded in Florence in 1583 with a mission to make Tuscan Italian the language of education and scholarship. The Académie française had been founded in Paris in 1635 to do the same for Parisian French. Although the Royal Society of London was not given a formal role in the reshaping of the English language, the prose style it encouraged was perfected in the eighteenth century by writers like Joseph Addison and Richard Steele.

A NEW BREED CALLED SCIENTISTS

But there was something more that needed to be done if the English language was to become a vehicle for every kind of knowledge. The word 'scientist' did not exist at the time of the Royal Society's founding, but that is the term that we now use to describe its Fellows. As well as finding a word to describe themselves, scientists have had a need since 1660 to find hundreds of thousands of words to describe the objects and actions of their ever-expanding areas of natural knowledge. Their words went on to fill scholarly papers, encyclopaedias, textbooks and translations from other languages. The scientific journal *Philosophical Transactions* was probably the first international science journal written in English. Its first issue was printed in 1665. Interestingly, when Isaac Newton published his treatise on mathematics, known as *Principia*, he did so in Latin. But his later work on light, *Opticks*, was written in English. Of course one of the reasons for Latin being used for scientific writing rather than English was that, at this stage, Latin was the better lingua franca for scholars from other countries.

Latin was also important as scientists all over Europe began to take words from it to build new vocabularies. Soon they were needing words for things that the Romans had never seen nor even imagined. Undeterred, scientists took to using parts of Latin words to make entirely new words. They used Ancient Greek in the same way. Today, it is estimated that 90 per cent of scientific terms have been created from recycled Latin and Greek. The result is called the International Scientific Vocabulary.

Remarkably, the language in which the majority of the world's scientists use this vocabulary is neither Italian nor French. It is English. The scientific papers that the Royal Society demanded of its members have become the worldwide way of presenting scientific results. Today, tens of thousands of English-language scientific journals complete the Society's circle of intuition, experiment and publication.

The nineteenth-century scientist Michael Faraday provided models of plain, clear scientific prose. Here is a sample from his *Chemical History of a Candle*:

> Then there is another point about these candles which will answer a question – that is, as to the way in which this fluid gets out of the cup, up the wick, and into the place of combustion. You know that the flames on these burning wicks in candles made of beeswax, stearin, or spermaceti, do not run down to the wax or other matter, and melt it all away, but keep to their own right place. They are fenced off from the fluid below, and do not encroach on the cup at the sides. I can not imagine a more beautiful example than the condition of adjustment under which a candle makes one part subserve to the other to the very end of its action. A combustible thing like that, burning away gradually, never being intruded upon by the flame, is a very beautiful sight, especially when you come to learn what a vigorous thing flame is – what power it has of destroying the wax itself when it gets hold of it, and of disturbing its proper form if it come only too near.

32 TRINITY COLLEGE – *English proverbs* (1670)

John Ray was a polymath and extraordinary scholar. He spent much of his life at Trinity College, Cambridge, where he held an array of different positions while undertaking his research. Best remembered for his pioneering work in rethinking the way biological species were classified, he was also a remarkable linguist. Indeed the words 'petal' and 'pollen' were first used by him.

Two books encapsulate his special contribution to English. The first is *A Collection of English Words*, which defines and groups dialect words according to the different regions of England. But the second is the book on which we are focusing here, *A Collection of English Proverbs*.

Proverbs memorably express a truth or seek to describe a common experience. The Preface to one of the later editions of *A Collection* puts it like this: 'The dignity also of proverbs is self-evident. They are not to be reckoned insignificant trifles only fit for schoolboys…they drive the nail home in discourse and clinch it with the strongest conviction.' Succinctly worded proverbs have the capacity to speak to us

The Great Court of Trinity College, Cambridge

memorably and profoundly. Many of them – such as 'the early bird catcheth the worm', first recorded by Ray – have entered the collective unconscious of English-language speakers.

PROVERBS OF AND BEYOND THEIR TIME

It is instructive to look at a selection of the proverbs chosen by Ray. A few are still in use now. Many express truths that are still very relevant. A few of them are very much of their time – the cough, which presumably presaged the plague, and the reference to hare coursing and wolves. But the vast majority do not take much investigation to yield their essential wisdom in a still intelligible pithy form. They are the English language at its most potent.

A   He that is angry is seldom at ease.
Long absent soon forgotten.

B   Be not a baker if your head be of butter.
The beggar is never out of his way.

C   Who never climbed never fell.
Care will kill a cat.
A dry cough is a trumpeter of death.

D   A good dog deserves a good bone.
Dogs wag their tails not so much in love to you as to your bread.

E   The early bird catcheth the worm.
In the end things will mend.

F Who hath a fair wife needs more than two eyes.
Faint heart ne'er won fair lady.
A fool and his money are soon parted.

G Look not a gift horse in the mouth.
All is not gold that glitters.

H What the heart thinketh the tongue speaketh.
Honey is sweet but the bee stings.

I Itch and ease can no man please.

K A knotty piece of timber must have smooth wedges.

L He liveth long that liveth well.
Love lives in cottages as well as in courts.

M He who marrieth for wealth selleth his liberty.
You must not let your mousetrap smell of cheese.

N It's more painful to nothing than something.

O One shrewd turn asks another.

P Poverty is the mother of health.

S Everything is good in its season.
One hour's sleep before midnight's worth two after.
A smiling boy seldom proves a good servant.

T The tide will fetch away what the ebb brings.

U No cut to unkindness.

V Valour can do little without discretion.

W Tread on a worm and it will turn.
The greatest wealth is contentment with a little.
Wolves lose their teeth but not their memory.
What is a workman without his tools.

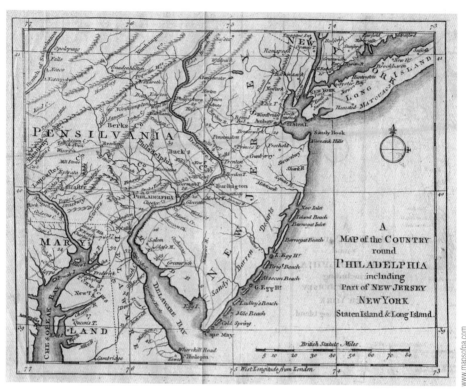

A map of the country around Philadelphia some one hundred years after it was founded

33 PHILADELPHIA – *the development of Midland American English* (1682)

In 1682, William Penn founded the city of Philadelphia in the colony that King Charles II insisted be called Pennsylvania. Penn was a Quaker, and his city welcomed Quakers, very many of them from the English Midlands. Subsequently, all manner of men and women escaping religious persecutions in Europe and New England made their homes in Pennsylvania.

Philadelphia is on the Schuylkill River, giving the city access to the Atlantic by way of Delaware Bay. Immigrants wishing to avoid Puritan-dominated New England colonies and slave-dominated Southern colonies found Pennsylvania and its surrounding territories to their liking. By 1776, Philadelphia had become the world's largest English-speaking city after London, and Pennsylvania's population was in place to play an important role in the development of American English in the Mississippi Valley.

Three regions on the eastern seaboard of North America have been identified as entry points for the English language: Massachusetts Bay, Delaware Bay and Chesapeake Bay. Three colonies in those regions are the homelands of the first American dialects. Massachusetts, Pennsylvania, and Virginia gave rise to the Yankee twang, the Midland burr, and the Southern drawl. A rich account of this story of origins is provided in David Hackett Fischer's *Albion's Seed*. He makes a case for what he calls the founder effect: the first group to settle a region provides a cultural template that is replicated by subsequent settlers. The seventeenth-century settler groups to Massachusetts, Pennsylvania and Virginia were, respectively, from England's East Anglia, Midlands, and West Country.

Fischer is a historian, not a linguist, but *Albion's Seed* works out a founder-effect thesis that has long been the standard explanation of America's dialectal groups. The argument is found in its fullest form in A. C. Baugh's magisterial *History of the English Language*. Recent scholarship contests Baugh and Fischer, but, whatever their origins, three great dialect regions can be identified on the American Atlantic seaboard: Northern, Midland and Southern. Midland is the name given to the speech of Pennsylvania, New Jersey, and southern New York State. (New York City is something of an exception, and upper New York State falls into the Northern dialectal region.)

THE IMPORTANCE OF MIDLAND AMERICAN

A special significance of Midland American is that it is the starting point of the dialect that Baugh called General American, the largest dialectal speech group in the world. As Americans moved west in the nineteenth century, Northern American clung to the shores of the Great Lakes, and Southern American dominated the former slave states, but Midland American provided the basis for the speech of a Middle America stretching from the Appalachians to the Rockies. General American is no longer a term that has much currency, but in the central Mississippi Valley there is a uniformity of speech that reflects the rapid nineteenth-century settlement by men and women from the Mid-Atlantic states. General American is the accent most favoured by American newsreaders on radio and television. In this accent, *caught* and *cot* sound alike. *Dance, glance* and *chance* sound like *manse* in British Received Punctuation. It is the accent of the film-star Fondas – Henry, Peter and Jane.

34 NÎMES – *using place names to make up new words* (1695)

What should a distinctively hardwearing cotton fabric made in the French town of Nîmes be called? The answer, of course, is denim. Originally referred to as 'serge de Nîmes', but shortened to denim over the years, denim is now the ubiquitous fashion and everyday wear of millions across the world. Sometime at the end of the seventeenth century, in 1695 according to the *Oxford English Dictionary*, denim entered the English language.

We do not know just how 'serge de Nîmes' got shortened to 'denim'. There is some speculation that denim might have been the word used to describe the cloth in England to assert its true provenance, just as we might do the same for 'champagne' today. The original serge from Nîmes was a twill weave made of silk and wool, but the denim we know today is a cotton product – the name has shifted as the fabric has been cheapened. An alternative name for denims is jeans. *Jean* is a twill weave cotton, a fabric that was originally said to come from Genoa. The medieval name for that was 'Jene', and so jeans. Today, neither jeans nor denims come from either Genoa or Nîmes, but the old names stick.

Words derived from place names are known as toponyms. And the coining of 'denim' is simply one example of how, when we are stuck for a new name for something, we often turn to the place most strongly associated with it for inspiration. The English language is full of them.

FROM PLACE TO IDEA

Here are a dozen toponyms, four of which continue the textile/clothes theme started with our focus on denim:

Badminton – a game with shuttlecocks invented in southwest England;

Bikini – a two-piece swimming costume using the name of a Pacific island where the atom bomb was tested, perhaps because such swimwear had a similarly explosive effect;

Bungalow – a corruption of 'Bengal', describing the kind of cottages built by European settlers in that part of India;

Calico – a coarse cotton cloth named in the sixteenth century after the town in India called Calicut where it originated;

Dijon – mustard made in this French city;

Hamburger – minced beef from the German city of Hamburg in the nineteenth century;

Jeans – originating from 'bleu de Gênes' (blue from Genoa), jeans was the name given to the hardwearing material associated with Genoan sailors;

Jersey – this Channel Island has given its name to both a distinctive sweater associated with it and to the island's breed of brown cows;

Lesbian – from the Greek island of Lesbos where, in the sixth century before Christ, the poet Sappho lived with a group of women with whom she was in love;

Limerick – popularized by Edward Lear, a limerick is a five-line nonsense poem with two rhyme sounds. Exactly how it was linked to a city or

county in Ireland has never been satisfactorily explained, though many
suggest that there was a group of local poets who enjoyed creating limer-
icks as a parlour game;

Magenta – the distinctive crimson colour which was discovered at the time
of the battle of Magenta in Italy;

Rugby – first used in 1864 and directly linked to the English public school
Rugby in Warwickshire where the game of rugby originated.

There are many other toponyms we might have chosen to define, of which the
following is just a sample: bedlam, bourbon, damask, Olympics, and tuxedo.

Sometimes a place name becomes so imbued with an event associated with it
that it seeps into our collective linguistic consciousness. Hiroshima and Camp David
are two contrasting examples – one associated with the horror of atomic war, and the
other with attempts to bring peace to the world.

35 BOSTON – *the development of New England English* (1704)

On 24 April 1704, John Campbell, the Boston postmaster, published the *Boston
News-Letter*. It was the first issue of the first North American English-language newspaper that did not fail as soon as it started. The *News-Letter* only ceased publication
when the British Army invaded Boston in 1776.

Newspapers played a major part in spreading the ideas that led to the American
Revolution, but when John Campbell established his paper it was with no revolutionary intent. It did, however, reflect the needs of the highly literate population of
the Commonwealth of Massachusetts, of which Boston was the capital. The lead
story in that first issue was based on a letter that had originally appeared in the
London *Flying Post* in December 1703. The *Flying Post* had taken four months to
reach Boston, but what it had to say was still highly newsworthy. The letter concerned
Scotland, unsettled by Jacobite threats. The *Post* reported 'that a great Number of
ill-affected persons are come over from *France*, under pretence of accepting her
Gracious Majesty's Indemnity; but in reality to increase divisions in the nation'.

John Campbell had been born in Scotland, but his Scots birthplace cannot be
guessed from the English that he employed in his newspaper. He was publishing in
America, but that fact cannot be guessed from the newspaper's English either. Campbell wrote an English that was in the process of becoming the standard form for
anyone claiming gentility. Educated American colonists, not yet calling themselves
Americans, wrote exactly like educated Londoners.

In the streets of Boston, the situation was different. Migration to Massachusetts
had begun in 1620, and by 1640 over 20,000 people had moved to the new colony.

They came mainly from the East Anglian counties of Norfolk, Suffolk, Cambridgeshire, and Essex. There the dominant speech was East Midland English; that had evolved from Old English Mercian.

First issue of the *Boston News-Letter*

YANKEE DOODLES

By 1700, East Anglians had peopled the colonies of Massachusetts, Rhode Island, Connecticut and New Hampshire. No one is sure where the word 'Yankee' comes from. It may have a Dutch or an American Indian origin, but it began to be used by the British of their opponents in the Revolutionary War, and in the nineteenth century New Englanders were happy to call themselves Yankees, from which the shortened form of 'Yank' derives. The Yankees created a speech community large enough for its characteristics to persist. New England English is most popularly known for what is called its Yankee twang, and the origins of that are to be found, many say, in East Anglia's Norfolk whine. The term was widely popularized through the song first sung by British troops in mockery of their opponents during the American War of Independence: 'Yankee Doodle'. In the nineteenth century the Yankee dialect greatly amused readers of Thomas Chandler Haliburton, who invented conversations with a Samuel Slick of Slickville, a supposedly typical Yankee:

> Mr. Slick said, Did you never mind, squire, how hard it is to get rid of 'a bad shillin', how everlastin'ly it keeps a-comin' back to you? – I said, I had never experienced any difficulty of that kind, never having endeavoured to pass one that I knew was spurious. – No, I suppose not, said he, because you are a careless kind of a man that way, and let your shillin's desart oftener than they had ought to. But what would I have been, had I been so stravagant? and as to passin' bad money, I see no harm in it, if you have given valy for it, and received it above boord handsum, in the regular way of swap, trade, or sale.

New England speech began moving west in the early nineteenth century, and the form of the English language that developed in New England is now called, by Americans, Northern English. It is to be found westward from Massachusetts through the Mohawk Gap along the shores of the Great Lakes through to parts of the Pacific Northwest. At the same time, the New England speech left in Boston itself was being hugely influenced by the mass migration of the Irish to that city after 1845.

6 THE STANDARDS AGENDA

LICHFIELD – 1709

TEMPLE – 1712

CANONGATE – 1760

SMOCK ALLEY – 1762

MONTREAL – 1763

KEW GARDENS – 1771

KOLKATA – 1786

MARYLEBONE – 1788

SYDNEY – 1788

ST MARY-LE-BOW – 1803

COUPVRAY – 1809

MONROVIA – 1822

Elliott Brown

Statue of Samuel Johnson in Lichfield today

36 LICHFIELD – *setting standards for the English language* (1709)

On 18 September 1709, in Lichfield in Staffordshire, a son was born to Michael and Sarah Johnson. The boy was called Samuel. He grew up surrounded by books because his father was a bookseller. Following education at Lichfield Grammar School and Pembroke College, Oxford, he continued a boyhood habit of voracious reading for the remainder of his life. He moved to London to become its leading literary critic in England's great age of criticism, but he is now best known as the author of a dictionary that gave the modern spellings of some 40,000 words and provided a set of rules for the writing of good English.

Staffordshire is 125 miles northwest of London, and the people of Lichfield had what Londoners would have considered a broad accent. By the time Johnson came to live in London, he had shed a great deal of that accent, but he noted, late in his life, that 'when people watch me narrowly, and I do not watch myself, they will find me out to be of a particular county'. He went on to say that once a man had mastered ninth-tenths of London speech, he would not be bothered to change the rest. Johnson's comments on his own accent show that a fashionable voice was emerging. It was the voice of the wealthy of the West End of London. The notion of a right and wrong way of speaking had entered English social thinking. As a result, many people, even today, believe that there is only one proper way to speak English.

THE IDEA OF PROPER ENGLISH

The development of the idea of a proper way of speaking had been preceded by the development of the idea of a proper way of writing. The process had begun in the late fifteenth century when the scribes of Chancellery were standardizing a way to write English language. Up till then, the records had been kept in Latin, and if not in Latin, then in French. Westminster's scribes needed a single system, and they based it on the East Midland English that the majority of them spoke. In 1476, the printing press came to Westminster. Printers, like scribes, had a professional interest in standardized forms, but whereas what Chancellery scribes wrote in Westminster stayed in Westminster, printers sold their work throughout England. By the seventeenth century, Westminster English was establishing itself as the English for anything printed.

Though printers were the messengers of printed English, they were not its arbiters. The arbiters were scholars, and they had serious concerns about the English that the printers were spreading. The first English grammars – they began to appear at the end of the sixteenth century – were modelled on Latin grammars. These made English appear to fall short in a number of ways. It is not possible to end a sentence with a preposition in Latin; double negatives make a positive in Latin; double comparatives are impossible in Latin; infinitives cannot be split in Latin. A sense that English was inferior became inbuilt. Even though English gradually superseded Latin, it continued to be thought second best. A Renaissance list of Latinate grammar rules was imposed on the English language. It has caused distress ever since. The rules are not observed in the majority of spoken dialects, and they are regularly broken whenever a writer nods.

It was a dictionary that gave the final seal to the new rules of the English language. It arrived in 1755 with Samuel Johnson's *Dictionary of the English language: in which the words are deduced from their originals, and illustrated in their different significations by examples from the best writers. To which are prefixed, a history of the language, and an English grammar.* It was so successful – so comprehensive, so authoritative – that it was evident that Johnson had set the standard and become the benchmark. The University of Oxford that had not awarded him an undergraduate degree now made him a Doctor of Law. Dictionary makers and grammarians took Johnson as their master.

Johnson's *Dictionary* included a section called 'A Grammar of the English Tongue'. It began: 'Grammar, which is the art of using words properly, comprises four parts; Orthography, Etymology, Syntax, and Prosody.' Syntax meant what it means today; Orthography meant spelling; Etymology meant the parts of speech; and Prosody meant pronunciation. Johnson's Grammar reinforced the Latinate rules.

 TEMPLE – *the idea of an English Language Academy* (1712)

On 12 May 1712, at Middle-Temple-Gate in the City of London, Jonathan Swift and his Tory patrons published *A Proposal for Correcting, Improving and Ascertaining the English Tongue*. The aim was to stimulate Parliament to establish an English Academy to correct the English language. Swift wanted an authority that would fix 'our language for ever, after such alterations are made in it as shall be thought requisite'.

The correction of English was not an isolated experiment, and the English were not the first to try to shape a standard form for their written language. The Accademia della Crusca had been founded in Florence in 1583 with a mission to maintain the purity of the Italian language. The Académie française had been founded in Paris in 1634 with a mission to establish a literary language based on the French of the Ile de France. The Academia Española had been founded in Madrid in 1713 with a mission to secure the Castilian language.

Jonathan Swift's call in 1712 for the foundation of an English Academy with the task of 'ascertaining the English Tongue' might have been taken as a sign that the English were merely catching up. If so, they did not catch up. Parliament never found time to consider the idea.

At the end of the eighteenth century, a plan similar to Swift's was proposed for the United States by a number of influential thinkers, including the then Vice-President John Adams. He believed that 'an academy instituted by the authority of Congress for correcting, improving, and fixing the English language would strike all the world with admiration and Great Britain with envy'. The American Congress, like the British Parliament, did not consider the idea.

None the less, English was corrected quite as effectively as Italian, French and Spanish. It was a job done by the work of the grammarians (see pages 71–2), by the members of the Royal Society (see pages 85–7), and by the lexicographers – especially the lexicographers. Dr Johnson's work on a *Dictionary of the English Language* has often been called the equivalent of the work of any Continental academy (see pages 97–9).

AN EVOLVING LANGUAGE

English was corrected, but, like Italian, French and Spanish, English continued to evolve, continued to change its grammar, continued to take on new words, continued to alter its pronunciations, and continued to feel the tension between energized versions of its spoken forms and the conservative version of its written form.

The tension between a wish to prescribe and fix English with clear rules and the power of the developing and changing language that is English continues today. English has continuing defects – unreformed spelling and hapless punctuation among them – but the written form has become the efficient and universal medium that the reader is reading at this moment. Many people want to call this 'correct English', but that is a social term – not a linguistic one. None the less, if you wish to impress people with your education and ability, it is best to be fluent in this form of the language.

 CANONGATE – *British Sign Language* (1760)

In 1760, Thomas Braidwood founded Braidwood's Academy for the Deaf and Dumb in Canongate, Edinburgh. It was the first British school of its kind. Following considerable success in Edinburgh, Braidwood moved to England to become headmaster of the London Asylum for the Deaf and Dumb. There, in 1815, Braidwood's son was visited by an American, Thomas Hopkins Gallaudet. Gallaudet was pioneering education for the deaf in the United States, but he fell out with Braidwood, and he went to Paris where he learned a sign language in use in schools there. He took that back to the United States. Today, it has become American Sign Language. The Braidwood system has become British Sign language. The two are separate languages, mutually unintelligible. There are linguistic and social lessons to be learned from this story.

It was the aim of English teachers to teach deaf children to communicate in English and, if possible, to teach them to speak English and to lip read. One result was a conflict between oralism, as it was called, and signing. Even those teachers willing to tolerate signing confined it to finger-spelling in which the letters of each word were spelled out by twenty-six finger positions. People could become quick at this, but it was no quicker than speaking to someone letter by letter.

Meanwhile, communities of deaf children were learning to sign to each other in ever quicker ways, using all manner of short cuts and symbols. They went far beyond finger-spelling. The children outpaced their teachers, and their teachers became hostile. The cane was used on anyone using signs other than finger-spelling.

Despite punishments, children developed sign language wonderfully, making it something by which people could communicate with ease, fluency, speed and joy.

A map of the Canongate area c.1930

Deaf people taught it to each other secretly and in defiance of authority. It was only in the 1940s that it came into the open and began to be an approved medium in British schools. The social lesson of sign is that educational systems can use language as a mode of repression as well as of expression. The linguistic lesson of sign is equally important.

A FORM OF ENGLISH OR A SEPARATE LANGUAGE?

In 2003, the British government recognized British Sign Language as a language in its own right. That means that British Sign is no longer the same language as the English language. How can that be? When Thomas Braidwood began to teach deaf children to communicate in Canongate in 1760, he could not have imagined that a new language would be added to the world's collection of languages. But that is what happened.

Linguistically, Braidwood was offering the children a 'pidgin', a cut-down speech that people use to bridge two different languages. But there is a magic to pidgins. If they are used by children to talk to other children, pidgins develop into natural languages with full grammars, capable of expressing any human thought. These newly formed languages are called creoles. They might lack vocabulary, but any language might lack vocabulary. Users simply invent new words in the many ways that words are always being invented.

Linguists had not thought that people could create a creole with their hands, but British deaf children had, over a period of some 200 years, created a new language. So had American deaf children. American Sign, too, is a language in its own right, different not only from American English but also from British Sign. Thomas Braidwood's Edinburgh academy is no longer in existence, but Thomas Hopkins Gallaudet's American Asylum for the Deaf, founded on his return to the United States, exists today as the American School for the Deaf. Also, he has given his name to Gallaudet University in Washington, DC. Its website describes it as a bilingual institution, teaching 'deaf and hard of hearing individuals through American Sign Language and English'.

39 SMOCK ALLEY – *English elocution* (1762)

Thomas Sheridan was born in Dublin in 1719. He first came to prominence as a Shakespearean actor playing roles such as Richard III at the Theatre Royal in Smock Alley, Dublin. Although he spent much of his life in London, he is uniquely part of the Irish literary and linguistic scene, being the godson of Jonathan Swift and the father of Richard Sheridan the playwright. Towards the end of his life, he returned to Dublin and resumed work at the Theatre Royal.

But Sheridan's contribution to the English language was not his undoubted prowess as an actor and theatre manager. He was the celebrity lecturer of his age on a topic clearly related to acting – elocution, or what he also referred to as 'eloquence'.

Sheridan's definition of elocution was 'the just and graceful management of the voice, countenance and gesture in speaking'. In the eighteenth century concerns with elocution paralleled the concerns with spelling exemplified by Dr Johnson's work on his dictionary (see pages 97–9), and contemporary grammarians' interest in the structures of the language.

If proper spelling was predominantly the concern of linguists, proper speaking had a much more obvious social imperative. If you pronounced a word in one way it suggested you were educated. Said differently, it indicated either your provincial origin or lack of education or both. So great was people's desire to improve themselves that there was a huge market in elocution courses. And the acknowledged master trainer was Thomas Sheridan. His courses sold out, with some 1,600 subscribers paying a guinea each, an astonishing amount.

Just as television celebrities do today, so, in 1762, Sheridan produced the book of the show, *A course of lectures on elocution: together with two dissertations on language; and some other tracts relative to those subjects*. It was a bestseller. You can get a sense of Sheridan's approach from an earlier work of his, *British Education*. Here he argues that 'a revival of the art of speaking and the study of our language' might help to cure 'the evils of immorality, ignorance and false taste'.

Sheridan set great importance by 'articulation', 'giving every letter in a syllable its due proportion of sound, according to the most approved custom of pronouncing it'. He wanted the listener's ear to be able to have no difficulty in hearing the 'number' of syllables in any word. He thought this would help people to spell, and to improve their comprehension and attention. Just as poor handwriting makes it difficult for the reader, so, he argued, poor elocution similarly disadvantages the listener.

Smock Alley Theatre

The Smock Alley Theatre today

SHERIDAN'S LEGACY

If only pronunciation or elocution were such a straightforward matter on which to adjudicate. Johnson himself was drawn into the debate about Sheridan's approaches through their mutual friend, James Boswell. Boswell records a conversation between Johnson and himself in which Johnson remarks: 'What entitles Sheridan to fix the pronunciation of English? He has, in the first place the disadvantage of being an Irishman; and if he says he will fix it after the example of the best company, why they differ among themselves.'

And that is, of course, the challenge. As Johnson warns us, Lord Chesterfield told him that 'great' should be pronounced to rhyme with 'state', while Sir William Yonge advised it must be spoken like 'seat' and that only an Irishman would pronounce it 'grait'.

But Sheridan did raise an important issue that had previously not been greatly discussed – that is, the way people speak. During the nineteenth century there was a great interest in elocution in the United States, with a growing number of people seeing better speaking as a route to advancement. In England, George Bernard Shaw famously explored the many social connotations of speaking properly in *Pygmalion* (see pages 171–2).

40 MONTREAL – *the English language in Canada* (1763)

In 1763, by way of the Treaty of Paris, the French crown conceded the city of Montreal and the province of Quebec to Great Britain. New France was no more. The French army withdrew from the Canadas, and the French navy left the Great Lakes. The treaty had long-term effects on the English language in North America.

There was a sufficient presence of the British army in Quebec to keep its 75,000 French speakers in subjection, but there was an insufficient presence of that army in North America to keep its 1,600,000 English speakers in subjection. Thirteen colonies rebelled and formed the United States of America. In 1783, a second Treaty of Paris acknowledged the victory of the new nation, and 60,000 men and women chose to leave it. Though many went to England, 50,000 relocated to Nova Scotia, New Brunswick and Quebec. Their way of speaking was the starting point of modern-day Canadian English.

The men and women moving north, Loyalists as they called themselves, came from all of the former colonies, but they came mainly from southern New York, New Jersey, Pennsylvania and Delaware – the Mid-Atlantic colonies, now states. There were relatively fewer from New England, where anti-British feeling had been strongest, and fewer still from the South. From there, it was as easy to go to England as to reach any Canadian province. Eastern seaboard speech was already divided into three dialects: Northern (the New England states), Midland (the Mid-Atlantic states) and Southern (see pages 77, 90 and 93). So it was Midland American English that came to dominate in the Canadas. The English were from the beginning more mobile than the French-speaking inhabitants of Quebec. As a result, it was the English language that later spread through the western provinces of the country that came to be called Canada. Canadian English shares a great deal with Lakeside American (the American English heard along the United States shores of the Great Lakes), but a keen ear can distinguish the

Canadian. Someone who calls a 'sofa' a 'chesterfield' and who pronounces 'about' as if it were 'a boot' is very likely to be from Canada.

CANADIAN ENGLISH TODAY

Today, the English language in Canada reflects a history that owes more to British English than does the English language in the United States. Canadians of Loyalist stock were fierce preservers of things English. They had no time for the spelling reforms introduced into American English in 1828 by Noah Webster. To this day, many will call the letter 'z' 'zed', not 'zee'. Particularly, written Canadian English has wanted to keep faith with British ways of doing things.

None the less, most books on sale in Canada have been printed in the United States. The 49th Parallel may divide the two countries politically, but it is linguistically permeable.

One result is that Canada is a country with two forms of Standard English, British and American. The library of the State University of New York at Buffalo (on the Canadian border) advises readers to use both British and American spellings when searching for Canadian documents. It also refers readers to a website that lists 'Differences between British, Canadian and American Spelling'. Although British spelling is demanded in many Canadian institutions, many also permit American spellings. The rule is not to mix them, but not everyone follows the rule.

It is perfectly possible at a garage to see a sign using the American 'tire' (rather than British 'tyre') and British 'centre' (not American 'center'). A particular Canadianism is the tendency to use the word 'eh' in the middle or at the end of a sentence, creating the feel of a question even when the words are really merely a statement with 'eh?' tagged on to check that the listener is paying attention: 'It's hot, eh, so let's open the window.'

American English is constantly encroaching, and Canadians are now as likely to say 'faucet' as they are to say 'tap', 'check' as 'bill', 'mom' as 'mum', 'frosting' as 'icing'. Canadians do not want to be mistaken for Americans, but young Canadians do not want to be thought old-fashioned. What most characterizes Canadian English, according to John Algeo, is 'the use of several possible variant pronunciations for the same word, sometimes even in the same sentence'.

 KEW GARDENS – *botanical English* (1771)

In 1771, Augusta, the Dowager Princess of Wales, agreed that one of her gardeners should be appointed a plant collector. Her garden was at Kew, and the gardener was Francis Masson. For over thirty years, he travelled the globe and brought home a thousand new species. On his final expedition, he froze to death in North America,

The original landscape design for Kew Gardens

but one of his potted plants is still alive in what is today the Royal Botanical Gardens, Kew.

A thousand new plants needed a thousand new names, and Francis Masson was not the only plant collector scouring the world to feed the English passion for gardening. Some 10,000 new plants were introduced to England in the course of the eighteenth and nineteenth centuries, and they all needed names.

At first, the naming had been chaotic. Native English plants had different names in various parts of the country; the same name was used for more than one plant; and many plants, especially herbs, had medieval Latin names in addition to local names. Among the plant names were Jerusalem cowslip, Jerusalem oak, Jerusalem sage, Jerusalem artichoke, Jerusalem cherry, Jerusalem corn. None of these had anything to do with the city of Jerusalem, but they were foreign – and so was Jerusalem.

More than one botanist attempted to sort things out, and the work of John Ray was the most admired, especially his *Methodus Plantarum Nova* in which he listed some 18,000 species in the final edition of 1703. His method for naming plants was a brave attempt, but was flawed by the classification system that he used to organize his species. He started by dividing them into Herbs and Trees, and he went on from there. It was a system that would not work.

What was needed was a scientifically organized, universal system, and it was provided not by an Englishman, but by a Swede, Carl Linnaeus. He rationalized the 'binomial nomenclature' that is the foundation of the modern scientific naming of all living things. Linnaeus insisted that every species should have two names: the first would identify the genus to which it belonged; the second would identify the species within the genus. The Linnean system works for animals as well as plants, and the binomial *Homo sapiens* is the best known of the Linnean names. Although the English did not like to admit it, Linnaeus's *System of Vegetables* did the job that John Ray's *Methodus* did not.

THE NAMING OF PLANTS

As a result, when Francis Masson set out for the South Seas in 1771 he had with him a logical system for the naming of any new plant of whatever kind that he might find. In recognition of his collecting and of his proper naming of his new species, Masson was elected to the Linnean Society in 1796. That was an honour for a gardener at a time when scientific work was largely the preserve of gentlemen, but the establishment, in London, of the Linnean Society itself was an even greater tribute to Linnaeus.

The Linnean Society had been founded in 1788 for 'the cultivation of the Science of Natural History in all its branches'. It is still actively engaged in the naming of plants and is still using the Latin language in the way that Linnaeus had done in the eighteenth century. Linnaeus chose Latin because it was still in his day the learned language of Europe. For a Swede, working in the Netherlands and England in the mid eighteenth century, Latin was one language that he could expect men of science to understand. Linnaeus's use of it as a lingua franca was already out of date; most Europeans were already using French for that purpose. None the less, the Latin basis of our modern plant names remains a final triumph of that ancient language.

Linnean plant names are part of the International Scientific Vocabulary (see pages 86–7). Scientific names may never seem as natural as 'rosemary,' 'pansy,' 'fennel,' 'columbine', 'daisy' and 'violet' – flowers that Ophelia presents to Laertes in *Hamlet* – but many Linnean names have entered the common speech of modern gardeners and as such have entered the English language.

42 KOLKATA – *the birth of linguistics and the origins of English* (1786)

In 1783, in the city that the British then called Calcutta and that Indians now call Kolkata, there arrived a remarkable man whose name was Sir William Jones. He was a lawyer by training, and he had come from London to take up a position on the Supreme Court of Bengal in West Bengal. Although Sir William was an able judge, it is for his work as a linguist rather than his work on the bench that he is remembered. Specifically he helped us to understand how the English language came to England via a global family of connected tongues.

Sir William learned languages the way other people learn operas. By the end of his life, he knew thirteen languages fluently and twenty-eight very well. Among those languages were a number of Indian ones. In particular, he had taught himself to read Sanskrit. Sanskrit holds the place in Indian culture that Latin and Greek hold in European culture. Having all three languages before him, he came to a remarkable conclusion. He reported it, on 2 February 1786, to the Asiatic Society of Bengal:

> The Sanscrit language, whatever be its antiquity, is of a wonderful structure; more perfect than the Greek, more copious than the Latin, and more exquisitely refined than either, yet bearing to both of them a stronger affinity, both in the roots of verbs and in the forms of grammar, than could possibly have been produced by accident, so strong indeed, that no philologer could examine them all three, without believing them to have sprung from some common source, which, perhaps, no longer exists: there is a similar reason, though not quite so forcible, for supposing that both the Gothick and the Celtick, though blended with a very different idiom, had the same origin with the Sanscrit.

HOW ENGLISH BEGAN

With that magnificent statement, the modern study of linguistics was born. It has now been determined that the majority of the languages of Europe and most of those of northern India have indeed 'sprung from some common source'. From Gaelic to Gujarati, from Albanian to Yagnobi, several hundreds of ancient and modern European and Indian languages have evolved over 6,000 years from an

The tomb of Sir William Jones in Kolkata

original language called Proto-Indo-European. It was, some say, the language of a tribe living on the Caspian steppes. It is the language from which English has come.

'Proto' is a term placed before a language that no one has ever heard or read, but that is constructed by working backwards from languages believed to be related. Informed conjecture produces a possible proto-type language, an ancestor language. Patterns have been identified that control sound changes between one language and another, and it was the great work of nineteenth-century linguists to show the relations between the languages that Sir William had so rightly guessed were in 'the same family'.

Sir William linked Sanscrit not only with Greek and Latin, but also with Gothick and Celtick. Those four language families are now seen to represent the great divisions of the languages of Western Europe; their modern names are Hellenic, Italic, Germanic and Celtic. Hellenes, Italics, Germanics and Celts began populating Western Europe about 4,000 years ago.

Some 3,000 years ago, people who spoke a language that we call Proto-Germanic arrived in the northern part of the Scandinavian Peninsula. They gradually increased in numbers and moved south along the coasts all the way to what is now Holland. They moved inland into parts of what is now north Germany. Over a thousand or so years, Proto-Germanic developed into North Germanic, West Germanic and East Germanic. East Germanic has disappeared. North Germanic has become Danish, Swedish, Norwegian and Icelandic. West Germanic has become Dutch, German and English.

Sir William Jones's inspired conjecture enables us to track the English language back some 6,000 years and to get a glimpse of how it came to Europe.

43 MARYLEBONE, LONDON – *the language of sport* (1788)

In 1787, the Marylebone Cricket Club was founded in Marylebone, London. The members of the MCC (as the club has come to be called) rented a field from a Mr Lord and established a set of rules to govern their game. Those they called *The Code of Laws*. Though the MCC left its original field long ago, it still calls its cricket ground 'Lords', and at the website @ *Lord's: The Home of Cricket* can be found *The Code of Laws*. Modified over the years, the rules of those eighteenth-century gentlemen now govern an international sport.

Cricket has spread, like the English language, round the world, but it is only found where British English is to be found. Australia, Barbados, India, Jamaica, New Zealand, Pakistan, South Africa and Trinidad are all great English-speaking and cricket-playing nations. The Americans never took to cricket, but baseball evolved from the very same village game that began on the downs of Sussex and Hampshire, and baseball means as much to an American as cricket does to the English.

British cricket and American baseball have made remarkable contributions not only to the health of their players, but also to their languages.

Cricketing terms are widely used in everyday speech. It is common to hear people, not all of them cricketers, say things like: 'It's not cricket', 'He stood up in the debate and bowled the Opposition a googly', 'He knocked his opponents for six and so won the contract', 'I've had a good innings; it's time to retire', 'He bats a straight bat; we should give him the job'. Cricket provides a DIY-idiom kit from balls through hat-trick to silly mid-on.

Baseball does the same for the American. The 'Baseball Lingo' page at Baseball Farming.com starts with 'Ace pitcher' and ends with 'Zinger'. In between, it provides a treasure-trove of terms begging to be used in the boardroom: 'walk', 'spit ball', 'sacrifice bunt', 'chin music', 'closer', 'curve ball', 'grounder', 'home plate', 'moon shot', 'pinch hitter'. You do not need to know what they mean to feel their linguistic potential.

Linguistic liveliness is not special to baseball and cricket. Every sport has its own vocabulary, and that vocabulary is ever ready to move into mainstream English. The English language is infused with sporting language, in idioms, metaphors and phrases.

The richness of the history and meanings of the word 'sport' gives some sense of why sporting English is also so rich. 'To sport' meant in the fourteenth century 'to take pleasure, to amuse oneself'. It came from the French 'desport' – a pastime, a pleasure. 'Sport' became associated with open-air games in the sixteenth century. 'To sport' took on the meaning of 'to wear' – as in 'he is sporting a fine coat' – at just about the same time that the MCC was drawing up its rules. The Americans gave the word a new twist when they began to refer to a lively fellow as a 'sport'; the British gave that an affectionate turn with their phrase 'a good sport', meaning 'a decent person'.

It is fair to say that there are any number of sports with which this discussion might be illustrated. Football fans (Australian, American or Association) could boast their sporting language as the equal of any, but since the first word has been given to cricket, it might as well be given the last word, too.

Cricket is played in the land of baseball where exiles and anglophiles like to strike willow against leather. For those who do, the website of the Rice Cricket Club of Houston, Texas, posts this legendary explanation of the MCC's *Code of Laws*:

You have two sides, one out in the field and one in. Each man that's in the side that's in goes out, and when he's out he comes in and the next man goes in until he's out. When they are all out, the side that's out comes in and the side that's been in goes out and tries to get those coming in, out. Sometimes you get men still in and not out. When a man goes out to go in, the men who are out try to get him out, and when he is out he goes in and the next man in goes out and goes in. There are two men called umpires who stay out all the time and they decide when the men who are in are out. When both sides have been in and all the men have been out, and both sides have been out twice after all the men have been in, including those who are not out, that is the end of the game.

SYDNEY – *the English language in Australia* (1788)

In 1788, 1,066 convicts were taken in a Royal Navy convoy from London to Port Jackson, the first British settlement in Australia. Port Jackson is today in the centre of Sydney, the largest English-speaking city in the Southern hemisphere.

At the beginning, there were two kinds of English spoken in Australia, the Cockney English of the convicts and the court English of their senior administrators. Twenty-first-century Australians no longer sound like either eighteenth-century Cockneys or eighteenth-century courtiers because the old dialects have evolved into Broad Australian and Formal Australian.

Between 1788 and 1868, the United Kingdom sent 160,000 convicts to Australia. The majority came from London's poorest classes, and they provided the linguistic basis of Broad Australian, a dialect condemned even as the convicts were creating it. In 1855, an Australian schools inspector was reporting that little care was being taken by teachers 'to correct vicious pronunciation or improper modulations of voice'.

Formal spoken Australian, like formal spoken English everywhere, takes care to avoid double negatives, double comparatives, and formulations like 'he don't', 'I seed', 'she know'd', and so on. Formal written English, in addition, avoids the ending of sentences with prepositions and the splitting of infinitives. All of those were features of what Samuel Pegge, in 1803, called 'the Cockney dialect', a spirited defence of which he mounted in *Anecdotes of the English Language: Chiefly Regarding the Local Dialect of London*.

It was not just from London that migrants took sail for Australia. In the 1850s, the first of many regional surges was caused by gold rushes. And all the while, Australian English was incorporating words from the Aboriginal languages, words like *kangaroo*, *wallaby*, *dingo* and *budgerigar*.

Map of Port Jackson a year after it was settled

AUSTRALIAN ENGLISH TODAY

One of the most noteworthy features of Australian English today is the lack of variation across such a vast country. If you listen to a speaker from Sydney or Perth or Melbourne, for example, you would not notice much difference in the way that they speak. Certainly the accent does not differ in the way that you would find between, say, Edinburgh and Truro in the United Kingdom.

There are, nevertheless, interesting social differences. Australia is not uncommon in having a division of dialects along class lines, but it is unusual in its widespread affection for its basilect: 'the variety of speech that is most remote from the prestige variety'. The popular name for it is 'Strine' (to rhyme with 'train'). Here is a sample: 'Aorta stop all these transistors from cummer ninner the country. Look what they doone to the weather. All this rine! Doan tell me it's not all these transistors – an all these hydrigen bombs too. Aorta stoppem!'

Politicians use Strine to curry favour with voters and, especially, to score points off opponents in the Houses of Parliament in Canberra. Broad Australian is supposed to reflect an Australian love of swear words, but it is more a willingness to permit that language in public discourse than a matter of a greater propensity for it. London Cockney easily matches Sydney Strine for swearing, but Cockney is not much used in the Houses of Parliament in Westminster.

In the twenty-first century, Australian English is as much influenced by American English as by British English, perhaps more so. That is partly a reflection of the role that American English has had as the language of a world superpower since 1945, and partly a reflection of the fact that British Empire policy during the Second World War made Australia realize it needed to look to the United States, not to the United Kingdom, for military and political support.

45 ST MARY-LE-BOW – *Cockney English* (1803)

People born within the sound of the bells of St Mary-le-Bow in Cheapside in the City of London were said to be Cockneys, and they had been called that since the seventeenth century at least. However, there was not a great deal said about the way they spoke until 1803 when Samuel Pegge published *Anecdotes of the English Language: Chiefly Regarding the Local Dialect of London and its Environs.*

Pegge does not call the local London dialect 'Cockney', but that is what it has come to be called, and his book is one of its first descriptions. It is the dialect of London's East End, and it was an English that was denounced and despised by language guardians in the nineteenth century and long into the twentieth century.

Cockney came to represent any dialect of English that pretentious speakers did not like. The dialect gap came to reflect a social gap, one exploited by Rudyard Kipling who made all his rankers speak like Cockneys and all his officers speak like public school boys. The division between London's West End and East End seemed then to stretch throughout the British Empire. (See the story of Australian English, pages 112–14, and that of New Zealand English, pages 129–32.)

In the fourteenth century, it is probable that all Londoners spoke alike whatever their rank. There is little reference or joking about higher or lower kinds of London speech in 1400 or 1500, or even 1600. Jokes and insults were made about rural, northern, Welsh and Scots dialects (especially in Shakespeare), but there were few jokes about London dialects. No one talked about Cockney until the beginning of the nineteenth century.

One reason that East End speech caught the attention of West End speakers at that point was the eighteenth century's concern with correct English. By 1700, 50 per cent of London women could read and write, with the male percentage even higher. That was a very large proportion, and it allowed a language separation to begin. People began to ask for rules for writing, spelling and grammar. Literate people began to model their speech on the new rules for writing and to describe as faults the use of the old rules.

Steve Cadman

St Mary-le-Bow today

THE CREATIVITY OF COCKNEY CRIMES

Those so-called faults are what Samuel Pegge listed, ironically, as the eighteen crimes of the local dialect of London (i.e. Cockney English). They included double negatives, double comparatives, split infinitives, misplaced modifiers, sentences that end with a preposition, many pronunciations, and word forms not found in Dr Johnson's *Dictionary* (see pages 97–9). Pegge did not have a high opinion of Samuel Johnson. 'I do not think,' said Pegge, 'that Lexicography was his *forte*.'

Pegge argued that the Cockney crimes could be defended on the grounds of ancient usage or authoritative usage. He showed that all of them could be found in the best writers, and he gave many examples, especially from Chaucer and Shakespeare.

The subtitle of *Anecdotes of the English Language* contains the statement: *Whence it will appear that the natives of the metropolis, and its vicinities, have not corrupted the language of their ancestors.* Though he did not use the terms, Pegge was asking his readers to ask themselves if good Mercian English could have become bad Cockney English.

Today, many people associate Cockney with its main export: rhyming slang in which everyday words are given new meanings:

Adam and Eve it = believe it
Apples and pears = stairs
China plate = mate
Butcher's hook = look
Christmas Eve = believe
Half inch = pinch
Porky pies = lies
Tea leaf = thief
Trouble and strife = wife
Whistle and flute = suit

Rhyming slang is said to have been developed by East End costermongers so they could talk to each other in front of their West End customers without being understood.

Like all languages, Cockney continues to evolve. The following are some recent examples of rhyming slang:

Britney Spears = tears
Calvin Klein = wine
Elsie Tanner = spanner
Posh and Becks = specs (spectacles)
Wallace and Gromit = vomit

COUPVRAY – *the English language in Braille* (1809)

In 1809, in Coupvray, a village 34 kilometres east of Paris, Louis Braille was born. At the age of three, he blinded himself in one eye with one of his father's leather-working tools. The treatment for his bad eye caused the infection of his good eye, and he became completely blind. At the age of ten, he was sent to a school for the blind in Paris. He did so well that, when it was time for him to leave, he was asked to stay on as a teacher. He accepted the position.

It was unusual in the nineteenth century for a blind person to be asked to teach the blind, but because he went from being a blind pupil to a blind teacher, he brought new thinking to the task. He was a musician and a skilled and popular organist; he was used to giving expression to his inner self through his keyboard-playing hands. He was also in the right city to develop what the French called 'écriture nocturne', night writing.

Night writing had been something that Napoleon had asked his military intelligence to develop so that his soldiers could read messages at night. People were amazed that night writing worked at all, but the first systems were inefficient because the unit of communication spread beyond a single fingertip. In the dark, soldiers lost their place in the messages.

Braille reworked the military's patterns of raised dots so that every sign – letter, number, punctuation mark or symbol – was represented by a small rectangle of six dots. Most importantly, the matrix of dots for any one sign could be read by a single fingertip.

We may not realize it, but printed English uses as many as 180 different signs. We talk about the twenty-six letters of the alphabet, but we immediately double the number of letter signs by having lower case letters and upper case letters. A glance at a keyboard will show how many other signs we use, and that is without calling on the symbols' menu of special characters.

Braille's six-dot grid proved exactly what was wanted to transcribe writing for the eye into writing for the fingertip, and Braille, as Braille's system has come to be called, arrived in the United States in 1860 when it was introduced at the St Louis School for the Blind, and in the United Kingdom in 1868, when it was adopted by the recently founded British and Foreign Blind Association.

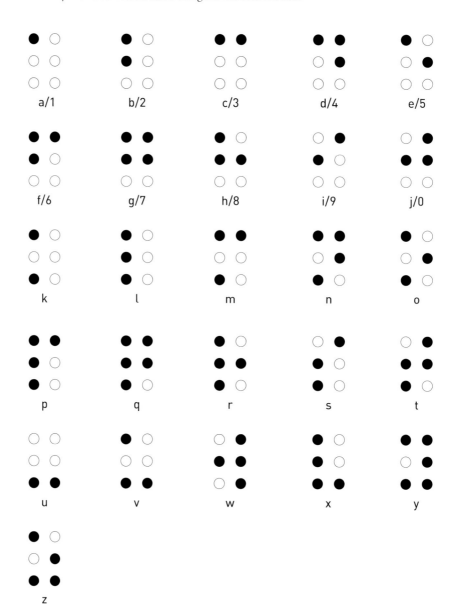

Braille's patterns of raised dots is still in use today

HOMO SAPIENS THE CODE-BREAKER

Braille can teach us a great deal about the way language works and about how deeply language is embedded in us. Writing had once seemed the province of the eye, but the French showed that it could also be the province of the fingertip. We are nature's code-breakers. So urgent is our need to communicate, we are able to do so by any means that the brain and body can use to create a message.

Analyzed at its basic level, Braille is a binary code consisting of embossed dots and blanks; it is astonishingly flexible and can be very fast. It has interested students of computing because, as David Salomon, an encoding expert, says, 'The contractions, short words, and other extensions of the Braille code are examples of intuitive, data compression.'

In *See It My Way*, Peter White, broadcaster, writer, world traveller and almost blind from birth, speaks of the joy he has had from reading. He reads Braille two handed, and he reads it as fast as a sighted person can read print. It may be that voice-recognition and print-reading software will displace Braille at some point, but it was the man from Coupvray who opened the book for the blind and gave the English language a remarkable new medium.

 MONROVIA – *the English language in West Africa* (1822)

In 1822, on the West Coast of Africa, the city of Monrovia was founded and named after the then President of the United States, James Monroe. A group of slave holders had formed the American Colonization Society. That aimed to solve what it saw as the race problem by returning Africans to Africa. Almost all the slaves who were to be sent back to Africa had in fact been born in the United States. They were not returning at all, but, in the hinterland of Monrovia and all along what was then called Gold Coast, those Africans from America found Africans speaking an unusual form of English.

One of the names given to that English is Kru and, through to the end of the nineteenth century, a people calling themselves the Kru worked as interpreters, guides and negotiators. The name 'Kru' may come from the English word 'crew'; certainly, these people had got their start by working on the boats of the English. Some say that Kru had been taken to the Americas by enslaved Africans. If so, it was being returned to Africa when freed American slaves began to inhabit Monrovia and the country that they created there – Liberia, the land of the free.

CREOLES AND PIDGINS

Kru is a creole language, and a creole originates from a pidgin. A pidgin is an artificial language created by adults who do not speak each other's languages, but need to

Wm Thornton Esqr

No. 1. JULY, 1820. Vol. I.

THE

African Intelligencer.

CONTENTS.

WASHINGTON:

Published by J. Ashmun, Pennsylvania Avenue.

....

DAVIS & FORCE PRINT.

—

1820.

The African Intelligencer, published by the Society for the Colonization of Free People of Color of America, which helped to found Monrovia

communicate to trade or work together. Some pidgins have no more than a hundred words and virtually no grammar, but pidgins become creoles when they are used by children as a mother tongue. Children turn the artificial language into a natural language with a full grammar and vocabulary.

Kru may have disappeared in the nineteenth century because it came into contact with the African American English of the Liberian. Large numbers of the ex-slaves could read and write, and that meant they could call upon a Standard English. That took on a prestige role in the new country. The African Americans intermarried with the Kru and so created the rich variety of English dialects of present-day Liberia.

Liberia's story is an unusual one in a number of ways, especially since its English is an American English, not a British English, but a parallel story is to be told of Sierra Leone where the British had established a city for released slaves. It was called Free Town, today Freetown. There arrived blacks from England and slaves from the Americas. A form of English called Krio developed.

Today, English is an official language in both Liberia and Sierra Leone as it is in Gambia, Ghana and Nigeria. English is also a lingua franca in these countries. Nigeria's inhabitants, for example, speak as many as 500 mother tongues and, as a result, English serves as an intermediary language for education, administration and commerce. In each nation, English plays a national role, though it would be hard to argue that there are different national dialects. However, distinct literatures in English have appeared in all of the anglophone West African nations, and these literatures reflect the nations' different histories.

7 THE INDUSTRIAL AGE

STOCKTON-ON-TEES – 1825

HARTFORD – 1828

CHENNAI – 1834

ST MARTIN-LE-GRAND – 1840

WAITANGI – 1840

THE STRAND – 1841

BALTIMORE – 1844

SALFORD – 1850

HANNIBAL – 1851

HYDE PARK – 1851

TIMES SQUARE – 1851

MANCHESTER – 1852

BERDICHEV – 1857

CHRISTCHURCH COLLEGE – 1865

LLANFAIRPWLLGWYNGYLL – 1868

EXETER PLACE – 1876

CAPE TOWN – 1881

DUBLIN – 1882

GISBORNE – 1894

48 **STOCKTON-ON-TEES** – *the English language and the steam engine* (1825)

In 1825, George Stephenson built a steam engine that he called *Locomotion* to haul a train from Stockton to Darlington. *Locomotion* was not the first self-moving steam engine, but it was the first passenger locomotive.

In October 1832, an Englishwoman, Fanny Kemble, travelled from New York to Philadelphia, making the journey by steamboats and stagecoaches and on what she called both the 'rail-way' and the 'rail-road'. Her hyphenated rail-way/rail-road doublet catches a moment when the two English-speaking nations were about to be separated by their common language. In his 1833 *Traveller's Guide through the Middle and Northern States, and the Provinces of Canada*, Gideon Davison, an American, also used rail-road and rail-way interchangeably, sometimes on the same page in the discussion of the same track. *Appletons' Illustrated Railway and Steam Navigation Guides*, issued two or three times monthly from the 1850s onwards and providing timetables for passenger railroads in the United States, invariably used the word 'railway'. To the end of the nineteenth century, 'railway' remained unexceptional for American users so that the Erie Railroad could be conveniently reorganized as the Erie Railway in 1861 after its bankruptcy in 1859 and re-reorganized as the Erie Rail-road again in 1895 after the Erie Railway's bankruptcy in 1893.

In 1832, Kemble talked about being seated in a carriage. 'Carriage' was a word that had once meant a wheeled vehicle generally, but by the nineteenth century its popular meaning had become limited to a private vehicle for carrying people. It then came to mean, in England, a railway vehicle designed to carry passengers, not goods, and so the Englishwoman wrote of the transfer from road to rail: 'Our coachful got into the first carriage of the train.' In 1833, the American Davison also used the word 'carriage' to describe the passenger vehicles of the Camden and Amboy Railroad, noting: 'The carriages are elegant, and among the best which have been constructed.' Despite Davison, the Americans were not going to use the word 'carriage' for this kind of vehicle. In the previous century, Edward Gibbon had been able to speak, exotically, of a Roman emperor 'reclining on a litter or car of ivory, drawn by two white mules', but as early as 1826 the word 'car' was appearing in Massachusetts rail-road legislation. 'Car' was in some respects preferable to 'carriage' since, by the 1820s, it had dropped out of common use and so was conveniently revived to describe a new kind of vehicle. 'Carriage' was, initially, a more obvious word since the passenger vehicles of the Camden and Amboy Railroad were scarcely different from stage coaches. The horse carriage took time to evolve into the railroad car holding fifty to sixty passengers.

Since the Americans had elected to call their railroad passenger vehicles 'cars', it did mean that at the end of the century they had to call their gas-driven, personal vehicles 'automobiles'. The British chose not to use that French word and used the yet-unused word 'car' instead for that kind of vehicle. By 1900, the railway/railroad industry was only one of many that had developed independently on both sides of the Atlantic, and in doing so had developed differing British and American vocabularies. The car/automobile industry was another.

FROM STEAM TO VIRTUAL TRAVEL VIA JET FUEL

British and American English continued to diverge until the arrival of the wireless/radio, film and television began to bring the languages together again. The invention of the aircraft and the development recently of cheap air travel have made the convergence even greater. That has narrowed the gaps between the different forms of English. American English has proved the dominant partner, and the British are at ease with a greater range of American accents than the Americans with British ones.

 HARTFORD – *establishing an American standard for English* (1828)

In 1828, *An American Dictionary of the English Language* was published by Noah Webster of Hartford, Connecticut. As a young man, he had believed that America 'should develop a form of English as distinctive as [its] government'. He saw the language as a rallying point for American identity. 'This country,' he said, 'must in some future time, be as distinguished by the superiority of her literary improvements, as she is already by the liberality of her civil and ecclesiastical constitutions.' In 1786, he retitled what he had been calling *The First Part of the Grammatical Institute of the English Language* with a more immediate name, *The American Spelling Book*. It became a best-seller.

They say that only the Bible and Mao's *Little Red Book* have sold more copies than *The American Spelling Book*, and as early as 1807 Webster was able to report that 2 million copies were in print. It was being used in every schoolroom, first in New England and then all along the East Coast. The little book was, at the same time, giving Webster the income to devote himself full time to lexicography, and he was already working on a project of greater scale and ambition, *A Compendious Dictionary of the English Language*. In time, that evolved into his two-volume *An American Dictionary of the English Language*. Where Samuel Johnson defined some 40,000 words, Noah Webster defined 70,000. *An American Dictionary* has never been out of print since its appearance in 1828.

On the occasion of Webster's death, Chancellor James Kent, the holder of New York State's highest legal office, made a comparison between Webster's work and the perished Pyramids of Egypt: 'This Dictionary, and the language which it embodies,

AN

AMERICAN DICTIONARY

OF THE

ENGLISH LANGUAGE:

INTENDED TO EXHIBIT,

I. The origin, affinities and primary signification of English words, as far as they have been ascertained.
II. The genuine orthography and pronunciation of words, according to general usage, or to just principles of analogy.
III. Accurate and discriminating definitions, with numerous authorities and illustrations.

TO WHICH ARE PREFIXED,

AN INTRODUCTORY DISSERTATION

ON THE

ORIGIN, HISTORY AND CONNECTION OF THE

LANGUAGES OF WESTERN ASIA AND OF EUROPE,

AND A CONCISE GRAMMAR

OF THE

ENGLISH LANGUAGE.

BY NOAH WEBSTER, LL. D.

IN TWO VOLUMES.

VOL. I.

He that wishes to be counted among the benefactors of posterity, must add, by his own toil, to the acquisitions of his ancestors.—*Rambler.*

NEW YORK:
PUBLISHED BY S. CONVERSE.
PRINTED BY HEZEKIAH HOWE—NEW HAVEN.
1828.

The title page of Webster's *An American Dictionary of the English Language*

will also perish; but it will not be with the gorgeous palaces. It will go with the solemn temples and the great globe itself.' That is a little strong, but, by 1867, a Webster's *Dictionary* could be had in twelve sizes from Royal Quarto to Pocket.

WEBSTER'S LEGACY

The most noticeable feature of Webster's *Dictionary* was that it included the spelling reforms that he had believed the English language needed. 'Honour' became 'honor';

'programme' became 'program'; 'centre' became 'center'; 'catalogue' became 'catalog'; 'advertise' became 'advertize'. Webster stuck to simplifying the spelling of a number of common words. He does not seem to have been thinking in terms of accents (either his own or anyone else's). According to David Crystal, Webster's spelling reforms only affected about 500 words of the 50,000 or so in educated usage, but the effect of those changes is dramatic because the words are so commonly used that they change completely the appearance of the American page. Readers are aware at once that it is not British English that they are reading. None the less, when we add up the differences between the two varieties, as David Crystal says, 'we are talking about a very small part of the language as a whole'.

Webster's *Dictionary*'s greatest impact has been that it has made the English language a completely American possession. While British English looks to the *Oxford English Dictionary*, American English looks to Webster without a second thought. There is none of the cultural misgivings of the kind that sometimes appear in Canadian English or Indian English. Webster gave the American people the linguistic independence that he felt they deserved. At the same time, he gave the English language two equally valid standards. The Indians say: 'There is no flag behind the English language.' That is only true because of Noah Webster's work.

Not all Americans liked what he did. Many refused to adopt what they thought were his curious and inelegant forms. As late as 1913, Edith Wharton was insisting that her New York publisher use British spellings if he were to continue to publish her novels. But Edith Wharton represented old New York. By 1913, most Americans were probably unaware that there were alternative British spellings.

CHENNAI – *the English language in India* (1834)

In 1834, Thomas Babington Macaulay landed at a city that today is called Chennai, but was then called Madras, a port in the Bay of Bengal. The British government had appointed him to the Council of India, and he took as his first point of business the subject of education. Within a year, he issued what has come to be called 'the infamous Minute of Lord Macaulay'. It recommended that English should be made the language of higher education, law and administration throughout India. His advice was adopted. Macaulay had set out a programme that would have profound effects in all three of the modern countries of India, Pakistan and Bangladesh.

The English language had already been in India for more than 300 years when Macaulay arrived. In 1600, a Company of London Merchants trading in the East Indies had been given a charter by Queen Elizabeth, and it is likely that the English were already in India by that date. English began to take words from Indian languages, and English traders initially learned enough of the local languages to enable them to do business and to make money.

The directors of what came to be called the East India Company were not settled on using English in India, and, through to the end of the eighteenth century, the Company's schools taught Sanskrit, Persian and Arabic. None the less, the fact that a trading company was concerning itself with education meant that it was involving itself with governing. At the same time, in order to maintain its supplies and to ensure their delivery, the East India Company took over the rule of one Indian state after another, creating an empire while making a market.

In 1857, after what the British call the Indian Mutiny but the Indians call the Indian Rebellion, the British government disbanded the Company and established direct British rule. However, there was no change in the English language policy that had been advised by Macaulay. In 1947, when India declared its independence of the United Kingdom, English was identified as one of the official languages of the new state with the provision that the official status of English would cease in 1965.

THE CONTINUING POWER OF ENGLISH IN INDIA

In 1965, there was insufficient political support to remove the official status of English. Too many Indians found it too useful for everyday communication. An Indian census in 1991 identified 114 Indian languages that had at least 10,000 speakers, and no Indian language could be found to replace the role that English still played. Despite its colonial taint, it continued to enable Indians from north, east, south and west of the country to talk to each other.

Indian English is not the English of London or Washington. Its sounds are different from British and American sounds. It constructs its words differently. It has its own vocabulary. It has its own sentence structures. In Indian English 'enthusiasm' becomes 'enthu': 'That guy has a lot of enthu'. That, in turn, leads to Indians saying 'He's a real enthu guy.' There are thousands of such differences in vocabulary and usage in modern Indian English.

Although most young Indians no longer harbour anti-colonial objections to English, there remains some internal prejudice against Indian English, with many speakers wishing to make Indian conform to British or American English standards. By contrast, the leading scholar on the subject, Braj B. Kachru, argues that speakers of Indian English must 'develop an identity with the local model of English without feeling that it is a "deficient" model'.

By some estimates, there are today 350 million people using the English language in India, Pakistan and Bangladesh. They vary in ability from complete fluency to stumbling words, but together they currently constitute the world's greatest English-speaking community. The future of English may be Asian.

51 ST MARTIN-LE-GRAND – *the English language and the Uniform Penny Post* (1840)

On 10 January 1840, Sir Rowland Hill refrained from visiting the General Post Office in St Martin-le-Grand in the City of London because that night the Uniform Penny Post was to begin and Hill expected that the post office would be besieged. He was right. His diary entry for the next day showed that 112,000 letters had been posted on 10 January 1840, three times the number of letters posted on 10 January 1839.

www.stampauctions.co.uk

The first postage stamp, a 'Penny Black'

What was remarkable about the Uniform Penny Post was that one price would apply not just to London, but to the whole of Great Britain. Whether a letter was to go from one street to the next, or from Truro to Aberdeen, the cost would be the same – one penny. The notion of distance was abolished. On 6 May 1840, paying for posting letters was made as simple as possible by the introduction of the first self-adhesive, pre-paid postage stamp, the Penny Black.

Rowland Hill, the man behind the new Penny Post and the postage stamp, induced Englishmen and Englishwomen to write hundreds of thousands of letters to one another. He had first had to persuade the British government to replace its antiquated, cumbersome, expensive and slow postal system with a modern, manageable, cheap and fast service. When he had done so, the flood of letters that resulted led to deliveries in cities like London being increased to many a day. The middle classes now had the resources that had once been the reserve of kings, popes and emperors and that had, up to 1840, been the prerogative of the noble and the wealthy.

THE GROWTH OF LETTER WRITING

It was not until the eighteenth century that letter writing in English had become widespread, and that was an age in which letter writing became an art. The letters of Horace Walpole fill thirty-four volumes. Their collection and editing was the life's work of Wilmarth Sheldon Lewis who began publishing Walpole's letters in 1939 and finished the job in 1971. Many twentieth-century scholars followed Lewis's lead in producing editions of letters complete with annotations, introductions, appendices and indexes. The work could take the lifetime of the scholar; sometimes, it was even longer – and another person would have to finish the publishing. Nineteenth-century novelists have been particularly well served. Often their letters are lengthy and powerful expositions of the writer's life and times; sometimes, they are short and bald business statements.

People who love collected letters often fear that the introduction of quick, cheap modes of communication will kill off the art of letter writing. That may not be the case. The Uniform Penny Post hugely increased the number of short notes that people sent to each other, but that did not stop the great writers from writing great letters. Charles Dickens, William Makepeace Thackeray and Anthony Trollope all produced thousands of magnificent letters.

It is usually only with the death of authors that their letters become public, and despite the fears that the telephone would kill the letter, the death of Ted Hughes and the publication of his letters showed that twentieth-century writers could easily match nineteenth-century ones as correspondents.

The twenty-first century must show whether or not the e-mail and the internet will kill off the letter as a masterpiece. But doubtless, somewhere, some wonderful writer is writing wonderful letters to someone, and we will only know about that many years hence.

Since the day of the Uniform Penny Post, the telegraph, the e-mail, texting, the social network and Twitter have provided ever more rapid means of exchanging written messages. With texting and Twitter, the speed of exchanges approaches the simultaneity of spoken, telephone or radio exchanges, but any text-based messaging system preserves a relation with one of the oldest of written forms, the letter.

52 WAITANGI – *the English language in New Zealand* (1840)

On 6 February 1840, at Waitangi, Aotearoa, Maori chiefs signed a treaty with the representatives of the British government. The Maori were agreeing to permanent white settlement in their islands. The Treaty of Waitangi signalled the moment when the British, not the French, asserted possession of what was renamed New Zealand; it was also the moment when English was destined to become the dominant European language of Aotearoa.

After 1840, European migration to New Zealand came almost exclusively from the British Isles. A census in 1871 showed that of these various migrants, 51 per cent came from England, 27 per cent from Scotland, and 22 per cent from Ireland. The majority spoke regional dialects unlike the upper-class English of the colony's

Bill Lucas

The lawn on which the treaty of Waitangi was signed in front of the Governor's residence

administrators. That division shaped linguistic attitudes and accents until the 1960s at least. At the same time, the Maori language provided many terms for local animals, plants and landscape features.

The proportions of the 1871 census suggest the founding elements of New Zealand English, but they do not take account of the fact that there was a continuous movement back and forth between New Zealand and Australia. Some 6 per cent of the 1871 white population was born in Australia, and very large numbers of those who came from the British Isles first landed in Australia before deciding to move to New Zealand. Australian English had then – and continues to have – a strong influence. (For the story of Australian English, see pages 112–14.)

As in Australia, school inspectors, administrators and leaders of opinion complained from the beginning about the kind of English that they found widespread in New Zealand. A major complaint was that many New Zealanders said 'in', not 'ing', at the ends of words; they added and dropped 'h's improperly; and generally sounded Cockney. (See pages 114–7 for Cockney.)

New Zealand linguists challenge the idea that there were large numbers of Londoners among the immigrants to New Zealand. Moreover, within England and the Empire, Cockney was the accent most disliked by upper-class English speakers,

A contemporary cartoon by Bob Brockie satirically depicting the treaty signing at Waitangi

and there was a tendency to label any disliked accent as Cockney. Arguing for a level-ling of the nineteenth-century English, Irish and Scottish immigrant dialects, New Zealand linguists claim that a distinctive voice appeared about 1900 and spread rapidly through the country. It was initially noted in derogatory terms as a colonial drawl or twang. However, modern-day New Zealanders have homogenized their speech, eroding the once unacceptable drawl as well as the once superior vowels.

DISTINCTIVELY NEW ZEALANDISH

A notable feature of New Zealand speech is a phenomenon called the High Rising Terminal. Speakers who are not asking questions will end on a rising note. Some-times called 'upspeak', the rising terminals delight young speakers and distress old listeners. The trend is a relatively recent one, and in England it is often thought to have been introduced by way of Australian soap operas. However, Australia may not be the land of origin of the High Rising Terminals. They were being noted by linguists in the northern half of New Zealand's North Island as early as 1966. From there, they may have spread wide across the English-speaking world.

How different is New Zealand English from Australian English? Linguists call the first NZE, and the second AusE, and they have devoted lengthy studies to discussions of their characteristics. *Comparative Studies in Australian and New Zealand English* provides over 400 pages on the matter. These studies mainly point to the likenesses between these two varieties of English by contrast with British English (BrE) and American English (AmE). But they say a great deal about the differences between NZE and AusE as well. However, these are quite subtle and are subject to many qualifications.

The great lexicographer of New Zealand English was Harry Orsman. His *Dictionary of New Zealandisms* contains almost 8,000 entries that track words particular to the country. Orsman also produced several collections of New Zealand slang. The blurb for one of them gives a flavour of the language that he loved: 'It's a well-known fact that Kiwis have their own way of talking, and without a guide you can easily come a greaser. Have a gink at this beaut little book, and you won't need to feel a nong any more. In fact, you'll be away laughing. You can put a ring around that!'

THE STRAND – *English as a language of satire* (1841)

Sometime in June 1841, Mark Lemon and Henry Mayhew met to talk about starting a new comic magazine which would combine humour with political commentary. During their discussion, so the story goes, someone remarked that a comic magazine, like good punch, needed lemon. Mayhew is reported to have been immediately taken by the name 'Punch'. So just over a month later when their new magazine was published, it bore the name *Punch*. It had a sub-title too – 'The London Charivari', an allusion to a successful satirical magazine already published in Paris. Between 1841 and 1992, and then briefly between 1996 and 2002, *Punch* magazine was one of the world's most influential English-language satirical publications.

In the first edition, Lemon argued that *Punch* would 'destroy the principle of evil by increasing the means of cultivating the good'. And in its early years the magazine did indeed became a scourge of authority, targeting the monarchy, leading politicians and promoting greater equality. It famously pointed out that the yearly stipend given to Prince Albert was, at £30,000, three times the total amount spent on educating the poor in England.

It used prose and poetry to make its points. So, in *The Song of the Shirt*, by Thomas Hood, *Punch* showed how it used rhyme to do what Charles Dickens was doing in prose to describe the impact of poverty:

With fingers weary and worn,
With eyelids heavy and red,
A woman sat in unwomanly rags,
Plying her needle and thread –
Stitch! Stitch! Stitch!
In poverty, hunger, and dirt,
And still with a voice of dolorous pitch
She sang 'The Song of the Shirt!'

But *Punch* did not confine its commentary to social issues; it was also at the forefront of thinking about language itself. In 1843 it created a new meaning for an old word, 'cartoon', as a humorous, often satirical, often caricatured illustration. The birth of this new meaning was occasioned by the overblown early sketches of the new designs for the Palace of Westminster. *Punch*'s John Leech poked great fun at these. His 'Cartoon no. 1: Substance and Shadow' mocked the overblown frescoes and the politicians' detachment from reality.

On 9 November 1895, *Punch* coined a new expression – 'a curate's egg' – to describe something that is good and bad in parts. In a cartoon by George du Maurier, the conversation went like this:

Right Reverend Host. 'I'm afraid you've got a bad Egg, Mr. Jones!'
The Curate. 'Oh no, my Lord, I assure you! Parts of it are excellent!'

Punch was always alert to the absurd or humorous in language. With its substantial London readership, it is not surprising that Cockney speech patterns came in from mockery – in particular, the East End habit of dropping the 'h' at the start of words such as 'hand', and sounding it at the beginning of words such as 'arm'. In a famous cartoon called 'Poor Letter H' in a collection called *Mr Punch's Cockney Humour*, the following appears:

COCKNEY HOBSERVATION – Cockneys are not the only people who drop or exasperate the 'h's'. It is done by common people in the provinces, and you may laugh at them for it. The deduction therefore is, that peasant, with an 'h', is fair game.

In the late twentieth century, *Punch* lost its punch. It ceased to publish in 2002, but cartoons in English-language newspapers trace their ancestry to *Punch*. In the United States, the *New Yorker* continues that tradition, as does *Private Eye* in Britain.

The morse code machine that sent a message between Baltimore and Washington

BALTIMORE – *the English language and the telegram* (1844)

On 24 May 1844, Samuel Finley Beese Morse sent a message from Baltimore to Washington. It was addressed to the President of the United States; it was in code and it travelled at the speed of light. When decoded, the message read: 'What hath God wrought.' The ancient forms of exchange, ones that required couriers or letters to cross land and sea, had been joined by the first electronic means of communication.

Morse had not only perfected the telegraph; he had also devised a binary encoding system – now called Morse code – to take full advantage of the electrical relaying that telegraphy permitted. His was a triumph of the new science of electricity, of encryption and of business. Telegraph stations began appearing right across the United States, following the routes of the expanding railroads.

Systems were quickly developed in Europe, and in 1851 a cable was laid across the English Channel. That was a great achievement, but the real challenge was to link Europe with America. After five attempts and huge expenditures, a permanent link was made, and on 27 July 1866 a message was sent from Cornwall to Newfoundland: 'Thank God, the cable is laid, and is in perfect working order.'

That message cost nothing beyond the millions of dollars spent on the cable. Transatlantic customers, however, found that they had to pay $150 for the first twenty words of a message and $4 for each additional word. Since labourers were then pleased to earn a dollar a day, the telegram, as the telegraph messages came to be called, was only for the rich. Telegrams were used to send urgent messages. Businesses and governments used them to seal deals and give orders; the general public used them to announce births, marriages and deaths.

THE LEGACY OF TELEGRAMMING

For 120 years, the telegram excited users. When Mark Twain heard that his obituary had been published, he sent a telegram saying: 'The report of my death was an exaggeration.' Oscar Wilde cabled his publisher to ask how his new book was doing. The message read: '?' The publisher cabled back: '!' W. C. Fields wired his dying friend John Barrymore the words: 'You can't do this to me.' A voter telegraphed President Herbert Hoover: 'Vote for Roosevelt and make it unanimous.'

Telegramming anticipated e-mailing and texting. It was the first example of simultaneously, long-distance messaging in which the exchange time of the written word began to approach the speed of the spoken word. Diplomats and journalists sent long telegrams, but mostly telegrams were short, blunt, to the point. The greatest number of them passed daily between the two great financial centres of the late nineteenth century: London and New York. Those were the metropoles of the English language, and the constant exchange of messages in the shared language predicted, though it did not bring about, the narrowing of the distance between British and American English. Since 1607, they had been separating; electronic communications were about to bring that linguistic Continental drift to a halt.

55 SALFORD – *literacy and free libraries* (1850)

In April 1850, the Royal Museum and Public Library opened in Salford. Located in Peel Park, the library held some 10,000 books on its shelves and had more than 1,200 visitors a day in its first year. In that same year, the Public Libraries Act was passed in England. Like the Museum Act five years earlier, the Act was a sign of the times, of industrial prosperity leading to pressure for greater access to cultural resources. Indeed the 1850s saw a pouring of energy into the building of museums, galleries and libraries.

The Public Libraries Act enabled boroughs to levy a tax to enable them to provide free public libraries. It was designed to raise levels of literacy, promoting self-improvement and education. Not everyone welcomed the new libraries. Some resented the cost they imposed on local residents who might not want to use them. Others feared that warm spaces would provide an environment in which the working classes might gather and make trouble. A sizeable proportion of people were anxious about the new power they would give ordinary people and, specifically, that they might end up engrossed in 'low' novels instead of reading 'improving' books.

But there are a number of places, other than Salford, that have a claim on the honour of creating the first free public library. In the United States, for example, the Peterborough Town Library, New Hampshire, was suggested at a public meeting in 1833, and Boston, Massachusetts, opened its public library in 1854 after discussions going back to 1848.

Closer to Salford, Chetham in Manchester has had an endowed library since 1653. Primarily aimed at the scholars attending Chetham School, it nevertheless argues its case as the first free public library. Following the founding in Edinburgh in 1821 of a Mechanics' Institute, many similar institutes had sprung up, often offering free or low-cost borrowing of books. Libraries were included in many museums. In the nineteenth century, the notion of the free library became widespread. With it came the encouragement of an ever-wider population to engage with the written word. Literacy spread the habit of reading, and reading spread the habit of literacy. By the end of the nineteenth century, English was already a world language, the majority of whose speakers were also readers. The influence of written English on spoken English that had begun with the printing press in the fifteenth century was, by 1900, leaving very few dialects of English unaffected.

Salford Museum and Library as it is today

Tom Jeffs

THE IMPACT OF LIBRARIES ON READING AND LEARNING

Public libraries, according to library historian Thomas Greenwood, were: 'centres of light and not only feed but create a taste for reading, and unquestionably, whatever does this is a benefit to the whole community and aids materially in the repressing and taming of the rougher and baser parts of human nature'.

Free public libraries were to the general public as schools were to children: they offered education through the medium of English. Just as the invention of printing (see pages 56–7) had enabled English books to be printed in some volume, so libraries enabled ordinary people to read everything from the technical English of reference works through to the reported speech of characters in novels or the dynamic language of Shakespeare's tragic heroes and heroines.

 HANNIBAL – *English comic writing* (1851)

On 16 January 1851, the Hannibal *Western Union* provided a short piece under the headline 'A Gallant Fireman'. It reported that a member of the newspaper's staff had saved 'the broom, an old mallet, the wash-pan and a dirty towel' and then ran to safety with them, declaring, on his return, 'If that thar fire hadn't bin put out, thar'd a' bin the greatest *confirmation* of the age!' 'A Gallant Fireman' shows that, at the age of sixteen, its author, Samuel Langhorne Clemens of Hannibal, Missouri, had an instinct for comic description. He grew up to become the writer who called himself Mark Twain.

Discussing 'Wit and Humour', William Hazlitt offered an explanation of what we find tragic and what we find comic: 'We weep at what thwarts or exceeds our desires in serious matters: we laugh at what only disappoints our expectations in trifles.' Comic writing moves towards the dangerous and disturbing, but makes sudden shifts to divert the meaning. Certainly Mark Twain's masterpiece, *The Adventures of Huckleberry Finn*, not only includes jokes, anecdotes and tall stories, but it also takes comic writing to the point where it borders on tragedy.

It is surprising to find that the only kind of laughter recorded in Old English literature is the mirthless laugh of a warrior who has killed an enemy. Swearing and bad language are also absent. It is likely that the Angles, Saxons and Jutes were as joke-loving and as foul-mouthed as we are today, but their writers did not think it a good idea to record the fact. Little English comic writing appears before the fourteenth century, but then with the delicate wit of the Gawayn poet and the wonderful comedy of Geoffrey Chaucer (see pages 20–24 and pages 45–7), English comic writing started strongly and has never ceased.

COMIC ENGLISH – STANDING THE TEST OF TIME

Some authors have been found funny by readers over the centuries, but there are strong patterns of fashion, and it is instructive to look back at comic writers who no longer amuse. Something that nineteenth-century American newspapers found very popular were anecdotalists writing up stories filled with comic dialect and published under a pseudonym, exactly the kind of material that Samuel Clemens wrote under the name of Mark Twain. But while his name remains known, those of Petroleum V. Nasby and Artemis Ward are forgotten.

The comic turn of Petroleum V. Nasby (born David Ross Locke) is shown in *Divers Views, Opinions, and Prophecies: Of Yoors Trooly* where he tells his reader: 'I yoost to go frum Pennsilvany to the cappytle wunst a year, to git my stock uv Dimocrisy recrootid, and to find out what we wuz expectid to bleeve doorin the cumin year, thus gettin full 6 munths ahed uv my nabers.' The comic turn of Artemis Ward (born Charles Farrar Browne) is shown in *Artemus Ward, His Book*: 'I manetane that wax figgers is more elevatin than awl the plays ever wroten. Take Shakespeer for instunse. Peple think heze grate things, kontend heze quite the reverse to the kontrary. What sort of sense is thare to King Leer who goze round cussin his darters, chawin hay and throin straw at folks, and larfin like a silly old koot and makin a ass of hisself generally?'

Petroleum V. Nasby, Artemus Ward and Mark Twain had the English-speaking world in fits of laughter in the 1860s. The humour of Nasby and Ward has lost its power; the humour of Twain remains.

 HYDE PARK – *industrialization and its impact on English* (1851)

On 1 May 1851, the Great Exhibition of the Works of Industry of all Nations, normally referred to as the Great Exhibition, opened its doors to the public in an enormous and intricate greenhouse-like structure in Hyde Park. A showcase for industrial and cultural artefacts from across the world, and especially its English-speaking parts, it was the block-buster exhibition of its era, attracting more than 6 million visitors. To understand the full extent of its popularity it is helpful to appreciate that the total population of Britain was only some 18 million people at this time.

The World Exhibition Building, designed by Joseph Paxton, at the Great Exhibition in Hyde Park. Known as the 'Crystal Palace' the building was dismantled and re-erected in South London where, sadly, it was later destroyed by fire

In her journal Queen Victoria records her own fascination:

We saw the first cotton machines from Oldham. Mr Whitworth's planing of iron tools, another for shearing and punching iron of just ½ inch thick, doing it as if it were bread!...What was particularly interesting was a printing machine on the vertical principle, by which a numbers of sheets are printed, dried and everything done in a second.

Walking through the extraordinary glasshouse, visitors would have been in no doubt that they were experiencing the hey-day of the Industrial Revolution.

The same industrialization that produced the inventions with which the Great Exhibition was full also marked a shift away from the countryside to the towns and cities. In the year of the Great Exhibition, about half of the population lived in rural areas, half in urban. By 1911, four-fifths of the population lived in towns and cities. This radical geographical shift marked a shift in linguistic power from the language of the large, rural estates to the language of factories and of technological invention.

THE GROWTH OF SPECIALIZED VOCABULARY

The kind of human creativity on show at the Great Exhibition was given full vent in an extraordinary outpouring of new words to describe new inventions and new concepts. David Crystal estimates that hundreds of thousands of new words entered the language as a consequence of the Industrial Revolution. He reminds us that words ending in '-ology', '-ography', '-metry', '-onomy' and '-ics' largely entered the language during the nineteenth century, in terms such as:

biology, palaeontology, entomology, morphology;
photography;
telemetry;
taxonomy;
mechanics; genetics.

In the period following the Great Exhibition, English became the pre-eminent language of science and technology. And even if some of the more curious words of this time – the daguerreotypes which were early forms of photographs, for example – are no longer in use, much of the technical language we employ today was the result of the same inventive, entrepreneurial, ambitious impulse that had produced the Crystal Palace itself and was captured in the language of the *Official Catalogue of the Great Exhibition of the Works of Industry of All Nations*.

Part of the fun, Melvyn Bragg speculates, must have been finding new names for new things. Here we find 'spinning-jennies', 'doubling machines', 'power looms', 'electro-plating', 'hair-trigger', 'lorry' and 'lithograph', all still intelligible today – even if, as Bragg points out, an 'anhydrohepseterion' (a machine for cooking potatoes) has not made it into the contemporary kitchen. New machines and gadgets have each required their own names, and as the pace of invention has increased since 1851, so has the need for new words.

That need can lead to strange developments. The pharmaceutical industry has had to turn to computer-generated words to provide unique nouns for thousands of new drugs, each requiring a patentable name. Before the computer, pharmacy had used more traditional practices for the invention of new names. When at the end of the nineteenth century, interesting and novel uses were invented for the leaves of the coca plant, two matching sets of new word processes were also invented. One product combined the coca leaf with the cola nut to produce Coca-Cola. Spin-off drinks not only imitated the taste, they also called themselves 'colas', so that a new common noun was born.

A second coca product was more chemically intensive, and its inventor followed the chemical industry's practice of adding the suffix '-ine' to the word 'coca'; '-ine', says the *Oxford English Dictionary*, means 'pertaining to'. Hence '-ine' and 'coca' produced 'cocaine'. As well as becoming a drug of choice, cocaine also proved to be a painkiller. From that, the pharmaceutical industry has derived a new suffix, '-aine', to be used to signify painkillers, producing names like amethocaine, bupivacaine, lidocaine, prilocaine and procaine. They are ugly words, but they are words none the less.

58 TIMES SQUARE – *The New York Times* (1851)

On 18 September 1851, the first edition of *The New York Daily Times* was produced at 113 Nassau Street in New York. In 1857, the editor, Henry Jarvis Raymond, changed the paper's name to *The New York Times* and moved its production to 41 Park Row. Then, in 1904, it moved to the famous square that now bears its name.

By renaming itself, *The New York Times* was both echoing and challenging the most powerful and prestigious newspaper in the English-speaking world: *The Times* of London. Since it was the first, that paper did not include its city of publication in its name, but since then newspapers throughout the world have so named themselves: *The Australian Times, The Calcutta Times, The Islamabad Times, The Los Angeles Times, Straits Times, The Wellington Times, The Zimbabwe Times.*

The word 'Times' has come to mean a newspaper. Moreover, adopting that title is to claim status, integrity and authority. That applies not only to the news that is reported, but also to the language in which it is written. Each of these newspapers likes to think of itself as 'a paper of record', providing an accurate chronicle of the times in a language that will stand the test of time. Visits to their websites show that despite the proliferation of street Englishes, *Times* English everywhere has a standard grammar.

This standard *Times* grammar is a conventional formulation. It was reached through the acceptance by the English upper class and the British educational elite of a set of rules for written English. The rules covered spelling, punctuation, grammar and usage. Those rules were formulated by the mid-eighteenth century and codified by Samuel Johnson's *Dictionary* (1795) and Lindley Murray's *English Grammar* (1755) – see page 98. Today, the major English-language newspapers throughout the world (as well as the major English-language publishing houses) have what are called stylebooks or style manuals. The London *Times* has *The Times Style and Usage Guide*. *The New York Times* has *The New York Times Manual*. There are a hundred such. They pride themselves on their local details, but on issues of English grammar there is little variation.

When Henry Jarvis Raymond renamed his paper in 1857, Americans were already aware of the prestige of *The Times* of London. In 1854, Nathaniel Hawthorne, America's unhappy Liverpool consul, noted that 'Every Englishman runs to *The Times* with his little grievance, as a child runs to his mother.' Three years later, *The New York Times* began to gain a similar reputation in the United States.

It was technology that gave newspapers extraordinary power. Steam-driven presses, first adopted by *The Times*, allowed the production of thousands of copies of every edition. When Samuel Morse perfected telegraph transmissions, daily news could be flashed over huge distances. That led to the formation of American wire services like the Associated Press in 1848. When a transatlantic cable was laid in 1866,

The New York Times Building in Times Square today

Andrea Puggioni

newspapers were ready to print daily news coming from another continent.

The New York Times matched *The Times* of London with every technological development, expanding its distribution, as well as expanding the depth and breadth of its coverage. In 1898, its masthead boasted 'All the News That's Fit to Print'. Wags rephrased that as 'All the news that fits the print'. No paper could hope to dominate a Continental-sized country the way *The Times* could dominate England. None the less, *The New York Times* is today as close to a national newspaper as the United States allows. Only *The Los Angeles Times* and *The Washington Post* can rival it.

A NEW KIND OF LANGUAGE GUIDE

Newspapers round the world follow either the New York or the London *Times* in matters of style. Sometimes, though, the English language throws up problems to which there is no easy solution. Spirits distilled from corn pose a corker. Scottish and Canadian producers spell their tipple without an 'e' as 'whisky', but Irish and American products tend to be spelled 'whiskey'. Eager to be consistent, *The New York Times Manual* tells writers to use the 'ey' spelling in all cases to avoid the distraction of alternative spellings in the same article. Scottish distilleries continue to complain, but the newspaper maintains its impressive but controlling uniformity.

'Now,' says the New York manual, 'everyone can find answers in the handy alphabetical guide used by the thousand journalists of the world's most authoritative newspaper.' *The Times* of London might disagree with that final claim.

59 MANCHESTER – *the vocabulary of English and the thesaurus* (1852)

In 1852, Peter Mark Roget, the Secretary of the Portico Library, Manchester, published *A Thesaurus of English Words and Phrases Classified and Arranged so as to Facilitate the Expression of Ideas and Assist in Literary Composition.* He had given ten years to collecting and arranging English synonyms – that is, words having the same, or nearly the same, meaning as other words.

His thesaurus was immediately popular. It went through twenty-eight printings in his lifetime. After his death, his son and his grandson continued to add to it. Now, it is known simply as *Roget's Thesaurus.* (The Rogets originally came from Switzerland, and their book to this day retains a Continental pronunciation – 'Rowshay'.)

Around the word 'collection', the Rogets grouped a set of synonyms that shows how their book worked: 'Collection, accumulation, heap, hoard, magazine, pile, rick, savings, bank, treasury, reservoir, repository, repertory, depository, depot, thesaurus, museum, storehouse, reservatory, conservatory, menagerie, receptacle, warehouse, dock, larder, garner, granary, storeroom, cistern, well, tank, armoury, arsenal, coffer.' From these, the word 'thesaurus' was chosen to describe the new kind of collection, accumulation, heap and hoard. Since then, 'thesaurus' has become the common noun for a dictionary of synonyms.

The list suggests the intellectual system that Peter Mark Roget had devised for arranging the thousands of words in his book. The alphabetical ordering of a dictionary would not do, and Roget, a capable scientist and natural philosopher, relied instead upon various ways for the ordering of ideas that had been developed since the Ancient Greeks.

Roget's groupings make for good browsing; none the less, most users of a thesaurus rely on the index to find what they want. The original index was a poor thing, but the indexes of modern thesauruses are often longer than the word collections themselves.

THE EXTRAORDINARY VARIETY OF ENGLISH VOCABULARY

'Thesaurus' (a word that comes to English from Greek by way of Latin) gives a first clue as to why the English language is rich in synonyms. Greek words did not begin to be imported in large numbers until the seventeenth century when they contributed particularly to the development of the scientific English (see pages 85–7). However, Greek words were easily absorbed by a language that had, since the ninth century, been continually invaded by words from other languages. Danish and French words arrived as a result of actual invasions (see pages 23–5 and 29–31).

Occupation by, and then intermarriage with, the Danes and the French led the English to expand their vocabulary with thousands of commonplace words – *kirk, dike, skirt, skin, die, ill* from Norse, and *carpenter, canon, kennel, catch, cattle, gaol, garden* from French. Those two sources of borrowings had two important consequences. First, English lost some of the reluctance that many languages show towards what are called variously foreign, loan or borrowed words.

Second, because so many of the early English borrowings were for words for which English already had a word, English began to accumulate synonyms. English had the word 'board', but it was happy to adopt the word 'table' as well. English had the word 'ditch', but it was happy to add the word 'dike'. Once the language had doublets of that kind, it tended to give them slightly different meanings.

The borrowing from Danish was intense, but it only went on for three centuries; the borrowings from French have gone on for a thousand years, and the same, though with a somewhat different pattern, is true of the borrowings from Latin (see pages 64–5).

Today, the English language is said to have over a million words. That is probably true, but it might also be true of some other languages. English speakers love to heap up what the Old English poets called 'word hoards'. Also, the authoritative dictionary of the English language, the *Oxford English Dictionary*, is much more inclusive than, say, the authoritative dictionary of the French language, the *Dictionnaire de l'Académie francaise*. Since the university-educated speaker of English has a vocabulary of 40,000 to 50,000 words, the million words of the language provide room for numerous synonyms.

 BERDICHEV – *exophonic English* (1857)

On 3 December 1857, Józef Teodor Konrad Korzeniowski was born in Berdichev, which was then in the Kiev Governorate (now Berdychiv, Ukraine). The boy would grow up to become Joseph Conrad, one of the most distinguished novelists in the English language. He had the benefit of a good education in a multilingual family, but his first language after Polish was not English. It was French, and quite as remarkable as his becoming an English-language novelist was the fact that he became a captain in the British Merchant Navy. At the age of sixteen, he left Poland and the Russian Empire, of which it was a part, and set out for Marseilles in order to become a sailor.

He didn't come to England until 1878 when he signed on to a coaster trading between Lowestoft and Newcastle. It was from its East Anglian crew that he began to learn English. They called him Polish Joe. In 1886, he became a Master Mariner and a British citizen. In 1895, he published his first novel, *Almayer's Folly: A Story of an Eastern River*. In the next eighteen years, he wrote eighteen more novels.

On hearing the news of his death in 1924, the *New York Times* wrote: 'Though he knew little English before he was 20, he became one of the master English stylists.' Perhaps an even greater tribute was the obituarist's final observation: 'Conrad's influence on later novelists has been profound.' It is not unusual for someone to become a fluent speaker of a foreign language; it is unusual for someone to become a fluent writer in a foreign language – and it is most unusual for someone to become a major writer in a foreign language. To become so great a writer of a foreign language that other great writers acknowledge that greatness is truly unusual.

Conrad's remarkable achievement speaks, first, to his own capacity, and, second, it speaks to the capacity of the English language in the nineteenth century. In *A Personal Record*, he said of his boyhood decision to go to sea that 'I had thought to myself that if I was to be a seaman then I would be a British seaman and no other.' Distant England, the British Empire and its language were strong in the Polish boy's mind.

John Peters

Joseph Conrad

EARLY INDICATION OF THE POTENTIAL OF ENGLISH AS A LINGUA FRANCA

Already, English had begun its movement beyond the many countries to which the English had taken their language. In 1850, French was the international language, and in the Middle Europe of Conrad's childhood, French shared with German the role of a lingua franca. But English was also one of the languages being adopted in Berdichev, something unimaginable in 1750.

A writer who writes in a language that is not his mother tongue is called an 'exophone' – a word created from Greek roots for 'foreign' and 'sound'. Joseph Conrad is the English language's most distinguished exophone, but he is joined by Luis Borges (an Argentinian who spoke fluent Old English and wrote exquisite Modern English), Vladimir Nabokov (whose English-language novels pose paradoxes matched only by those in his translation of *Alice in Wonderland* into his native Russian – said to be the finest translation of *Alice* into any language), Joseph Brodsky (a Russian poet expelled by the Soviet Union and made poet laureate by the United States) and Winfried Georg Sebald (who came to England from Germany as a student and stayed to write novels about an East Anglia distilled through an astonishing English). It is also worth noting that great exophones are not only found in the English language. Geoffrey Chaucer, Samuel Beckett and Julien Green, an Englishman, an Irishman and an American, have made major contributions to French literature.

CHRISTCHURCH COLLEGE – *English nonsense* (1865)

> Alice was beginning to get very tired of sitting by her sister on the bank, and of having nothing to do: once or twice she had peeped into the book her sister was reading, but it had no pictures or conversations in it, 'and what is the use of a book,' thought Alice 'without pictures or conversation?'

So began, in 1865, Lewis Carroll's tale of a girl who falls down a rabbit hole into a world of fantasy, distortion and strangeness. Lewis Carroll was the nom-de-plume of Charles Lutwidge Dodgson, a mathematician and a fellow of Christchurch College, Oxford. He called the tale *Alice's Adventures in Wonderland* and its sequel was *Through the Looking Glass and What Alice Found There*.

The second of the Alice books contains the poem 'Jabberwocky'. While Alice is talking to two talking chess pieces – the White King and the White Queen – she finds a book that she can only read by looking at its words in a mirror. The poem starts:

> *Twas brillig, and the slithy toves*
> *Did gyre and gimble in the wabe;*
> *All mimsy were the borogoves,*
> *And the mome raths outgrabe.*

Written while Carroll was staying near Sunderland and possibly influenced by local legends of the Lambton Worm, the poem is an extraordinarily evocative ballad-like story. Its newly coined nonsense words leap from the page. Many of them have crept into the *Oxford English Dictionary* where they have been given solemn definitions:

bandersnatch – a fierce fantasy creature
chortle – a chuckle with a bit of a snort
frabjous – fair and joyous
galumph – move noisily and clumsily
outgrabe – make a strange noise
wabe – a wet hillside

The imposing façade of Christchurch College, Oxford

Alice puzzles over the poem's meaning and then concludes: 'Somehow it seems to fill my head with ideas – only I don't exactly know what they are! However, somebody killed something: that's clear, at any rate.'

Humpty Dumpty, a character from an English nursery rhyme, pops up to tell Alice that he can explain the poem (which he attempts to do). And as he does so he introduces the concept of 'portmanteau' words to describe words that are blends of two other words. 'Slithy', for example, combines 'lithe' and 'slimy'. He also makes a nonsensical remark that linguists have subsequently taken very seriously: '"When I use a word," Humpty Dumpty said, in rather a scornful tone, "it means just what I choose it to mean – neither more nor less."'

In 1846, Edward Lear, a poet and illustrator, had published *A Book of Nonsense*. In 1889, it was being republished as *A Book of Nonsense: Twenty-Seventh Edition*, and its immense popularity shows how attractive nonsense was for the Victorian reader. Lear's poem 'The Owl and the Pussycat', written in 1867, two years after *Alice's Adventures in Wonderland*, has become as enduring as *Alice*, and it too has given the *Oxford English Dictionary* a word: 'runcible':

They dined on mince, and slices of quince
Which they ate with a runcible spoon.

THE STUFF OF NONSENSE

The great Edwardian commentator on the great Victorians, G. K. Chesterton, pointed out that Edward Lear and Lewis Carroll were doing something new with the English language. They were not the first writers to use nonsense, he said, but they were the first writers who used it to mean 'absolutely nothing'. Aristophanes, Rabelais and Sterne had all used nonsense, but it was nonsense with a point. Theirs was nonsense intended to expose politicians, clerics, academics, anyone who used language in overblown, pompous, deceptive ways. The nonsense of Lear and Carroll seemed to have no purpose in mind beyond the joy of indulging in language itself, in showing the extraordinary, sonorous, intoxicating power of words.

Nonsense can also expose the underlying power of grammar and the human mind's instinct for meaning. In 1957, the word sequence 'Colorless green ideas sleep furiously' was made famous in linguistics by Noam Chomsky. He labelled it Sentence 1. He contrasted it with 'Furiously sleep ideas green colorless'. He labelled that Sentence 2. 'It is fair to assume,' said Chomsky, 'that neither sentence (1) nor (2) (nor indeed any part of these sentences) has ever occurred in an English discourse. Hence, in any statistical model for grammaticalness, these sentences will be ruled out on identical grounds as equally "remote" from English. Yet (1), though nonsensical, is grammatical, while (2) is not grammatical.' Upon that distinction, Chomsky developed his theory of transformational grammar and the relationship of language to the deep structures of the human brain. English nonsense can tell us a great deal.

LLANFAIRPWLLGWYNGYLL – *English place names* (1868)

In 1868, Anglesey Central Railway opened a new station to serve the people who lived in the village of Llanfairpwllgwyngyll. In English, that means 'St Mary's Church in the Hollow of the White Hazel'. Since so few visitors got off at Llanfairpwllgwyngyll, the villagers expanded the name to Llanfairpwllgwyngyllgogerychwyrndrobwllllan-tysiliogogogoch – 'St Mary's Church in the Hollow of the White Hazel near the Rapid Whirlpool of St Tysilio of the Red Cave'. Travellers then came in large numbers to visit a place with a name almost as long as its platform. The ruse has worked well ever since. Though the railway was closed in 1968, people still go to have their photos taken at Llanfairpwllgwyngyllgogerychwyrndrobwllllantysiliogogogoch.

The villagers themselves call it Llanfair PG, but like to challenge visitors to attempt the fifty-eight-letter form. Maoris have given some of their villages longer names in order to outdo the Welsh, but Llanfair PG at full length is still the longest, official place name in Europe.

Llanfairpwllgwyngyll can tell us some interesting things about place names. First of all, they are words that are invented and accepted in a conscious fashion in a way

The railway station with the longest English name in the world

that is not the pattern with other words. When people deliberately invent new words, they are normally rejected by other speakers, and they will only insinuate themselves into the language in an unconscious or unacknowledged way if there is a felt need for them. Place names are more readily accepted; their artificiality is not held against them.

Second, Llanfairpwllgwyngyll contains a meaning of sorts ('St Mary's Church in the Hollow of the White Hazel'), but that kind of meaning gets lost. With use, it becomes more of a signpost than a normal word. In fact, place names are in the category of proper nouns – names of places, persons and things – and most dictionaries do not include them. Lexicographers now say that the English language contains a million or so words, but that does not include proper nouns, and so it does not include the hundred of thousands of the world's place names.

Third, it is questionable as to whether or not Llanfairpwllgwyngyll is part of the English language. But Llanfairpwllgwyngyll is appearing quite easily in these English sentences and not as a foreign word, but simply as the name of a place.

EVERY PLACE NAME TELLS A STORY
In the British Isles, there are some 40,000 place names. Most of them are very old, and many are Celtic in origin, like Llanfairpwllgwyngyll. *Brewer's Britain and Ireland*

provides the etymologies of about 7,500, and it shows that numerous Welsh place names begin with 'Llan'. It means 'church-site'. *Brewer's Britain* also points out that periodically other Welsh villages try to give themselves longer names than Llanfair-pwllgwyngyllgogerychwyrndrobwllllantysiliogogogoch.

The shortest place name in the British Isles is Ae, a village in Dumfries and Galloway. 'Ae' is Celtic for river, as are Avon, Ouse and Wey. Many place names owe something to the Romans, particularly those ending in '-chester'. That comes from the Latin word *castrum* – fort. Those are places where Roman armies set up camps that later became cities. Places ending in '-by', '-thorp', '-beck', '-dale' and '-thwaite' were originally Danish settlements and are usually found on the east coast and in the north.

Very many place names in England originate from Angle, Saxon and Jute settlements of the fifth through to the seventh centuries, and those names are often repeated in every county and then recycled to be given to new settlements, and finally exported to become the names of places in North America, Africa and Oceana.

Over time, place names can change greatly. A name can chart a place's passage from Britonic through Roman, Saxon, Norman to modern possession. Until the nineteenth century, there was very little signposting and most people knew the names of places by having heard them. On the rare occasions when place names were written down, spellings varied greatly. Winchester may have begun as a Celtic place name, Caergwinntguic. If so, that evolved to become Cair-Guntin, Caerg-wintwg, Caer Gwent, Venta Belgarum, Venta Castra, Wintanceastre, Wincestre, Vincestre (with over a hundred different spellings), until finally it became Winchester.

 EXETER PLACE – *the English language and the telephone* (1876)

On 10 March 1876, Alexander Graham Bell said, 'Mr Watson, come here, I want to see you.' Remarkably, Thomas A. Watson went to Mr Bell, and they saw each other. What Watson had done was walk from one room to another at 5 Exeter Place, Boston. The event was remarkable because Bell had just sent Watson the world's first telephone message. Watson had heard it and reacted accordingly.

Since Samuel Morse had made the telegraph work in 1844 (see pages 134–5), inventors, electricians, mechanics and theorists had been struggling to achieve what they called audible telegraphy. They wanted to send the human voice down the wire, and not just the short and long pulses (the dots and dashes) of Morse code. They wanted to invent the telephone, which was a word first used to mean what it means today, by Alexander Graham Bell in an address to the American Academy of the Arts and Sciences in May 1876. The word had up till then been used to describe various

Alexander Graham Bell's laboratory

kinds of long-distance communication systems relying on string or air, none of which worked.

By 1900, there were nearly 1 million telephones in operation in the United States, and by 1920 the number had risen to nearly 12 million. In 2007, there were over 3 billion mobile phones and 1 billion fixed phones for a world population of 6 billion. Since 2007, the number of phones has increased even more rapidly than the number of people.

The telephone had the capacity to unite users of the English language into a single community, but to do that telephone calls would have to cover thousands of miles, and long-distance telephony proved difficult to perfect. It was not until 1927 that the first public transatlantic system was developed. It was expensive, but people in London and New York could then speak to each other from the comfort of their offices. If they were still 'separated by a common language', the separation had begun to reduce.

THE INFLUENCE OF THE TELEPHONE ON ENGLISH

Telephone users in the two countries had already established their own conventions. Both might say 'Hello' when picking up the phone, but the American might say 'Who is this?' while the Briton might say 'Who is that?' British users into the 1960s might answer the phone by giving their telephone number: 'Chorley Wood double two' or 'Prospect 9314'. Another British answering pattern, mainly male, would be to respond to a call with a last name: 'Curmudgeon here'. Americans could find those openings surprising.

Today, with cheap international telephone calls and the advent of smart and Skype phones, North Americans, Britons, Australians, New Zealanders, South Africans, West Indians, and English-using Indians, Pakistanis and Bangladeshis are engaging in daily conversations. Those conversations are one of the centripetal forces that maintain the mutual intelligibility of global English.

Calling call centres trains us all in international English. Though it is characteristic of phone users to engage the facial expressions and body language that they employ in a face-to-face conversation, phone users know that those are not part of the communication of a telephone call. Consequently, and especially when talking to strangers, phone users speak more clearly and they tend to avoid words and phrases that they know to be local.

The British and American telephone dialects began to mesh in 1927, and today we are used to hearing a range of the world's English accents. The telephone has made us adept at tuning our ears to them.

 CAPE TOWN – *the English language in South Africa* (1881)

In 1881, Olive Schreiner set sail from Cape Town. In her luggage, she had a number of manuscripts, and in 1883 a novel appeared in London called *The Story of an African Farm*. The title page gave the author's name as Ralph Iron. Its author was in fact Olive Schreiner, and it was the first English-language novel to be written by someone born in Africa. Schreiner was the daughter of an English woman and a German missionary. She was born in the Karoo, the dry tableland north of Cape Town, and the Karoo figures in her novel as the landscape that shapes her characters and their lives. The word 'karoo' came to the English language by way of Afrikaans, the language of Dutch settlers who called themselves Afrikaners. The Afrikaners had taken the word 'karoo' from Khoikhoi, the language of the original settlers of the tableland.

Though the English language had come to Africa as early as the sixteenth century, it was not until the beginning of the nineteenth century that any large community of European speakers of English began to develop on the continent of Africa, and it did so in Southern Africa.

AAPTE

The South African landscape of Olive Schreiner's writing

The British had needed to secure a route to India, and Cape Town provided a good base, one that the British declared theirs in 1814. Wanting to protect Cape Town from inland attack and discovering the fine climate of Southern Africa, the British took control of more and more of the territory.

By the time Olive Schreiner was born in 1855, a dialect called Cape Settler English had emerged as children of people from all over the British Isles began to shape a common speech. The British would not intermarry with Africans, but they did intermarry with Afrikaners, the descendants of seventeenth-century Dutch settlers in the Cape. That introduced Dutch vowels and vocabulary into Cape Settler English, the dialect that is the basis of the English spoken today in South Africa, Namibia, Botswana, Zimbabwe and Zambia.

FORMS OF SOUTH AFRICAN ENGLISH

The new dialect had developed in a hierarchical, colonial world, and three forms of Cape Settler English came to be identified: Extreme South African English, Respectable South African English, and Conservative South African English. Extreme South African English showed the greatest influence of Afrikaans. Conservative South African English showed the greatest influence of British Received

Pronunciation. A book called *South African English Pronunciation*, published in Cape Town in 1929, expressed a fear that South African speech was deviating from the best British standard and moving towards Cockney English, a dialect that was denounced in South Africa, just as it was in Australia (see page 112).

Another fear was that English was being invaded by Afrikaans, and *South African English Pronunciation* cited the examples of *kraal, drift, stoep, springbok, ouispan, trek, spoor, donga, kloof* and *veldt*. South African English was indeed borrowing many words from Afrikaans, and many of those words had been borrowed in turn from the Bantu and Khosian languages spoken in Southern Africa.

Rather than see these words as invading English, modern linguists see them as enriching English, and the *Oxford Dictionary of the English of South Africa* today boasts that it provides over 2,000 etymologies of words that have entered the English language in South Africa.

 DUBLIN – *extreme English* (1882)

On 2 February 1882, in the Dublin suburb of Rathgar, James Augustine Joyce was born, the first surviving child of John and May Joyce. He was a boy on whom the father lavished affection and favour, sending him to private Jesuit schools and finally to University College, Dublin.

With his classical and conventional education, James Joyce became fluent in several languages, learned in the arts and literature, and rebellious against his family, his country and his Church. Joyce's thoughts on his upbringing found expression in *A Portrait of the Artist as a Young Man*, an autobiographical novel. Significantly, Stephen Dedalus, poet hero of the novel, declares that the English language, 'so familiar and so foreign, will always be for me an acquired speech. I have not made or accepted its words. My voice holds them at bay.' But Stephen Dedalus cannot speak Gaelic. English would have to be the medium of his art.

PUSHING THE BOUNDARIES OF ENGLISH

Joyce, like Dedalus, unable to speak Gaelic, was forced to write in English and, in a series of ever-increasing linguistic experiments, pushed against the limits of the language 'so familiar and so foreign'. A movement towards an extreme English can be seen in the progression of his novels.

A Portrait of the Artist as a Young Man, published in 1916, catches the thought of the child Dedalus: 'Once upon a time and a very good time it was there was a moocow coming down along the road and this moocow that was coming down along the road met a nicens little boy named baby tuckoo...'

© Dave Walsh

Statue of James Joyce in Dublin

Ulysses, published in 1921 and often identified as the greatest novel of the twentieth century, catches the thought of the adult Dedalus:

> My Latin quarter hat. God, we simply must dress the character. I want puce gloves. You were a student, weren't you? Of what in the other devil's name? Paysayenn. P. C. N., you know: physiques, chimiques et naturelles. Aha. Eating your groatsworth of mou en civet, fleshpots of Egypt, elbowed by belching cabmen. Just say in the most natural tone: when I was in Paris, boul' Mich', I used to…

Finnegans Wake, published in 1939, catches the thought of a man through a single night. Joyce reworks punctuation, reshapes words, and bends syntax to force buried meanings to the surface and expose layers of reference. The novel opens with a refracted telling of the story of Tristram and Iseult:

> riverrun, past Eve and Adam's, from swerve of shore to bend of bay, brings us by a commodius vicus of recirculation back to Howth Castle and Environs.
>
> Sir Tristram, violer d'amores, fr'over the short sea, had passencore rearrived from North Armorica on this side the scraggy isthmus of Europe Minor to wielderfight his penisolate war: nor had topsawyer's rocks by the stream Oconee exaggerated themselse to Laurens County's gorgios while they went doublin their mumper all the time

The last line of the novel supplies the missing half of the first line – 'A way a lone a last a loved a long the' – so that *Finnegans Wake* ends with its beginning. Joyce devoted his life to writing his novels, and he wanted his readers to devote their lives to reading them.

There are a very few writers whose work has a profound effect on the English language itself, such is their power of expression and the limits to which they drive words and meanings. Geoffrey Chaucer, William Tyndale, William Shakespeare, Samuel Johnson are examples. So too James Joyce. Readers encountering his work have to rethink their idea of what the English language is and of what it is capable.

GISBORNE – *English slang* (1894)

Eric Partridge was born near Gisborne in New Zealand. When Eric was seven his father, a sheep farmer, taught him how to use a dictionary and encouraged him to write stories. This event seems to have been significant in first triggering Eric's lifelong curiosity with words – although, ironically, the words that really caught his interest were those that did *not* necessarily appear in dictionaries of the time.

For Partridge's main interest was in slang, that kind of informal English that lies below the surface of more formal vocabulary. Slang is language of a highly colloquial type, often used by people who share a common interest. It is the kind of English we may use when we are speaking with friends. Above all, it is a powerful means of people staking out their identity by developing words that are synonyms for more formal ones, but well understood within the group. Partridge's mighty *Dictionary of Slang and Unconventional English*, first published in 1937, has gone through many subsequent editions and is still in print today.

Partridge provided fifteen categories of slang, among them: expressions of high spirits; exercises in humour; enrichments of the language; deflations of pomposity; exposures of those not 'in the swim'; protections of secrets.

Criminals and teenagers are great users of slang, and the first references to it in the English language come with comments on what was called criminal cant . Many recent discussions of slang have been provoked by the spread of Teen Speak, a phenomenon for which television and mobile phones are blamed but in fact is a perennial linguistic phenomenon (see pages 218–19).

THE POWER OF SLANG

Slang is an expression of our creativity. At the same time it allows us to be different *and* proclaim our identity as part of a group. Look online today and there are hundreds of dictionaries and word lists of different slangs, of which the many urban dictionaries are good examples of how, when we live cheek by jowl with others, we love to coin new words. And in the internet age these words can travel fast and be quickly documented.

The English Project has published a book of family words, *Kitchen Table Lingo*, words that are a form of home-brewed slang. Criteria for entry included the word being used by at least three people and its *not* appearing in any authoritative dictionary. Contributions included:

Floordrobe = the place that untidy teenagers use to store their clothes;
Hodgey = disgruntled, out of sorts;
Scrudgings = the burnt-on remains of delicious home-cooked dishes that
    can be scraped off and fought over after the dish has been served.

Kitchen Table Lingo turned up more than sixty words for the television remote control – from 'blapper' to 'donker', and from 'kadumpher' to tinky-toot'. The popularity of the many different lingos that exist are a testament to the vibrancy of English as she is spoken the world over.

The aim of people using and creating slang is to make up words that are not in the dictionary in order to shock, delight, amaze, intrigue and mystify. Friends and enemies alike can be the objects of this verbal gaming, but slang users have to contend with the online glossaries that are being constantly updated. The best of these is *Urban Dictionary*; it boasts over 6 million definitions. Hard copy slang dictionaries are far behind; the *Oxford Dictionary of Slang* (2003) can boast no more than 10,000 slang words and phrases. Moreover, as a word moves from speech to print and from print to dictionary, its slanginess must steadily decrease.

8 THE TWENTIETH CENTURY

POLDHU – 1901

NEWGATE – 1902

NEW ORLEANS – 1902

FLEET STREET – 1903

NEW YORK – 1913

HAYMARKET – 1914

GUERNSEY – 1926

PORTLAND PLACE –1926

OXFORD – 1928

BLETCHLEY PARK – 1939

THE EMPIRE STATE BUILDING – 1941

ISLINGTON – 1946

ETON – 1956

LIVERPOOL – 1963

ATLANTIC CITY – 1968

67 POLDHU – *the English language and the radio* (1901)

In 1901, at Poldhu at the furthest reach of Cornwall, Guglielmo Marconi made the very first transatlantic radio transmission. It was received at St John's, Newfoundland. The message was 'S'. It was sent in Morse code (see pages 134–5), three dots heard as three brief clicks 1,800 miles away. The content of the message was small, but the promise was great.

Marconi said: 'I now felt for the first time absolutely certain that the day would come when mankind would be able to send messages without wires not only across the Atlantic but between the farthermost ends of the Earth.' He was right. Today, radio criss-crosses the globe, and not only the globe. Radio messages have been exchanged with men on the moon (see pages 193–5), and they have been beamed to outer space to try to contact alien life.

Initially, Marconi's invention was used by governments and the armed forces. President Theodore Roosevelt of the United States sent King Edward VII of Great

Marconi's Wireless Telephone Company station at Poldhu in Cornwall where the first transatlantic radio transmission was made

Britain a radio message of greeting in January 1902. The world's navies were also quick to develop such an aid to shipping. At the same time, improvements in technology, along with reductions in the size and cost of equipment, meant that radios – wireless sets as they were first called – began to appear everywhere.

By 1922, there were sufficient home wirelesses in the United Kingdom for six radio companies to start a service for them. It was called the British Broadcasting Company. It was so successful that it received a Royal Charter in 1927, becoming the British Broadcasting Corporation, better known as the BBC. The BBC has a special place in our story and you can read more about its particular role with regard to English on pages 174–6. In the United States, the first radio station was KDKA, and by 1923 there were more than 500 stations across the country.

The word 'radio' was first used in 1897, but for a long while it was known by the more descriptive term 'wireless', although 'radio' was commonly used by the 1920s. (See page 186 for some of the implications of choosing to use the word 'wireless' rather than 'radio'.) In the 1950s and 1960s pop music filled the airwaves. And these days the word 'wireless' is making a return as a popular choice because wireless internet access means that, among other services, we can now have radio streamed to us whenever we are in range of a local wireless hub. Globally we can achieve this via various hand-held devices, some going via satellite.

A SIGNIFICANT SHIFT TO THE SPOKEN WORD

We should not underestimate the significance of having a radio in the home. Suddenly, for leisure activity, there was an alternative to the book. If the nineteenth century was the age of the novel, the first half of the twentieth century was the era of radio and the start of the mass media revolution. Once its price became affordable, almost every household could own a radio. By the 1930s, two out of three homes had a radio in the United States. By the end of the Second World War, 95 per cent of homes in the States had a radio. There are comparable statistics across the developed world. The emphasis shifted from the written word to the spoken word. Radio was to usher in comedians, playwrights, musicians and singers, where before novelists and non-fiction writers had prevailed. It was also able to empower ordinary people. So, political historians agree that radio (and then television) played a significant role in the American Civil Rights Movement.

E. B. White put his finger on the cultural impact of radio in 1933 when he said:

I live in a strictly rural community and people here speak of 'The Radio' in the large sense with an over-meaning. When they say 'The Radio' they do not mean a cabinet, an electrical phenomenon or a man in a studio, they refer to a pervading and somewhat godlike presence which has come into their lives and homes.

Whether you were listening to the radio in rural America or urban Britain, its potency was undeniable. Whether you deemed it divine or not, few would dispute that it profoundly emphasized the spoken English word. In so doing, it broadened at a stroke the cultural horizons of ordinary people, giving them opportunities that were previously tied to the written word.

68 NEWGATE – *the English language and prison patter* (1902)

In 1902, Newgate Prison closed, and two years later the building was demolished. Its first prisoner had entered in 1188; tens of thousands of men, women and children passed through its terrible gate, many to die by the rope, with many more to die of jail fever in its rat-infested dungeons.

Newgate had its own English, variously called prison patter, prison lingo, prison slang. Versions are today found in every prison in the United Kingdom, the United States, Australia, everywhere in the English-speaking world. Prison patter is primarily a spoken language, and much of it is cant: 'the secret language […] used by gipsies, thieves, professional beggars, etc' as the *Oxford English Dictionary* defines it. Prison patter overlaps with the trade talk of lawyers and warders so that terms like 'wing' and 'block', and 'ABH' ('actual bodily harm') and 'GBH' ('grievous bodily harm'), are part of the prison vocabulary. Some terms, like 'association', 'parole' and

© Museum of London

Newgate Prison from the garden of St Sepulchre's Church in a painting of 1901

'segregation', are part of the general vocabulary of English, but have special meanings within the prison system.

American prison lingo is the best documented, especially on the internet, and it has a large African American element in the Northern prisons and a large Latin American element in the Southern prisons. 'Despite such regionalism,' says Patrick Ellis, 'there is a lasting and remarkably diffuse presence of certain archaic slang and cant terms, if not entire cant languages, in prison environments across the country.' The same is true of Australian prison lingo, especially since Australian English owes so much to Cockney English.

Prison patter is said to be 'charged with cynicism, suspicion, gloom and coercion', but prison humour is seen in the phrase 'bomb squad': it is the name given to the prisoners set to clean an area into which excrement has been thrown. It pokes fun at the police force's elite as much as it does at prison inmates. Prison patter releases emotion; it expresses violence without being violent. It teases and it jokes. As an HMP Winchester prisoner said, 'It's easy enough to learn; you soon pick it up.'

PRISON AS A BREEDING GROUND FOR NEW FORMS OF ENGLISH

Prison is a rich place for talk. Randy Kearse, an American convict, spent nine years in prison compiling a dictionary that he called *Street Talk*. He planned to collect 1,001 terms, and he ended up with 10,000. Randy Hearse was not making a dictionary of prison lingo exclusively, but prison is a good place, he says, to collect words. 'Guys have nothing but time on their hands in prison. So being able to talk witty, being able to talk slick, really highlights you as an individual.'

Examples of prison patter from Her Majesty's Prison Winchester include:

A four = a four-year sentence
A two = a two-year sentence
An eight = an eight-year sentence
Bacon, bacon head = a paedophile (Rhyming Slang, bonce (head) > nonce)
Bang weights = to work out in the gym
Bang-out, banging-out = to beat up
Bang-up, banging-up = to lock in a cell
Bash = to masturbate
Beast = a paedophile
Bend-up, bending-up = to restrain a prisoner in his cell, prior to moving him
Bin = a prison
Bird = time in prison (Rhyming Slang, bird-lime)
Bird, doing bird = to spend time in prison
Block = the punishment block

Bomb squad = prisoners set to clean an area into which excrement has been
    thrown from the windows of the prison

Brew = alcohol

Burn = tobacco

Burn cat = a tobacco addict

Carpet = a sentence of three years

Cat = a convict

Down the brink = segregated, put in segregation

Drum = a house

Drum, drumming = to burgle

Echo = an exercise yard

Ghost, to be ghosted = to go to the visitor centre and find that your visitor
    has not turned up

Gov = a prison officer

Grass = an informer

Hench = big, well-built

Jam (jam roll) = parole

Jammer = a knife, usually a homemade one

Kite = a cheque

Marga = small, skinny (a Jamaican word)

Nicker = a chaplain (Rhyming Slang, vicar)

Nonce = a paedophile

Peter = a cell

Raze-up, razing-up = to cut with a razor

Ride, riding my bang = to spend time in prison

Rub-down, rubbing down = to search a cell

Salmon = tobacco

Screw = prison officer

Shank = a knife, usually a homemade one

Shiv = a knife, usually a homemade one

Skins = cigarette papers

Snitch = an informer

Snout = tobacco

Sweeper = someone who collects cigarette butts

Tear-up, tearing-up = to beat up

Vanilla = a judge (Rhyming Slang, vanilla fudge)

Vera = cigarette paper (Rhyming Slang, Vera Lynn = a skin)

Visit, visiting = to leave the prison, as in: 'I'm going visiting'

Winda warrior = someone who shouts out of windows

69 NEW ORLEANS – *African American English* (1902)

I stood on the corner, my feet was dripping wet,
Stood on the corner, my feet was dripping wet,
I asked every man I met.

Can't give me a dollar, give me a lousy dime,
If you can't give me a dollar, give me a lousy dime,
Just to feed that hungry man of mine.

I got a husband, and I got a kid man too,
I got a husband, I got a kid man too,
My husband can't do what my kid man can do.

Jelly Roll Morton heard those words sung by a woman in the streets of New Orleans in 1902. It was the first time that he had encountered what he came to know as 'the blues'. The singer was an African American artist named Mamie Desdoume. Many years later, Morton repeated the words to Alan Lomax, the great American folk music collector, and they are now lodged in the Library of Congress. What was once the possession of a street singer is now part of the treasury of the English language. Perhaps the most remarkable aspect of the blues is its music, but its words are truly worth attention.

Though Jelly Roll Morton first heard the blues in 1902, they had probably been around for twenty years before that. Blues emerged in the African American community of the Deep South after the Civil War and Emancipation. They were an expression of a freed people, but a people who continued to experience repression as slavery was replaced by segregation. Blues language is a powerful tribute to artists deprived of academic training. Rhythmic and verbal structuring created a genre as formal and as beautiful as the Renaissance sonnet. They were a flowering of African American English.

A FULLY FLEDGED DIALECT OF ENGLISH

African American English may not have become a fully formed dialect until some time after 1700 because the large-scale importation of Africans to North America did not begin until the end of the seventeenth century. But by the end of the eighteenth century, travellers were beginning to notice African features in Southern speech. Although black and white Southern English have a great deal in common, they are distinct.

African American English is in origin a dialect or variant of Southern English (see pages 77–9), but it has evolved very differently in the 300 years of its existence. Some argue that the slaves first created a pidgin language based on an amalgam of African languages; others argue that the slaves created an English creole, combining directly imports from African languages with Southern English. However, it may have been African American English began its separation from Southern English 300 years ago because there was no intermarriage between black and white. As a result, culture served the function usually played by geography in creating separate dialects.

When African American English moved out of the South in the great northward and westward migrations of African American people in the first half of the twentieth century, it spread with its people to the cities of the north and the west. To this day it has retained a remarkable uniformity across the United States. By contrast, Southern whites migrating north and west lost their accents. Southern blacks took their accents with them, and they did not lose them because they did not intermarry with Northern whites.

FLEET STREET – *tabloid English* (1903)

On 2 November 1903, *The Daily Mirror* was published by Alfred Harmsworth. It is generally considered to be the first mass-market, British tabloid. Initially it was aimed at women and intended to be 'a mirror of feminine life as well on its grave as on its lighter sides'. It was conservative in outlook and only modestly successful until the 1930s. At the end of the 1930s it shifted its allegiances and targeted a left-wing male readership. *The Mirror* concentrated on sordid scandal, trivia and gossip. It adopted a clipped, simplistic sensational style of English prose. Although there are tabloid newspapers throughout the world, we have selected British tabloids as being of significance because of their extraordinarily distinct and lively style of English.

There had, of course, been sensational newspapers before *The Mirror*. From the seventeenth century onwards, broadside ballads were sold as single sheets and as pamphlets. They were full of murders, disasters and strange events – the stuff of tabloids today. In the 1830s, the United States introduced cheap newspapers appealing to a mass market. The *New York Sun* and *The Penny Press* are two good examples. Reflecting the fact that many of their readers were only partly literate, these newspapers went for dynamic everyday language, broken up into very short sentences and paragraphs.

In Britain, immediately preceding *The Mirror*, *The Mail* had been launched in 1896. Pitched as the 'busy man's' paper, *The Mail* was popular and undoubtedly easier to read than the broadsheets, but not yet a sensational and distinctive tabloid like *The Mirror*.

THE VITALITY OF TABLOID ENGLISH

Of all the recent British tabloids, it is perhaps *The Sun*, first published on 17 November 1969, which epitomizes the British tabloid tradition. For inventiveness, verbal dexterity and tastelessness, *Sun* headlines are in a league of their own:

> SUPER CALEY GO BALLISTIC, CELTIC ARE ATROCIOUS (describing a poor performance from Celtic football team and invoking a Julie Andrews song)
>
> FREDDIE STARR ATE MY HAMSTER (a complete fabrication which certainly enhanced Freddie Starr's career)
>
> ZIP ME UP BEFORE YOU GO-GO (alluding to a song and an indiscretion in a lavatory in Los Angeles by singer George Michael)

Tabloids remind us of the power of brevity, of exaggeration and of onomatopoeia. 'Row' is preferred to 'controversy', 'scrap' rather than 'cancel', 'slam' or 'blast' for 'criticize', 'spilt' for 'division', 'snub' for 'fail to attend', 'riddle' for 'mystery', 'quit' for 'resign', 'soar' for 'rise' and, favourite of all, 'sex romp' for 'sexual infidelity'. Their writers, often criticized for producing material of a low reading age, nevertheless consistently manage to stick to short sentences with few words. Three-letter words predominate: axe, ban, bid, hit, row.

A tabloid, which originally meant a compressed tablet, is a newspaper that is half the size of a broadsheet. A broadsheet was the original form of the newspaper – a large, broad sheet of paper printed on one side only. It was *The Times* of London that developed the technology to print on both sides of the page using high-speed presses in the 1820s. Papers like *The Times* came to be called broadsheets, and the name referred not only to the size of the paper but also to the quality of the paper, meaning its fine style and its accuracy of reporting (see pages 141–2). Such high-minded papers came to be called high-brow.

By folding the broadsheet in half, speeding up the steam-driven presses and aiming at the low-brow market, the tabloid was created, ready for its dominance in the twentieth century. It was the fate of many broadsheets to fold and become tabloids.

Marxist analysis tells us that popular culture embraces 'bad taste, offensiveness to officialdom, comic verbal compositions, vulgar language, ritualistic degradation and parody, emphasis on laughter, and excessiveness of all forms, but especially of the body'. That exactly describes the tabloids. In them, the English language shows itself in carnival mode.

The United Kingdom and the United States are famed for their tabloids. Australia is too, and the Australian-born American newspaperman Rupert Murdoch was the owner of British newspaper *The Sun*. He was also the owner of *The Times* of London.

Front page of *The Sun* with a provocatively eye-catching headline

The profits from the 'low-brow' paper are said to keep the 'high-brow' paper in business. Technically, *The Times* is itself now a tabloid since its broadsheets were folded in half on 30 October 2004 – as the broadsheet *Guardian* was pleased to report. Will tabloid shape lead one day to tabloid English?

71 NEW YORK – *the language of crosswords* (1913)

On 21 December 1913, the *New York World* included a new kind of word game. It was created by Arthur Wynne and was called a 'word-cross' puzzle. It is generally thought to have been the first published version of what, since 1924, we have called a crossword. The first crossword in Britain appeared in *Pearson's Magazine* in February 1922, and the first *Times* crossword was published on 1 February 1930.

Wynne's puzzle (see below) was in the shape of a cross, and not the square more familiar to us now. It had no black squares, although he invented this idea later, as well as experimenting with its overall shape.

2-3.	What bargain hunters enjoy.	6-22.	What we all should be.
4-5.	A written acknowledgment.	4-26.	A day dream.
6-7.	Such and nothing more.	2-11.	A talon.
10-11.	A bird.	19-28.	A pigeon.
14-15.	Opposed to less.	F-7.	Part of your head.
18-19.	What this puzzle is.	23-30.	A river in Russia.
22-23.	An animal of prey.	1-32.	To govern.
26-27.	The close of a day.	33-34.	An aromatic plant.
28-29.	To elude.	N-8.	A fist.
30-31.	The plural of is.	24-31.	To agree with.
8-9.	To cultivate.	3-12.	Part of a ship.
12-13.	A bar of wood or iron.	20-29.	One.
16-17.	What artists learn to do.	5-27.	Exchanging.
20-21.	Fastened.	9-25.	To sink in mud.
24-25.	Found on the seashore.	13-21.	A boy.
10-18.	The fibre of the gomuti palm.		

PUZZLE SOLUTION

The first crossword by Arthur Wynne as it appeared in *The New York World*,
21 December 1913

There are many variations of crossword layout. In North America there tends to be more white space with fewer black squares than in Britain. Most crosswords are symmetrical to the eye. Within this there are two basic kinds of clue, simple or cryptic. The simple version is a set of definitions which, if solved, produce the correct word. Cryptic clues make the game more tricky. They read as sentences (although not always ones that make logical sense) and tend to have two halves. One gives a kind of definition, while the other hints at the answer (hence 'cryptic', i.e. hidden). Often the trick is to work out which part is the definition and which the clue. Each kind of clue tells you the number of letters as a further prompt.

A common aspect of a cryptic clue is an anagram. So if the clue were 'Unusually remote celestial body (6)'. The answer would be 'METEOR'. The letters REMOTE ordered in an unusual way (i.e. as an anagram) can be rearranged to spell the word METEOR. And a meteor is a kind of celestial body. Crypticisms are loved by many, loathed in equal measure by those who enjoy the simple kind of clue, and derided by people who think that the whole business of crossword puzzling is a waste of time.

THE STRANGE ATTRACTION OF WORDS

Although Wynne's word-cross can be seen as the first formal example of a cross-word, written word puzzles have been around for a long while. When the ruins of Pompeii were excavated, archaeologists found a primitive form of crossword which has subsequently been called a word square. The game required the same word to go across and down and all to connect together so that every across and every down word is a real word. In nineteenth-century England, word squares were set as puzzles for children to solve as a means of helping them build their vocabulary.

Doing crossword puzzles can become strangely addictive. Indeed, in 1924, *The New York Times* bemoaned the 'sinful waste in the utterly futile finding of words the letters of which will fit into a prearranged pattern, more or less complex'. It went on to dismiss the activity as a 'primitive form of mental exercise', with success or failure in any given attempt 'irrelevant to mental development'. This was the high-brow reaction to a popular pursuit. There must have been sardonic smiles when, in 1942, *The New York Times* finally caved in to popular pressure and began publishing a crossword on a Sunday.

Crossword puzzles are the tip of a linguistic iceberg. There are hundreds of other word puzzles or games in common use of which the following are examples: acrostics, word searches, word polygons, hangman, Scrabble, Upwords and charades. Sometimes word games make it to the television screen, as in *Blankety Blank*, *Call my Bluff*, *Spelling Bee* and *Countdown*.

There is even a scholarly publication exploring the phenomenon of our playful interest in language – *Word Ways: The Journal of Recreational Linguistics*. Words are a source of endless fun, and word games are powerful evidence of the deep attraction of the building blocks of the English language.

 72 HAYMARKET – *rude English* (1914)

On 11 April 1914, the audience for George Bernard Shaw's *Pygmalion*, playing at His Majesty's Theatre, Haymarket, heard the following exchange:

> FREDDY: Are you walking across the Park, Miss Doolittle? If so—
> LIZA: Walk! Not bloody likely. [Sensation.] I am going in a taxi. [She goes out.]

Sensation. Shock. Eliza Doolittle's 'Not bloody likely' was a watershed in public taste in England. For the first time in the theatre, the word 'bloody' had been used. That morning, the London *Daily Sketch* had run a teasing headline:

> TONIGHT'S 'PYGMALION', IN WHICH MRS. PATRICK CAMPBELL IS EXPECTED TO CAUSE THE GREATEST THEATRICAL SENSATION FOR YEARS.

Mrs Patrick Campbell had used the rude word, but the prediction of a sensation was exaggerated. Even the Lord Chamberlain's office, the licensing body, described the incident as 'merely funny' rather than offensive and clearly saw how appropriate it was in the context of Shaw's play. Wags for the remainder of the year went around saying 'not pygmalion likely'.

The *Oxford English Dictionary* calls 'bloody' 'a vague epithet expressing anger, resentment'. 'Bloody' may be a contraction of 'By Our Lady'. If so, it takes its place with other religious oaths like 'Zounds', much used in Shakespeare and meaning 'God's wounds', or 'Marry', meaning 'By the Virgin Mary'. Swearing by sacred persons and things begins as a solemn and religious practice, but it regularly degenerates into a formula for emotional release, expression of repression, eruptions from the psyche.

Chaucer and Shakespeare filled their writing with religious oaths, and the dropping of such oaths in the seventeenth century was matched by a weakening in Catholic beliefs. With the decline in respect for Mary came a decline in insulting her. Certainly, the English came more and more to rely on the potential shock force of sexual language. That had always been a source of humour in pre-modern literature, but as society became more sexually inhibited foul language became more forceful.

The eighteenth century put mounting emphasis on good speech and conduct. Delicacy became increasingly praised and, with it, coyness. In *Tristram Shandy*, Laurence Sterne tickled his readers by having two nuns say 'bugger' while, none the less, preserving their modesty. They needed to get two mules moving, so one says 'bou, bou, bou' and the other says 'ger, ger, ger'. At the same date, Samuel Johnson kept his dictionary clean by omitting the word 'shit'.

The title *5,000 Adult Sex Words & Phrases* shows how rich is the rude-word field, and it is these words that have steadily been moving into the public domain since Eliza Doolittle said 'bloody'. A rude word with its origin in religion and not sex, it was the more allowable in 1911, but Shaw's challenge to British hypocrisy was a beginning for more blunt language. In 1936, Hector Thaxter, a music hall comedian, said 'arse' on the radio. In 1965, Kenneth Tynan said 'fuck' on television. That broke the final taboo. However, though 'arse' is now commonplace, 'fuck' is not.

What had broken the barriers between 1936 and 1965 was the publication of D.H. Lawrence's *Lady Chatterley's Lover*. The words 'fuck' and 'cunt' occur often in the conversations of the gamekeeper hero and the lady he loves. The words, however, are used with tenderness and with care. As Lawrence was striving to redeem the regional dialect of his beloved Nottinghamshire, so he was striving to redeem words that he believed were improperly banished from the English language (see British regional dialects, pages 114–17). It took a court case in 1960 to make *Lady Chatterley's Lover* a book that was openly on sale. But the widespread reading of this work did nothing to improve the social status of the rude words.

A MORE PERMISSIVE WORLD

In 1972, the *Oxford English Dictionary* included the words 'fuck' and 'cunt' for the first time, and, in 2004, the BBC televised *Jerry Springer: The Opera*. It is a show that boasts some 8,000 swear words. The BBC was stormed with complaints. In the twenty-first century, swear words, rude words, foul language and bad language retain their power to shock. That may be a good thing.

Rude words are both acts of verbal aggression and releases of strong emotion. When they appear in plays and musicals, they come from the conscious sources of language creation, but there is evidence to show that rude words are often released involuntarily. They are close to screams and cries. In 1900, attacked by a Belgian anarchist, the Prince of Wales grunted, 'Fuck it, I've taken a bullet.' It would be difficult to blame him for that.

73 GUERNSEY – *modern English usage* (1926)

In 1903, an unknown ex-teacher called Henry Fowler moved to live in Guernsey with his younger brother, Frank. The Channel Island environment seems to have had a positive impact on his creativity, for, after an undistinguished career to date, within three years he had published, with his brother, *The King's English*.

The book was well received. It tried to do two things: 'to pass by all rules, of whatever absolute importance, that are shown by observation to be seldom or never broken', and 'to illustrate by living examples, with the name of a reputable authority attached to each, all blunders that observation shows to be common'. In other words, Fowler was trying to do something bolder than Victorian linguists and grammarians: he was seeking to combine an understanding of tradition with a recognition of the realities of current usage.

Fowler's time in Guernsey set him on a trajectory that peaked with the publication in 1926 of his landmark text, *Dictionary of Modern English Usage*. This extraordinary book, reprinted many times since, seems to have first been mooted in 1911. Progress was then interrupted by the First World War. To understand Fowler's work you have to realize that at the time of its writing there was a head of steam building to 'control' spoken English. In 1913, the Society for Pure English was launched at the suggestion of the then Poet Laureate, Robert Bridges. An early supporter was Thomas Hardy, and Fowler himself was quick to follow. The Society sought to ensure that both tradition and contemporary linguistic forces were managed effectively as the importance of spoken English grew with the growth of radio and film. (The BBC, newly created, was at the forefront of the call for Pure English, see pages 174–6.)

Fowler explores a number of burning topics, including the use of the split infinitive and the use of prepositions at the end of sentences. Of the split infinitive ('To boldly go'), Fowler wrote:

> The English-speaking world may be divided into (1) those who neither know nor care what a split infinitive is; (2) those who do not know, but care very much; (3) those who know and condemn; (4) those who know and approve; and (5) those who know and distinguish.

He concluded, 'those who neither know nor care are the vast majority, and are happy folk, to be envied by the minority classes'.

On prepositions at the end of sentences Fowler dismissed the so-called rule that made it 'wrong' to end a sentence with a preposition, reminding his readers that many great writers end their sentences with prepositions. The latter style point is supposed to have provoked Winston Churchill to say, 'This is the kind of tedious nonsense up with which I will not put.' Fowler went on to point out that the preposition is, in any case, often the adverbial particle of a phrasal verb and, therefore, needs to stay with its verb.

FOWLER'S ENDURING INFLUENCE

In a recent edition of the *Dictionary of Modern Usage*, David Crystal is clear that earlier views of Fowler as a highly prescriptive work are overly simplistic: 'He turns out to be far more sophisticated in his analysis of language than most people realise. Several of his entries display a concern for descriptive accuracy which would do any modern linguist proud.' Crystal points out how his name became synonymous with his approach to language (as in 'Look it up in Fowler' and spawned adjectives such as 'fowlerian', 'fowlerish' and 'fowleresque').

Fowler's influence on language had a long run. In 2008, William F. Buckley titled a New York *Sun* piece on verbal failures of Bill Clinton and Barack Obama 'A Fowler's of Politics'. But liberal as Henry Watson Fowler was on matters of English usage, such is English speakers' and English writers' fear of falling into errors of language that Fowler is remembered more as a rule enforcer than a rule relaxer.

74 PORTLAND PLACE – *BBC English* (1926)

For much of the last century, possibly the single most important influence on the way English was spoken was the BBC. Initially through the power of radio and then via television, the BBC way of speaking was looked to by many as the *right* way.

This was not accidental. For, mindful of his responsibilities, John Reith, the first director-general of the BBC, set up an Advisory Committee on Spoken English. Initially chaired by the poet laureate Robert Bridges and then later by George Bernard Shaw, and with some of the leading linguists of the day as members, it was an influential group. Later on, it was to count the distinguished broadcaster Alistair Cooke as a member.

The committee had responsibility for making recommendations to BBC announcers about how they should pronounce new or unfamiliar words and also, more contentiously, how to pronounce words where there were different, competing, pronunciations.

In the 16 July 1926 edition of the *Radio Times*, the Committee published a list of words and their guidance on pronunciation. The list included:

Acoustics = a-coó-sticks
Courtesy = cúrtesy
Gala = gáhla
Idyll = idill
Char-a-banc = shárrabang
Garage = garage (French) *not* garridge
Mozart = Moze-art
Southampton = Soúth-hámpton

Two years earlier, Reith had published a book called *Broadcast over Britain*, in which he had written: 'We have made a special effort to secure in our stations men who, in the presentation of programme items, the reading of news bulletins and so on, can be relied upon to employ the correct pronunciation of the English tongue.'

He goes on to say:

> I have frequently heard that disputes as to the right pronunciation of words have been settled by reference to the manner in which they have been spoken on the wireless. No one would deny the great advantage of a standard pronunciation of the language, not only in theory but in practice. Our responsibilities in this matter are obvious, since in talking to so vast a multitude, mistakes are likely to be promulgated to a much greater extent than was ever possible before.

Although the Advisory Committee on Spoken English maintained that its job was not to say that other pronunciations were wrong, when one of its members, Arthur Lloyd James, came to publish a book called *The Broadcast Word*, he was happy to say that 'we may conveniently uses the terms right and wrong'. Given John Reith's influence, it is difficult to square assurances of apparent linguistic neutrality with a line from *Broadcast over Britain*: 'One hears the most appalling travesties of vowel pronunciation.'

The starting point of BBC English is an accent that became known as 'Received Pronunciation', or RP. It was a new name for a speech pattern developed in English public schools in the nineteenth century. Its intention was to ensure that it was not possible to detect the birthplace of a speaker.

The term 'Received Pronunciation' is normally credited to Daniel Jones, who used it widely in his *Outline of English Phonetics*, first published in England in 1922. That was just as plans for a national broadcasting corporation were getting underway, and Jones was promptly asked to join the BBC's Advisory Committee on Spoken English.

In 1926, there were several names for what came to be called 'BBC English'. The most ancient was, of course, 'the King's English'. Whatever that might have meant in the eighteenth century, in the nineteenth century it came to mean Public School English. The vulgar name for this accent was 'Posh English'. Daniel Jones also used the name 'Received English'. Scholars have largely settled on 'Received Pronunciation'. Like all the other names, it raises problems – 'received by whom'? It is regularly contracted to 'RP'.

Keriluamox

The home of 'BBC English', Broadcasting House in Portland Place today

75 OXFORD – *the Oxford English Dictionary* (1928)

In Oxford, on 6 June 1928, scholars and friends held a celebration at which the *Oxford English Dictionary* was declared completed and published. It was in twelve volumes and work on it had begun over forty years earlier. At the Oxford University

By permission of the Secretary to the Delegates of Oxford University Press

Photograph of the *Oxford English Dictionary* editor, Sir James A.H. Murray, in the Scriptorium. From the Oxford University Press Archive.

Press, they say that a boy, who had begun working as a compositor's assistant at the start of the project, spent his whole life on the same title, retiring when the first edition was done.

The boy compositor could have spent another lifetime on the *Oxford English Dictionary* because updating was needed immediately. New words continued to be collected, and after years of producing supplements, the whole dictionary was republished in 1989 – this time, with twenty volumes and 22,000 pages. Although new words are accumulating faster than ever, there will not be a third, hard-copy edition. In 1928, the *Oxford English Dictionary* listed over 100,000 headwords. In 1989, it listed 291,500. In 2000, the *Oxford English Dictionary* went online, and it is in the process of a complete rewriting. Some 4,000 new words are being added every year. What will be called *OED3* is promised for 2037; meanwhile, the digital *OED* lists over 600,000 headwords.

That number represents the latest count in an accumulation that began in 1582. It was then that Richard Mulcaster, first headmaster of Merchant Taylors' School in the City of London, published a list of 8,000 English words that boys found difficult to spell. In 1604, Robert Cawdrey published *A Table Alphabeticall of Hard Usual English Words*. He included only 2,500 words, but he provided definitions, and it is generally regarded as the first monolingual English dictionary. In 1623, Henry Cockeram's *English Dictionarie* was the first to call itself a dictionary. In 1681, Thomas Blount published his *Glossographia: or A Dictionary Interpreting the Hard Words of Whatsoever Language, Now Used in Our Refined English Tongue*. Blount identified and discussed over 11,000 words, and, with him, the list had become a dictionary in which spelling was secondary to etymology and meaning.

In 1755 came Dr Johnson's *Dictionary of the English Language* (see pages 97–9). It contained over 40,000 headwords, with their multiple meanings clearly distinguished, and it is the first modern dictionary. What makes Johnson modern is the fact that though he provided definitions, he did not prescribe meanings. Instead, he illustrated the meanings of words by way of quotations – 118,000 quotations. Those allowed readers to determine for themselves what the words in his dictionary meant.

THE HISTORICAL PRINCIPLES APPROACH

The descriptive principle that Johnson introduced is the key to the making of the *Oxford English Dictionary*. In 1928, it was called *A New English Dictionary on Historical Principles*. For every word, it provided an etymological history, spelling variants, and then dated first instances of the word's first discovered appearances in manuscript or print, supported by quotations to show how English writers have used that word.

Within each entry, as a word's meanings evolve over time, each new meaning was given a definition and a set of demonstrating quotations. The word 'set', itself, occupying twenty-five, double-column pages in the print editions, is the prime example of the process. 'Set', the verb, has had 155 separate meanings, with 'set up' alone showing 70 subordinate meanings. 'Set', the noun, has many more.

The first written appearance of the word dates from around 888. A quotation from King Alfred shows how it was used. That first instance is the key to the 'historical principles' of the *OED*. Words are included if they have appeared in the written language. 'Set' was in the language long before the ninth century, but the dictionary provides the earliest quotation readers have found. That gives the first meaning or 'usage' of the word. Subsequent meanings are given in the date order in which they are found.

For a new word to gain entrance to the dictionary, it must first be found in five separate printed publications, none of which explain the meaning of the word. While 'blog' was being explained as a web-log or an online diary, it was not included in the *OED*. But after 1999, 'blog' had appeared sufficiently often and sufficiently independently to be accepted as part of the language. Once included in the dictionary, a word is not likely to be excluded, though some words, long unused, are marked as obsolete.

The historical principles of the *OED* enable it to avoid making judgments about whether or not a word should be included. It avoids issues of taste, propriety, slang or vulgarity. It provides evidence in relation to a word and leaves matters of usage to its readers. At the same time, as an institution, the *Oxford English Dictionary* serves the role of the unfounded English Academy (see page 99).

76 BLETCHLEY PARK – *English language and code* (1939)

On 15 August 1939, the United Kingdom's Government Code and Cypher School was secretly moved from the centre of London to an estate in the countryside called Bletchley Park. Two weeks later, war was declared on Germany and, for the next six years, the staff at Bletchley Park intercepted the radio communications of enemy armed forces – first those of Germany and Italy, and later those of Japan. Bletchley Park was midway between Oxford and Cambridge at the point where the rail line between the two universities was crossed by the line coming north from London.

Except in extreme circumstances, wartime military communications are sent in code, and it was the job of Bletchley Park to decode enemy messages sufficiently quickly to anticipate enemy moves. In the course of the war, allied decoders dealt with radio messages in over 150 languages. Messages came in a great range of military, diplomatic and commercial codes. It was a huge task, and the staff at Bletchley grew from fifty in 1939 to 5,000 by 1945.

The degree of decryption difficulty varies with the level of the code, and that level depends upon the importance of the message and the skill of the encoder. The most well-known codes of the Second World War were those encrypted by German Enigma machines, and, though there were more complex codes, the Enigma codes posed Bletchley Park with its first, great challenge.

Helping them to undertake the almost impossible work of breaking the German codes was the world's first programmable, electronic, digital computer, a massive machine called Colossus. It was the size of a room and could read some 5,000 letters a second.

Intelligence from enemy-encrypted code in the Second World War became known as 'ultra'. Ordinary attempts at secrecy had been broken. Ultra was a badge of honour. Without the efforts of such code-breakers, England and its allies might have suffered a very different fate.

THE BEGINNING OF THE INFORMATION AGE

Sometimes extraordinary feats happen because men and women are placed in extraordinarily challenging circumstances. This was the case with Bletchley Park. Those working at Bletchley seem to have had a curious blend of mathematical and linguistic skill, perhaps personified in the person of Alan Turing, a key figure behind the creation of the modern computer. When recruiting staff, one test was the ability to solve the *Daily Telegraph* crossword in fewer than twelve minutes!

Code-breakers also needed to understand important aspects of language such as the frequency of letters and the most common combinations of letters in any language. In German, for example, the ten most frequent letters are: e n i s t r a d h u. In English, they are: e t a o i n s r h l. The British National Museum of Computing is now based at Bletchley Park, a fitting tribute to its contribution to our understanding of the mathematics of language and, so most historians agree, in shortening the Second World War by some two years. Bletchley's claim to shaping the English language is summed up by British author and actor Stephen Fry: 'Not only did these people change the very course of history by helping to secure the allied victory, thereby quietly and modestly providing us with the free world, they also gave birth to the Information Age which underpins the way we all live today.' The work done at Bletchley Park holds several lessons for the student of the English language.

A first Bletchley Park lesson is that it tells us that all languages are interchangeable, and that, while the English language sat at the centre of an operation that was deciphering meanings in 150 languages, any one of those languages could have been at the centre. All human languages, different as they are, can be translated into all other human languages. All the messages in those 150 languages could be rendered in English. Vocabulary could make for a difficulty because some languages have many more words than others, but that difficulty has always been solved by borrowing words. English has borrowed words from over 350 languages.

A second Bletchley Park lesson is that it shows the difference between code and language. Code preserves a one-on-one relation between a sign and a meaning. Code words have only one meaning. Vervet monkeys are said to have ten different grunts, but each grunt has only one meaning. The vervet code aims to reduce ambiguity to zero. Human languages do not. A single word can have several meanings. 'Set' has at least 150 (see pages 178–9). Human language explores and exploits ambiguity. That was one reason that the human beings at Bletchley were able to crack machine codes.

 EMPIRE STATE BUILDING – *the language of advertising* (1941)

At 2.30 p.m. on 1 July, WX2XBS broadcast the first television advertisements from its transmitter on the Empire State Building in New York. The occasion was a baseball game between Brooklyn and Philadelphia. The advertisement was placed by a luxury watchmaker, Bulova. It consisted of their watch face image appearing in the bottom right-hand corner of the screen. They paid $9 for the privilege. WX2XBS (later NBC) was one of the first television stations to be granted a commercial licence.

So began television advertising. In the Middle Ages, shops advertised their wares to their illiterate customers by using an image associated with their trade: a boot, a hat, a clock, a diamond, a horse shoe, a candle and so on. With the arrival of printing and literacy, advertising became more verbal. By the nineteenth century, advertisements were many and fluent. In the 1920s, radio stations started advertising, and for many years aeroplane banner advertising was popular. Today, it is the internet that is the place to be for advertisers – streamed not just to computers, but to an array of hand-held devices.

When English – spoken or written – is used to sell ideas, services or products it has to be carefully honed to give the right messages. Photos, films or videos can attract and excite, but words are equally powerful. Words, of course, can carry many, sometimes conflicting, associations, and advertisers have become adept at concentrating on the meanings, sometimes subliminal, that they want us to take.

The Empire State Building

THE IMPACT OF ADVERTISING

The English language is the medium of most of the world's advertising, and that advertising has given English many new words:

Affluenza = a sickness from having too much money

Alcopops = alcohol aimed at young drinkers and disguised with fruit juice

Chick lit = books with female characters written by women mainly for women

Fashionista = someone who wears the latest branded items

Gastropub = a pub that serves good food

The trade names of products have themselves become words hoover, xerox, sellotape, thermos and, most recently, google, tweet and facebook. Such words are also known as eponyms.

Advertisers have to have a nose for what words work, but there are many guides for the trade. In the 1960s, Geoffrey Leech showed that the most popular adjectives used in advertising were:

new, good/better/best, free, fresh, delicious, full, sure, clean, wonderful, special, crisp, fine, big, great, real, easy, bright, extra, safe and rich.

This still seems to be a surprisingly contemporary list, with many of the same words much used today.

Where they cannot either use an existing word or coin a simple word, advertisers create compound words. Top-quality, economy-size, good-looking, hard-wearing, long-lasting, mouth-watering, chocolate-flavoured, feather-light and longer-lasting are all good examples.

Another linguistic trick of the advertising trade is the use of memorable slogans:

'The ultimate driving machine' (BMW)

'It's the real thing' (Coca-Cola)

'Guinness is good for you' (Guinness)

'Snap! Crackle! Pop!' (Kellogg's Rice Krispies)

'Let your fingers do the walking' (Yellow Pages).

Advertisers are linguistically inventive. That can lead to flashes of genius and flashes of stupidity, as Pepsi's copywriters demonstrated when they coined:

lipsmackinthirstquenchinacetastinmotivatingoodbuzzincooltalkinhighwalkinfastlivinevergivincoolfizzin.

That is not a word that is going to enter the English language, but it is a demonstration of the way that words can be worked into the most unexpected shapes. The verbal inventiveness of advertising is driven by money, but when advertisers invent a word like 'gastropub', we are all enriched.

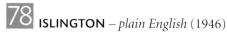 ISLINGTON – *plain English* (1946)

In 1946, George Orwell was living in Islington, and he was not far from the end of his life. He had just finished *Animal Farm*, but before he got started on *Nineteen Eighty-Four*, there was something that he wanted to tell the world:

> The great enemy of clear language is insincerity. When there is a gap between one's real and one's declared aims, one turns as it were instinctively to long words and exhausted idioms, like a cuttlefish spurting out.

In *Politics and the English Language*, Orwell explored a central theme of his novels: the relationship between language and truth. He hammered home his point by translating a passage from the Bible (Ecclesiastes 9:11) into a kind of doublespeak:

> I returned and saw under the sun, that the race is not to the swift, nor the battle to the strong, neither yet bread to the wise, nor yet riches to men of understanding, nor yet favour to men of skill; but time and chance happeneth to them all

becomes:

> Objective consideration of contemporary phenomena compels the conclusion that success or failure in competitive activities exhibits no tendency to be commensurate with innate capacity, but that a considerable element of the unpredictable must invariably be taken into account

Orwell went on to give instructions to anyone who wants to write well. By well, he meant clearly. He warned against imagery, long words, passive voices, foreign phrases and jargon. Above all, he advised writers to cut out anything they could cut.

THE POWER OF SIMPLICITY

In the years after the Second World War, Orwell's arguments hit home in England. The British Treasury commissioned Sir Ernest Gowers to advise the civil service on how to use English to best effect, and in 1954 Gowers brought his thinking together in *The Complete Plain Words*, a style guide to plain writing.

And, in 1979, the Plain English Campaign was launched in London. This organization seeks to celebrate the best kinds of simple and effective written communication with its kite-mark for high standards, the Crystal Mark, and to keep the issue of plain English in the public eye by orchestrating an annual Plain English Day.

In the United States, beginning in the 1970s, there have been parallel concerns with language, culminating in the enactment of the Plain Writing Act of 2010. There is now a website – www.plainlanguage.gov – dedicated to the use of effective communication by the federal government. There are similar initiatives in Australia and Canada. The concept of plain English has wide acceptance across the world.

While the glories of the English language include its capacity for imagery, for coining new words and for the development of jargon and private languages of all kinds, its continuing effectiveness has in part to be judged by its ability to convey meaning effectively. What started as Orwellian polemic has found roots as an enduring concern to avoid gobbledegook and to strive for clarity.

 ETON – *the English of the English upper class* (1956)

Some miles west of London in the Thames Valley, there is a school that has educated more prime ministers of England than any other. It is Eton College. Boys who go there are taught to speak in a particular kind of way if they do not already do so. Founded in 1440 by King Henry VI, the 'King's College of Our Lady of Eton besides Wyndsor' is emblematic of a social feature of language that is particularly English.

Many languages have a prestige dialect, a form of the language associated with power and rule. In London, a prestige dialect emerged in the eighteenth century (see pages 99–100). Written English had already been moulded into a Latinized and standard form, and those who could read began to speak as far as possible as they were taught to write. The accent to be adopted was that of Westminster where the royal court and high society were to be found. People strove to speak eloquently and fluently and fashionably.

What was true of England was true of other countries in Europe. By the eighteenth century, Spain, Italy, France and Germany had developed standardized forms of their written languages and, with them, prestige dialects. The English went a stage further.

In nineteenth-century England, ever-increasing numbers of the wealthy middle class began to imitate the upper class by sending their boys to boarding schools. For historical reasons, these were called 'public schools', though they were expensive and exclusive private establishments. The Westminster way of speaking was taught in schools that spread across England. All traces of any local accent had to be erased.

An aerial view of Eton College

An upper-class, non-regional accent became a prized thing. It is now called Received Pronunciation, or RP (see pages 175–6). The number of people who learn RP at home – that is, as children – is about 5 per cent of the population, roughly coinciding with the percentage of people receiving private education. That is why RP was initially called Public-School English. It has also been called BBC English, because once upon a time the BBC would only employ people who spoke like public-school boys.

Upper-class English is a matter of vocabulary and accent, not grammar and syntax. Upper-class pronunciation produces many differences: *fórmidable* not *formídable*; *int'resting*, not *interesting*; *marse*, not *mass*; and *Cartholic*, not *Catholic*; *jest*, not *just* – as in 'jest in time'; *cetch*, not *catch*; *forrid*, not *fore-head*; *tortoise*, not *tortoys*; *clart*, not *claret*. And upper-class vocabulary produces an equally long list: *lunch*, not *dinner*; *sick*, not *ill*; *wireless*, not *radio*; *rich*, not *wealthy*; *lavatory-paper*, not *toilet-paper*; *note-paper*, not *writing paper*; *pudding*, not *sweet*; *false teeth*, not *dentures*; *spectacles*, not *glasses*. These examples come from a paper published by Professor Alan Ross in 1954. He used the shorthand 'U' and 'non-U' to distinguish these differences.

U AND NON-U ENGLISH

In 1956, Nancy Mitford, an aristocrat, caused a storm when she included the U and non-U linguistic material in a book that she called *Noblesse Oblige*. To Ross's scholarly piece, she added her own humorous essay, along with those of Evelyn Waugh and John Betjeman. The butt of their satire was the speech of the English middle classes. They insisted that non-U speakers spoke badly. They also insisted that non-U speakers could never learn to speak properly. As Mitford said: 'One U-speaker recognizes another U-speaker almost as soon as he opens his mouth.' That is true of any accent, but it had a particular implication for Mitford.

The upper-class accent has come under attack since the 1960s, and it is opposed by a speech called Estuary English or Estuarian. Estuarian contradicts the elitist assumptions of RP. It is an accent that deliberately talks down, not up. It is an accent of younger people adopting London lower-class speech patterns. Estuarian is a modified form of Cockney, a mock Cockney, sometimes called 'Mockney'. In 2008, *The Times* claimed that an MP with ambitions to become Chancellor of the Exchequer was taking Mockney lessons to cure his 'irritable vowel syndrome'. He had been educated at a public school and needed to erase the too obvious evidence of that fact. He succeeded. He has subsequently, if not consequently, become the United Kingdom's Chancellor of the Exchequer.

 LIVERPOOL – *British urban English* (1963)

In 'Annus Mirabilis', Philip Larkin says that sexual intercourse began between the publishing of *Lady Chatterley's Lover* in 1960 and the issuing of the song 'Please, Please Me' in 1963. D.H. Lawrence was responsible for *Lady Chatterley* and the Beatles for 'Please, Please Me'. These artists were responsible for more than the release of English sexual intercourse, however; they were responsible for the release of English regional accents – the Beatles more so than Lawrence.

Lawrence, a man from Nottinghamshire, writes in Standard English (see pages 97–9) and gives his upper-class characters upper-class speech (see pages 185–7). To Oliver Mellors, the gamekeeper hero of *Lady Chatterley's Lover*, Lawrence gives a formal English except when Mellors is intimate with his beloved Lady Chatterley, Connie. Then Mellors speaks in Nottinghamshire dialect:

'Coom then tha mun goo!' he said. 'Mun I?' she said. 'Maun Ah!' he corrected. 'Why should I say maun when you said mun' she protested. 'You're not playing fair.'
'Arena Ah!' he said, leaning forward and softly stroking her face.

Traditionally, regional dialect in the English novel was used to suggest social inferiority, lack of education, low manners or inexperience. But Lawrence used Nottinghamshire English to establish the power of Mellors, his grace, his depth, his understanding. Connie tries to speak the dialect, but she discovers that, like Standard English, it has its rules and she needs to learn them.

Lawrence's tutorials on regional English were not what most readers took from *Lady Chatterley's Lover*, and it was the Beatles who had to give the United Kingdom linguistic shock treatment. When they moved from Liverpool to London, they continued to speak as they spoke in Liverpool. They did not attempt southern speech patterns; they continued to use Liverpool English. That was a bolt from the blue for the capital.

Inside The Cavern Club in Liverpool where The Beatles first performed as The Quarrymen

Successful people were expected to abandon regional English when they reached London. Joan Bakewell from Cheshire and Kate Adie from Sunderland had adopted BBC English and were doing very well with the BBC.

THE RISE AND RISE OF LIVERPUDLIAN ENGLISH

John Lennon, Paul McCartney, George Harrison and Ringo Starr, all from Liverpool, were expected to do the same. They did not. They continued to talk like Liverpudlians. In 1964, in *Hard Day's Night*, the film that celebrated their London arrival and success, the vowels of Liverpool are loud and clear. Paul McCartney had sought out the Welsh writer Alun Owen to write the script because he knew that Owen could catch their way of talking. For his part, Owen feared that their 'Scouse wit' would be blunted by over-rehearsed dialogue.

Scouse is the name given to the speech of Liverpool. Like Cockney, Brummie, Mancunian and Geordie, it is one of those terms, partly affectionate, partly contemptuous, that are given to the highly distinct speech patterns of Britain's great cities. In the 1950s, those were the dialects that speakers of Standard English found most objectionable. By contrast, they tended to regard rural dialects less with dislike and more as sources of an older, more 'pure' English.

Urban dialects are usually subject to greater change than rural ones, and Scouse is a good example of that pattern. Liverpool, a village in the eighteenth century, became England's greatest seaport in the nineteenth. It initially attracted people from the Lancashire countryside. Those migrants were followed in the middle of the century by Irish immigrants, the majority from Dublin. Scouse is the result of that mixing of English and Irish dialects. The Liverpool accent stretches in a 10-mile radius from the city centre and, as Paul McCartney says, outside that 10 miles it is 'deep Lancashire, lad'.

The Beatles are called Scouse speakers, but it is their accent that is Scouse, not their grammar. George, Paul and John had all gone to Merseyside Grammar School; there they learned Standard English grammar (see pages 71–2). That education removed distinct dialectal features. The Beatles would not say, as Oliver Mellors says, 'Coom then tha mun goo!', but, since the Beatles, Standard English spoken with a pronounced urban accent has become fashionable.

The Beatles had astonishing language skills and, with the release of *Sgt. Pepper's Lonely Hearts Club Band* in 1967, John Lennon and Paul McCartney showed themselves not only to be musicians of the first order, but lyric writers of the first order too.

Members of the National Women's Liberation Party protest against the Miss America Pageant in Atlantic City in 1968

Associated Press

81 ATLANTIC CITY – *sexist English* (1968)

Sometime in the 1960s the term 'sexism' was coined. It is not clear exactly who first used it, but the Miss America Pageant in Atlantic City, New Jersey, in September 1968, was a good and early occasion, location and date for using new words. Women, angry at the belittling of their gender by such pageants, took to the streets. In their conversations and in the subsequent press coverage, the terms 'sexism' and 'sexist' began to be used.

Sexism describes the bias against women to be found in boardrooms, in government, in the media, in advertising and in communities. Language, too, can be sexist. In some languages, nouns are either masculine or feminine and it is clear from other linguistic features as to whether a pronoun, idea, thing or concept is male or female. This is not so with English, although some words are undoubtedly associated with different genders – such as boats, which are feminine, for example.

English does not have gender-neutral, single, third-person pronouns. Traditional English drives speakers to select either 'she' or 'he', and to say things like 'Everyone must collect his ticket from the front office' when that 'everyone' includes women as well as men. The masculine pronoun is made to serve as the default. Generalizations about the human race speak about 'man' or 'mankind'. The Linnean name for our species is *Homo sapiens*, and *homo* is Latin for man. Our language tends to make women linguistically invisible.

Or worse. Certain key jobs just shout their gender. So 'nurse' for most speakers means female nurse, so that if the nurse is a man he will be called explicitly a 'male nurse'. By contrast, a surgeon means a male surgeon for most speakers, and so if the surgeon is a woman, she will find herself called 'female surgeon'. For some while this urban fable was doing the rounds:

> A young man and his father have a car accident. The father is tragically killed and the son is rushed to hospital. On seeing the child the surgeon immediately exclaims: 'I can't possibly operate. It's my son!'

The question is then posed: how can this be? Strangely, many people cannot make the obvious deduction that the surgeon is, of course, the boy's mother. (Maybe you even fell for it, gentle reader!)

Proverbs and jokes are often full of sexism (although female comics are ensuring that there are many good laughs to be had at men's expense these days).

A SUBTLE BUT PERCEPTIBLE SHIFT

Since the late 1960s there have been many attempts at consciously changing the course of the English language. Although subject to local variation, for the most part English has become genuinely less sexist. Many organizations have guidelines on language use, and it is gradually becoming unacceptable to be sexist.

Most people know how to say 'people' rather than 'men'. 'Ms' has become a widely used alternative for 'Miss' where a woman prefers not to give any indication of marital status. We have 'flight attendants' or 'crew' on aeroplanes at least as often as we have 'stewardesses'. Meetings and organizations often have 'chairs' rather than 'chairmen', without causing silly jokes about chairs being items of furniture. 'Chair' is a good match to 'board', as in the 'Chair of the Board'. There are congressmen and congresswomen in Washington DC.

And, if we are in doubt or simply striving for even-handedness, it is common for speakers to refer to 'men and women' instead of just 'men'. Such shifts take time, though. There are still sexist people alive, many of them. Language simply reflects this. But, as Albert Baugh points out, 'Efforts to eliminate sexism from English, though having met with resistance, have been more successful than most attempts at reform.'

9 THE TECHNOLOGICAL REVOLUTION

82 SEA OF TRANQUILLITY – *English on the moon* (1969)

On 21 July 1969, the world held its breath as Apollo 11's lunar module descended to the surface of the moon. The spider-like craft looked impossibly fragile. Once safely touched down, Neil Armstrong spoke to those back in Cape Kennedy, saying, 'Houston, Tranquility Base here. The Eagle has landed finally.' A few hours later, Armstrong opened the hatch and climbed down to the surface of the moon. Here Armstrong said: 'That's one small step for man, one giant leap for mankind.' They are the first words to have been spoken on the moon, and they were in English. The global language was going universal.

Some people think that the first words on the moon were actually 'for a man' rather than 'for man'. Armstrong, they argue, fluffed his lines in the heat of the moment. Clearly 'a man' makes more sense, contrasting the puny individual stride with the scientific and technological one that might be said to be mankind's achievement. Since it is not clear from the recording what Armstrong said, his exact words remain a source of speculation.

Before the moon landing, the most popular book about it was written by Jules Verne in 1865 – *De la terre à la lune* (*From the Earth to the Moon*). In it, two Americans vie with each other to create a space cannon to blast themselves to the moon. In 1901, H.G. Wells published a science fiction novel, *The First Men in the Moon*, in which two Englishmen travel to the moon. On their way there in an impressive piece of scientific imagination, they even experience weightlessness. On the moon, they encounter strange creatures, including 5-foot-high Selenites (named after the moon goddess Selena) who live underground in a highly technologically developed community. The moon landers are captured by the Selenites, but one of them, Mr Bedford, the story's narrator, escapes and manages to get back to Earth. The other, Mr Cavor, remains on the moon. Interestingly, while there, partly as a necessary device of the plot, he teaches two of the Selenites to speak English.

From the beginning of time, human beings have seen the full moon shining brightly in the night sky and imagined what it must be like. With powerful telescopes, we have mapped its surface. We have gradually discovered its extraordinary influence on, among other things, our tides. We have included it in our stories and nursery rhymes. For a long while, we have longed to be able to travel to it. When Armstrong stepped out on to the lunar surface, fact and fiction came together in an extraordinary way.

A LEGACY OF THE LUNAR LANDING

At the peak of the space race, when the battle between Russia and the United States to put the first man on the moon was at its height, there was an extraordinary global interest in space travel. This has left its trace on the English language in a significant number of words and phrases, including:

blast-off;
booster;
heatshield;
it's not rocket science;
lift-off;
mission control;
shuttle;
soft landing;
space station;
unmanned.

As a consequence, children can travel safely in the back of our cars on 'booster' seats. The world's (or a business's) economy can be poised for 'lift-off' (recovery) or (if accomplished in a planned and controlled way) have a 'soft landing' if slowing down. When we want to imply that something is not complicated, we may remark 'it's not rocket science'.

Armstrong and all the men and women who made his moon landing possible have left a modest trace on our words and a giant leap for our imaginations.

LOS ANGELES – *the language of e-mail* (1969)

An hour and a half before midnight on 29 October 1969, a computer in Los Angeles sent a message to a computer 360 miles away in Stanford. The plan had been for the message to read 'login', but in fact it only actually transmitted the first two letters – 'lo' – as the system crashed.

Unsurprisingly, across the world computer scientists had been grappling with the new communications opportunity afforded them by increasingly powerful computers. In the 1960s, computers were all built differently, and they used different languages and programs. What was needed was a linking network and shared soft-ware. The United States Defense Department built the network and called it the ARPANET. In 1966, a file was sent from one computer to another. A set of rules was developed for anyone who wanted to use the ARPANET. Those rules were called a File Transfer Protocol, or FTP.

FTP operators soon began to hitch personal messages to their FTP files. The Defense Department was not happy about this messing with its system, and work was put in hand to devise a protocol for personal messages. It was called SMTP – Simple Mail Transfer Protocol. SMTP hugely increased the traffic on the ARPANET, fuelled by everyone with access to an ARPANET-linked computer. It was one of the reasons the American government let the ARPANET go public in 1990. Its legacy is today's internet.

From the beginning, the transfer protocols were international because they were devised by American and British teams. One outcome was the 'dot' of the final e-mail addressing system. All were agreed on the technicalities, but the Americans were calling the sign a 'period' and the British were calling it a 'full stop'. Calling it a 'dot' was the transatlantic solution. Meanwhile, a symbol had to be found to separate the e-mailer's name from the e-mailer's location in the e-mailer's address. The man working on this, Ray Tomlinson, says that he looked at his keyboard for his least used key, and @ was it. The fact that it says 'someone at somewhere' seems to be a wonderful chance. With the @, the e-mail format had been perfected, and it gradu-ally spread across the world.

Human beings love to talk to one another. We love to natter, prattle, chatter, witter, rabbit, rattle, chat, jaw. Just for the sake of it. Sometimes, we make an excuse and pretend that we have something important to say, but most of the time it is, in the words of BT, 'Good to talk'. And talk and talk is what people have done with e-mail. It was the first of the electronic systems that facilitate written communication, the predecessor of the chat, the text and the tweet.

These are all new forms of communication, intermediate between the telephone and the letter. Send and store systems – they send the message instantly but store it indefinitely. They can allow for something close to the immediacy of the phone, but they can allow also for the pausing and re-reading of the letter. E-mailers who reply too quickly or too wildly or 'To All' are legendary. A whole book has been written about that: *Send: Why People Email So Badly and How To Do It Better.*

@ HOME OR @ WORK

By 1996, people in the United States were using e-mail more than traditional mail. Like texting and Twitter (see pages 209–11 and 216–17), an e-mail invites informality. Abbreviations abound – FYI (For Your Information), IMO (In My Opinion), FWIW (For What It's Worth), IIRC (If I Remember Correctly).

'Noisy' e-mailers send their messages in capitals to suggest REALLY STRONG FEELINGS ABOUT SOMETHING! Other e-mailers amuse themselves with the non-alphabetic keys such as .... / - \ and *. From that has grown emoticons. They say what traditional punctuation can't say: :-), :), <:o). E-mail encourages writers to develop their own voice, to use expressions known only to them and those to whom they write, to be colloquial, irreverent and playful.

Linguists advise against making dramatic claims for the influence of e-mail on the English language, but David Crystal imagines a world in which students will be encouraged to explore the stylistic features of e-mail just as they once were taught the correct formats for personal and business letters. However, those e-mails might indeed be classics, since SMTP may have had its heyday. For the under-45s, text, Facebook and Twitter have become preferred means of electronic send-and-store messaging.

84 BELMOPAN – *the English language in Belize* (1970)

The part of the world where English has made least penetration is Latin America. The dominant language of this continent is Spanish, though Portuguese is the language of the largest country, Brazil. From Mexico to Chile, the Spanish-speaking countries of Latin America vary greatly in the degree to which English is used and, outside the cities, in many places it is not used at all.

Spanish and English are in some kind of competition. Spanish, like English, is a world language; it claims to have more native speakers than English; it is the language that its advocates predict will take over in North America. That is not an impossible scenario, but it is an unlikely one.

Mexico, technically part of North America, is heavily penetrated by the language of its giant neighbour to the north. Latin America counters by the great northwards thrust of Spanish. The Spanish-speaking population of the United States numbers 20 million, and that Spanish-speaking population is growing at a faster rate than the English-speaking population.

There are some real points of competition between English and Spanish in the Americas, and the city of Belmopan in Belize in Central America is an interesting pressure point. Belmopan was founded as recently as 1970 to become the new Belizean capital when Belize City, the old capital, was destroyed by a hurricane in 1961. Rather than rebuild, the government and many inhabitants decided to relocate.

Belize was once called British Honduras, and today it is the only Central American country in which English is the official language. In South America, Guyana (once called British Guiana) stands out for the same reason: English is its official language. As the old names suggest, both Belize and Guyana were once British colonies, and so the official language was English for both. But in Belize that official language designation is becoming every day more anomalous.

Ever since Belmopan's foundation, the percentage of native speakers of English has been falling. Belize is not a densely populated country; at the millennium, the count was under 200,000, but only 4 per cent counted English as their first language, against 33 per cent who considered Spanish to be their first language. The percentage of Spanish speakers continues to increase. With that, agitation grows to remove the status of official language from English. If that happens, Belize would have moved in the opposite direction from Rwanda, which made English an official language in 2008 (see pages 219–21). If losing official status meant that English ceased to be taught in Belize's schools, then it would have a big impact.

The role of English as a first language tells one story. However, the role of English as a second language in Belize tells a different story. Adding in the second-language speakers puts English as a language used by 53 per cent of the population. Significantly, there are no second-language Spanish speakers listed. This tiny country, with its small population, tells a big fact about English and about Spanish as world languages. Spanish remains regularly a first language, but English is being increasingly adopted as a second language, one which people believe it is worth investing the time, labour and expense necessary to learn.

However, the Spanish speaker might argue that Belize at least does not speak so strongly in favour of English as a second language as might first appear. The fact is that the 40 per cent of Belizeans who claim English as a second language give Kriol as their first language. Now, Belizean Kriol is a close relative of Jamaican Labrish, Barbadian Bajan and Trinidadian Patois (see pages 79–81).

Kriol is a creole, the kind of natural language that arises with children who have two linguistic sources from which to draw their speech. Kriol, Labrish, Bajan and Patois draw their phonology, vocabulary and grammar from English and a mix of African languages. Belize Kriol shows its affinity with English:

Weh yu nayhn? = what is your name?
Gud maanin = good morning.
Da how yu di du? = how are you?
Aarait = fine, thank you.
Humoch dis kaas? = how much does this cost?
Ah mi gat wahn gud gud taim = I've had a wonderful time.

The Spanish speaker might point out that moving from Creole English to Standard English is nothing like learning a foreign language. But that is not the whole story of English and Spanish in Latin America. Aarait.

85 ST PANCRAS – *the British Library* (1973)

The date of 1 July 1973 marks the official beginning of the British Library. It was brought into being by the 1972 British Library Act. But a long time before then, there were various institutions that played the role of a national library. Best known of these was the British Museum's Department of Printed Books, which was founded in 1753. With its glorious domed reading-room, the British Museum's library was already one of the world's largest on account of it being a legal deposit library entitled to receive a copy of every book, periodical or newspaper published in the United Kingdom.

The new British Library was formally opened in June 1998 after considerable delays in its designing and building. Anyone who has a permanent address in Britain can apply for a reader's pass. The British Library serves as a memory bank for the English language. In 2010 the British Library held a stunning exhibition – 'Evolving English: One Language, Many Voices'. Examples of the great Reformation Bibles were sitting open side by side (see pages 73–4). Nearby was the Undley Bracteate (see pages 17–19). There, too, was the *Anglo-Saxon Chronicle* (see pages 35–6). *Sumer is icumen in* could be heard (see pages 37–9). William Caxton's *Recuyell of the Histories of Troye* was open, ready to be read (see pages 56–7). Linguists could move between Ben Jonson's *English Grammar* (see pages 81–3), Samuel Johnson's *A Dictionary of the English Language* (see pages 97–9), the BBC's guidelines on

Amber Newland

The new British Library today

pronunciation (see pages 174–6), and George Bernard Shaw's *Pygmalion* (see pages 171–2). On show was a stunning fraction of the riches held in one of the world's greatest libraries.

THE WORLD'S ENGLISH-LANGUAGE TREASURE HOUSES

The British Library is a model of the English-language treasure houses to be found around the English-speaking world. According to the French geographer Jean Gottmann, 'the greatest concentration of large libraries in the world' is on the East Coast of the United States. In the continuous urban development that runs from Boston to Washington are located forty-four giant libraries, each of which contains over a million books. The greatest of these is the Library of Congress in Washington, with 30 million books. Next is the New York Public Library, with over 15 million books. Scattered through the region are what have to be called lesser libraries, but they are still enormous repositories of books in superbly ordered collections – Harvard University's Widener Library, Yale University's Sterling Library, Columbia University's Butler Library, Princeton University's Firestone Library.

Those libraries, like the British Library, contain books in every language, but they are first of all English-language libraries. The notion of their collective English-language riches is overwhelming even as they stand scattered over the region that Jean Gottmann called 'Megalopolis'. The bricks-and-mortar library reaches its apogee there.

However, the twenty-first century is promising to unite the scattered contents of these English-language treasure houses. Steadily the collections are being digitized, and their limitless resources are being made accessible to more and more readers. Already, the *Library Journal* reports, Google has digitized 12 million books. There is as yet limited access to many of them, and the scanning (done at the rate of a thousand pages an hour) leaves much to be desired. None the less, for the poor scholar who cannot afford to fly to Megalopolis, a Universal Virtual Library is becoming a reality.

Everything is messy to begin with. Look at any page of most books printed in the sixteenth century. Gradually, technologies improve; gradually, standards are raised. Look at any page of most books printed in the twentieth century. The technology for first-class book digitizing is already available. The riches of the British Library are coming to every desk top.

86 ISLAMABAD – *the English language in Pakistan* (1973)

In 1947, Pakistan became an independent state, Karachi was named its first capital, and the British Raj (or Reign) was over. The withdrawal of the British did not, however, mean that they took their language with them. Though the provinces that were to make up Pakistan had not come under the rule of the Raj until the middle of the nineteenth century, the British imposed their language along with their rule, and it became the medium not only of government and politics, but also of upper-class and educated culture. English also served as a lingua franca in territories where over seventy languages were (and are) spoken.

There was, none the less, much hostility to the English language in the new nation, and it might have been expected to be officially discouraged, but the opposite happened. Pakistan was anxious to 'remake' itself, and in particular to find a new site for its capital. In the 1960s, that was moved from Karachi to the newly created city of Islamabad. In 1973, a new constitution was agreed, and it was at that date that English, along with Urdu, was declared an official language of the Islamic Republic of Pakistan. There are other 'recognized languages', but English is accorded a special status in a land in which very few have it as a mother tongue. The constitution did say that English was only to have that status until 1988, but in 1988 no change was made.

There was pressure in the early years of the new nation to make Urdu the single national language. In the 1950s, a Pakistani Committee for the Official Language worked to make Urdu a language of international learning. Urdu took thousands of words from English, exactly as the English had taken thousands of words from Latin in the sixteenth and the seventeenth centuries (see pages 64–5). The Urdu enrichment policy had some unexpected results.

The Pakistani government's language policy was one of the grievances that led the Bengali-speaking people in the eastern section of the divided country to declare their independence. In 1971, the Pakistani province of Bengal became the People's Republic of Bangladesh. There, the official language is Bengali. English is not given any status. The politics of language can be fierce, and the English language has become entangled in post-colonial politics on every continent.

PAKISTANI ENGLISH – A SPECIAL KIND?

A number of Pakistani linguists argue that Pakistani English is a distinct form of the language. Their point is that it is an English influenced by the many languages spoken in Sindh, the Punjab, Baluchistan, Khyber Pakhtunkhwa and the tribal zones. The impact is not only on the phonology of Pakistani English, it has also provided a distinct vocabulary and, to some extent, a grammar.

On its website, Pakistan Research Repository, the Higher Education Commission of Pakistan presents a thesis entitled 'The Form and Functions of English' by Mubina Talaat. Talaat makes the case for the special character of Pakistani English. She quotes a passage from *Mag*, a woman's weekly magazine, to show this English at work:

> Just last month, Moin faced bitter reality during the Andherey Dareechey show at Bahriya Auditorium, when during the show quite few artists gave him crisp repartes to chew, frequently, as Moin tried desperately to hold on to a mixture of decency and wit. Unfortunately, the man has become such an alien to witty remarks after insisting on playing the host and compere, that he couldn't come up with any quick thinking or kerara remark.

Talaat points to 'crisp repartes' (repartees) as an example of a tendency to duplicate meaning and to 'kerara remark' as an example of the use of an Urdu word, again repeating a meaning since 'quick thinking' amounts to 'kerara remark'. She explains the special features of Pakistani English as instances of 'code-mixing and code-switching' by writers who are thinking in Urdu as well as in English. That results in parts of speech changing their function, in the frequent omission of the definite article, and in the creation of phrases such as 'Eve-teasing', 'monkey justice', 'pindrop silence'.

Talaat suggests that Urdu is the language that most influences Pakistani English. If true, that reflects an interesting political and social overlap of English and Urdu. English is spoken by about 10 per cent of the population of Pakistan. Urdu is spoken by no more than 8 per cent. However, an Urdu- and English-speaking elite rules the country.

In 1947, at the time of the Partition, it is estimated that no more than 2 per cent spoke English, so the number of English speakers has greatly increased. In 1947, English was an imperial language; today, it is a global language. Despite the calls of nationalists, Pakistan never did abandon English, and it is unlikely to do so in the twenty-first century.

87 THE BRONX – *the language of rap* (1973)

Sometime in the 1970s, the words 'rap' and 'hip hop' began to be used to describe a type of music. Busy Bee Starski, DJ Hollywood and DJ Afrika Bambaataa are the three artists who are accorded the honour of founding hip hop and rap – though other artists make other claims.

However, all agree that, in the dance clubs of the Bronx in New York in the 1970s, DJs (Disc Jockeys) began to play a different kind of music that involved 'sampling' (recording elements of disco and funk music of the previous decade and then playing them differently). Often DJs had two turntables to enable them to provide greater varieties of sound (called 'scratchings'). The new music had a strong beat, a distinctive feel, and no vocals. DJs who were good at deejaying were in demand. Consequently they were treated as if they were performing artists and were increasingly introduced by an MC (Master of Ceremony). MCs told stories and developed a rhyming patter that gradually came to be referred to as rapping, just as their role was referred to as mc-ing.

Hip hop initially described the music, and rap the distinctively rhythmic patter, but increasingly the two terms have become interchangeable. Hip hop typically also applies to other aspects of behaviour, such as a particular style of dressing, the creation of graffiti, and breakdancing.

THE INFLUENCE OF RAP

'Rap' has for a very long time meant a knock or a stroke, and it has long meant fast talking or banter in African American English (see pages 164–5). It came to mean fast-talking, fast-beating music by way of an easy progression, a progression that shows how and why English creates new words from old ones.

The online *Rap Dictionary* lists close to 3,000 terms. Remarkably, the first 136 are all numbers, starting with '007' and ending with 98.7. '007' means, lame'y, 'James Bond'; '98.7' means, intriguingly, either 'WRKS KISS FM, a NYC radio station that helped bring hip-hop to the radio' or 'WILD 98.7, a Tampa Bay radio station that claims to be blazing the most music'. There is a great deal of joking and faking in this kind of language (and this kind of dictionary). 'AK' figures in a number of rap terms and reflects the love of violence that gives drive to the form. 'Beanpie' means unprotected sex with someone else's woman, as in 'That devil got beanpie from ma ho'. In the plural, 'beanpies' means 'bags of crack cocaine'. Guns, sex and drugs make up a large part of the life and language of the rapper. Rap's wild language overlaps with street slang, prison patter, jive talk and drug cant, all of which give and take words from one another.

THE SUCCESS OF RAP

Just as much of the language of rap comes from the rich street English of the American ghetto, so rap in turn supplies ripe terms to American Teen Speak (see pages 218–19). And rap is not only used by teenagers. The huge success of rap music brought its language into mainstream English. On 5 February 1999, *Time* magazine made rap its cover story with the headline 'Hip Hop Nation: After 20 Years How It's Changed America'. President Barack Obama has talked of 'dissing' an opponent. A member of the British royal family has used 'wicked' to mean 'great news'. 'Bling' is widely used to describe the gold jewellery beloved of rappers and now worn by all fashionistas.

Rap glorifies violence, portrays women as sexual objects, and promotes drugs. But ironic twists make reading rap a complex linguistic exercise. Tricia Rose, in *Black Noise*, talks about rap's 'hidden transcripts'. She sees in the violence of its language coding for political repression, economic need and sexual desire. She links rap to carnivalesque exuberance and excess – the mark of worldwide popular culture.

 SAN JOSE – *the English language and text preservation* (1975)

In 1975, IBM moved Charles Goldfarb from its research centre in Cambridge, Massachusetts, to its research centre at San Jose, California. Goldfarb had created something big, and IBM wanted him to develop it from an in-house system to an international standard.

Goldfarb, with his colleagues Ed Mosher and Ray Lorie, had devised a means of enabling legal documents to be printed on different computer systems. The key had been to see any document as made up of two kinds of information: content and format. Goldfarb and his team called the document's content, its data, and the document's format, its mark-up. It was a way of looking at a text that came from the printing industry: copy-editors, marking format instructions on a manuscript, call those instructions 'mark-up'. These instructions need to be tagged as mark-up to ensure that they are not included in the printed text.

The first name that Goldfarb, Mosher and Lorie gave to their document processing software was Integrated Text System. But the crucial insight lay in removing from any text all formatting and replacing it with a series of mark-up tags.

Even paragraphing was to be removed in the text going from the computer to the printer. In its place would be a tag, <p>, to show that a paragraph should start. A second tag, </p>, would be inserted to show that the paragraph had ended. The tag <i> would mean that italicizing should start; </i> would mean that italicizing should stop. Beyond that, things get complicated.

The mark-up tags are so central to its operation that Goldfarb renamed the system Generalized Markup Language. It was generalized because it could work on any computer platform. It was mark-up because formatting was shown through the tags. It was a computer language that humans could read. Generalized Markup Language was reduced to its head letters, GML, which were also the initials of Goldfarb, Mosher and Lorie.

American industry, government and defence were quick to see the advantages of GML and were eager to see it standardized across the United States for document processing. In 1983, Generalized Markup Language became Standard Generalized Markup Language, or SGML, recognized by the American National Standard Institute. A year later, it was recognized by the International Organization for Standardization, as a worldwide standard for computer document preparation and output (to screen, printer or printing press).

THE ADVANTAGES OF SGML

SGML is a language that can be read by computers as easily as it can be read by humans. Its open-ended tagging system allows users to structure documents in the most intelligent manner and allows documents to be made intelligent. It is a document-processing system, and that includes word processing, but it is rather too heavy duty for amateurs to use. Microsoft *Word* does well enough for most people, but *Word* does not have SGML's power, intelligence and flexibility.

The great strength of SGML, and the reason that IBM called for its development in the first place, is its independence of platforms. It operates on all computer systems. It can talk to any of them. Moreover, it is designed to work on computing systems not yet designed. Therein lies its genius, and therein lies its great promise for those who love the English language. A special application of SGML has been written for the electronic encoding of literature. It is called the TEI.

TEI is short for the Text Encoding Initiative – 'an international organization founded in 1987 to develop guidelines for encoding machine-readable texts in the humanities and social sciences'. Within the SGML protocols, TEI has developed the document definitions and mark-up tags for the electronic encoding of every form of literary genre from the anecdote to the epic, from the novel to the history. TEI can ensure the highest level of accuracy for the reproduction of the texts and its super software guarantees their preservation and incorruptibility. TEI is being used by universities throughout the world to encode the riches of English literature. *The*

Scholars Lab at the University of Virginia has already encoded 45,000 classic texts. *The Orlando Project* at the University of Alberta is encoding 'Women Writers in the British Isles'. *Documenting the American South* at the University of North Carolina is encoding texts that relate to 'southern literature, history and culture'. The great work of encoding the world's written heritage is well underway. SGML-TEI safe-keeps literature for ever.

There is one other application of SGML that reaches us all – SGML-HTML. HTML, HyperText Markup Language, is a specialized SGML application that Tim Berners-Lee wrote to create the World Wide Web (see pages 207–9).

89 SINGAPORE – *English in Singapore* (1987)

In 1987, the government of Singapore ordered that all education, from primary school to university, should be in English. One result is that today almost everyone in Singapore speaks English, and it is the only Asian country of which that can be said.

The English language has a privileged status in Singapore, but it is also part of the language policy of the government of Singapore that English should not be the mother tongue of any of the citizens of this island state. The mother tongues are Chinese, Malay and Tamil. English is, in the phrase of Anthea Fraser Gupta, 'the step-tongue'.

A home-grown advertisement written in Singlish outside a cafe on Pulau Ubin in Singapore

The Singapore language policy dates back to the beginning of the Republic of Singapore and the thinking of its first prime minister, Lee Kuan Yew. He had it written into the constitution that 'Malay, Mandarin, Tamil and English shall be the four official languages in Singapore.' Lee promoted English not as the global language that it has since become, but in order to make it a unifying factor in a linguistically divided country. English was to be a neutral tongue, owned by none, spoken by all.

From being an impoverished country at its foundation in 1965, Singapore is today one of the world's most prosperous, with a population of 5 million people living on an island no more than twice the size of the Isle of Wight. (The Isle of Wight has a population of 150,000.)

A LANGUAGE DILEMMA

There is one respect in which the Singapore government has been, in its own view, less than successful in its language policy. And that is a result of the extraordinary success of the neutral tongue. There are 3 million people of Chinese origin in Singapore, the majority of whom are equally at ease with Chinese and English. In fact, there is evidence that some Chinese families hardly use Chinese in the home.

The first problem is that English threatens to become a mother tongue, not a 'step-tongue'. But a greater anxiety for the government is the fact that a new form of English has developed – the language that the world knows as 'Singlish'. Singaporean Malay, Chinese and Tamil children are all fluent English speakers, they go to school together, and they often live in communities in which the government has deliberately mixed the three groups. The result is that the children created their own language. Singlish is an English creole of a kind that is found wherever children in mixed-language worlds need to try to understand one another (see pages 196–8).

Singaporeans love to blog and the net is a rich source of Singlish:

> OK lah, bye bye. Don't like that lah. You are going there ah? No parking lots here, what. The price is too high for me lah. And then how many rooms ah? It is very troublesome ley. Don't be like that ley! I'm not at home lah. That's why ah.

The added 'lah's, 'ley's and 'ah's make it seem an exotic English to those who have learned their English elsewhere. The Singlish vocabulary suggests the multiple languages that inform it: *habis* – finished; *makan* – eat; *chope* – reserve something; *cheem* – difficult, *ang mo* – a white person; *rojak* – mixed; *liao* – the end; *kiasu* – afraid to lose face.

Linguists love Singlish, and *Singlish* is the title of enthusiastic books by Ida Catherine Larsen, Lambert M. Surhone, and Doug Case. However, Singlish is disliked by the Singapore government and by many in places of authority. It is condemned as a corrupt form that humiliates the state. An official 'Speak Good English Movement' wages war on it.

It is probably impossible to stop young Singaporeans doing what they want to do with English, and the struggle between Singlish and Good English is only a more focused form of problems found everywhere that the English language is used. Like most creoles, Singlish is essentially a spoken language. It is true that Singapore is a blogger-mad city with tens of thousands of youngsters blogging in Singlish every day, but the blog is its own linguistic realm (see pages 211–12), one that thrives on Teen Speak (see pages 218–19). But language users are skilled at keeping separate the different registers of their language, knowing when and where to use street, home or formal talk. People are diglossic (as linguists say) and will know to use 'Good English' if it pays to do so.

'Good English' is an alternative term for Standard English, and Anthea Fraser Gupta, in *A Standard for Written Singapore English?*, points up the issues that challenge writers. The Singapore state exerts its usual pressure for conformity, but a question yet to be answered is whether Singapore should take British or American English as its standard. Will Singapore plump for one or the other? Will it follow Canada and have two standards (see pages 164–5). Will it take the Indian route and move towards its own standard (see pages 126–7)?

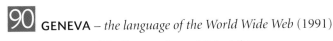

90 GENEVA – *the language of the World Wide Web* (1991)

On 6 August 1991, Tim Berners-Lee published this message:

> The WorldWideWeb (WWW) project aims to allow all links to be made to any information anywhere…The WWW project was started to allow high energy physicists to share data, news, and documentation. We are very interested in spreading the web to other areas, and having gateway servers for other data. Collaborators welcome!

Berners-Lee was a contractor working at the European Organization for Nuclear Research, more popularly known as CERN, in Geneva, Switzerland. For more than a decade, he and his colleagues had been considering how the power of the internet could be best harnessed.

By 1991, what had started as a project to enable physicists to share data across the internet was beginning to attract wider interest. The internet is a gigantic network of computers that can talk to each other using communication protocols. Berners-Lee created a protocol that he called HTML for 'Hypertext Markup Language'. It was a brilliantly simplified form of SGML (see pages 203–5). The 'hypertext' is the link in blue that enables a reader to jump from one text (or webpage) to another across the web. The 'markup' is a set of codes that enables webpages to be written and posted with ease.

In 1994, a young programmer called Marc Andreessen gave the world Netscape, a web browser designed to be used by people who knew nothing about web browsers. With HTML, WWW and Netscape, the web exploded. The decade ended with what became known as the dot.com bubble. Over-ambitious digital business start-ups crashed, while a few took off spectacularly. Microsoft, Google, Amazon, Wikipedia and eBay were the successful ones. To create a new, huge web business was the dream of every web entrepreneur. Facebook and Twitter showed that it could still be done ten years later.

2010: TOP 5 WEB LANGUAGES		
Language	Users	%
English	565m	27
Chinese	510m	24
Spanish	165m	8
Japanese	100m	5
Portuguese	82m	4

It is now hard to imagine life before the web. It has utterly transformed trade, warfare, science, technology and, above all, communication. In 2010, English was the language most used on the web. Chinese was not far behind. A difference in language use between English and Chinese is that while most Chinese-language users live in China, English-language users are spread across the world. The web has reinforced the worldwide use of English and has contributed to the fact that English has become the global lingua franca (see pags 226–7).

THE IMPACT OF THE WORLD WIDE WEB ON THE ENGLISH LANGUAGE
There are many words that owe their existence or a new meaning to the web, among them:

> attachment, bookmark, broadband, blog, browser, byte, chip, cookie, crash, cyber, debug, digital, domain, dotcom, download, e-commerce, e-book, e-mail, engine, file, folder, google, home, link, modem, mouse, multi-tasking, offline, online, password, plug-in, refresh, rickroll, search, thread, tweet, upload, wiki, www, zip.

But the web's influence is of a much larger magnitude. It is changing the way we communicate, research, buy, sell, travel, read. Linguists are uncertain as to how the web will affect languages in general and English in particular.

Most consider that it is too early to be sure how English might be changed by the web. Will the way people communicate in chat rooms and by text, for example, change the way that they write and the language they use in other linguistic contexts – in their formal speech, their formal writing? Will ebooks and e-learning transform education, affect grammar, change our notions of Standard English? Does the web's unique blend of written and spoken English suggest a new approach to style? And what of the virtual world, will we be able to apply this to our actual one in new ways?

 HELSINKI – *the English language and texting* (1993)

In 1993, Riku Pihkonen of the Nokia Research Centre in Helsinki may have been the very first person to have sent a mobile phone to mobile phone SMS text message. There are other claimants for the sending of the first SMS text message, and the first person to send an SMS text message to a mobile phone seems to have been Neil Papworth using a Vodafone network. On 3 December 1992, he sent a message to the mobile phone of his friend Richard Jarvis. It read 'Merry Christmas'. However, the seasonal greeting was sent not from a phone, but from a computer.

Riku Pihkonen has as good a claim as any to be called the first true SMSer because SMS is a communications protocol that permits the exchange of short text messages between mobile telephones. (SMS is the abbreviation for 'Systems Management Server', and a communications protocol is a set of digital instructions for exchanging messages. Another commonly used communications protocol is SMTP – 'Simple Mail Transfer Protocol'. That handles e-mail messages (see pages 195–6).)

Crucially, SMS in its first form could only handle very short messages – 160 characters maximum, including spaces and punctuation. But vitally, it used a very limited broadband and so was very, very cheap. Soon millions and then billions of people were sending SMS text messages. The practice came to be called 'texting' or 'txting', and the verb 'to text' was born.

Its speediness, cheapness and brevity soon generated its own language, a form of English immensely dependent upon and enlivened by abbreviations, contractions, acronyms and substitutions. Net glossaries such as Lingo2Word's 'Popular Texting TxT Lingo' abound with entries like: *ans* – answer; *asslp* – asleep; *ata2ud* – attitude; *attn* – attention; *avg* – average; *aw8* – await; *awcigo* – and where can I get one?

THE JOY OF TEXT

Texters have new terms for themselves and their activity. An SMSer is a texter. SMSing is to text messages. SMSD is 'to SMS dump' – to break up with someone by text message. SMSex is sex by mobile text. SMSL means 'I shit myself laughing', and so on. In March 2001, *The Sunday Times* reported that there was a teenage girl who was sending a thousand text messages a month: 'grammar and spelling were totally irrelevant'. Then on 3 March 2003, the *Daily Telegraph* ran the headline, 'Girl Writes English Essay in Phone Text Shorthand.' Her teacher said: 'I could not believe what I was seeing. The page was riddled with hieroglyphics, many of which I simply could not translate.'

Not only was the United Kingdom dismayed; it seems that the world was as well. A scholarly study in the *Journal of Computer-Mediated Communication* reported that the story was posted on at least 1,630 websites across the world. Major English-language newspapers repeated and raised the level of shock and horror. By contrast, *Computer-Mediated Communication* believed that the 13-year-old had shown 'creativity, wit, and "new literacy" wit' in her account of her summer holiday in txt. She began:

> My smmr hols wr CWOT. B4, we used 2 go 2 NY 2C my bro, his GF & thr 3 :-@ kds FTF. ILNY, its gr8.

The *Guardian* in London translated that as:

> My summer holidays were a complete waste of time. Before, we used to go to New York to see my brother, his girlfriend and their three screaming kids face to face. I love New York, it's a great place.

Like Singlish (see pages 205–7) and Teen Speak (see pages 218–19), txt causes distress to the supporters of Good English Movements. However, like Singlish and Teen Speak, txt is a special language register to be used to make friends and traumatize teachers. It is probably true to say that it is now gradually disappearing, and 2003 may have been its high point. In 2002, the first BlackBerries arrived, and they were followed by the iPhone leading a host of smartphones. Providing a full keyboard and allowing unlimited message length, the new phones have made the magnificent contractions and substitutions of classical texting an anachronism.

Despite the newness of txt-speak in the 1990s, there are not many things new in language. In their turn, the telegraph and the telegram, both of which put a price on the length of a message, saw the introduction of clipped and reduced words. Telegraphese and telegramese gave us OK and PDQ, and it may be that txt will make a similar long-term contribution to the English language. Two contenders are LOL and OMG. A problem with LOL is that mothers think it means 'Lots of Love', but daughters know it means 'Laugh Out Loud'. That might leave us with only OMG when the txting rage is over. OMG.

92 SWARTHMORE – *the language of the blog* (1994)

Swarthmore College is set in rolling acres of land next to Scott Arboretum, some 11 miles southwest of Philadelphia. Sometime in 1994, a student called Justin Hall started to keep a web-based diary – *Justin's Links from the Underground.* According to the *New York Times Magazine* in 2004, Hall was the 'founding father of personal blogging'. There are others who doubtless claim the honour, but Hall's claim is a good one. His blog is now simply called *Justin's Links.* Since 1994, the blog has come above ground.

A blog is a web-based log or diary, and a blogger is the person who writes the blog. It seems strange to explain these terms, so widespread have they become. But Justin Hall's diary or log first had to be dubbed a 'weblog' and then contracted to 'blog' before the new word was born. A brilliant word carried a viral idea. Blogs proliferated, and 'blog' spawned 'blogging', 'blogger' and 'to blog'.

Initially, it required a certain amount of technical capability to post and design blogs. But the world of blogging dramatically expanded in 1999 when websites like LiveJournal and Blogger were launched. Today, blogging is so common that Rachel Blood can remind us that 'an old weblog dates from the year 2000; an ancient one was started in the last millennium'.

Of course, the practice of keeping diaries and journals is not new, and in England they began to appear at the end of the sixteenth century. They were aided by the spread of literacy and the falling prices of paper, pen and ink, but they also required a new attitude towards the self. Why record your daily doings? The developing religious practice of the daily examination of the conscience, and the making of daily records of income and expenditure, both contributed to the diary habit. In the seventeenth century, that habit grew rapidly.

Samuel Pepys is the most famous of the seventeenth-century diarists, and his records range from domestic detail to public policy. One day, he writes: 'Blessed be God, at the end of the last year I was in very good health, without any sense of my old pain but upon taking of cold. I lived in Axe yard, having my wife and servant Jane, and no more in family than us three.' Another day, he writes: 'But, Lord! how sad a sight it is to see the streets empty of people, and very few upon the 'Change. Jealous of every door that one sees shut up, lest it should be the plague; and about us two shops in three, if not more, generally shut up.'

Pepys began his diary entries on 1 January 1660, and he ended them on 31 May

A seventeen-century painting by John Hayls of Samuel Pepys, the original blogger!

1669. Deteriorating eyesight forced him to save his eyes for his public duties. Though Pepys wanted to write down intimate details of his private life, he also wanted to keep those details secret. He devised a code so that no one, particularly not Mrs Pepys, could read what he wrote. The code was not broken until the nineteenth century. But he would have made a magnificent blogger and, in a nice twist, decoded and available for all to read, Pepys's diary now appears as a blog at www.pepysdiary.com.

THE IMPACT OF BLOGGING

How different is blogging from hard-copy diary writing? Psychologically, the difference is complete. Pepys's private, encoded diary is the opposite of www.pepysdiary.com. The diary is secret; the blog is public. None the less, the act of writing a blog at the end of the day (as so many bloggers do) is exactly like that of writing a diary. And the contents of many blogs show it. People pour their souls and their secrets into them. Their fear, however, is the opposite of Pepys's. He dreaded anyone finding his diary; the blogger dreads no one finding it.

The blog's pull is its connectedness with others, and its ability to let mere mortals walk tall. Reading the best blogs shows their enormous pride in the craft of writing. At the same time, blogs do something strange with time. They start with today and work backwards. They are in effect diaries organized in reverse order. Evan Williams, the creator of *Blogger*, puts his finger on a key feature of the blog, one that makes its writing distinctive: 'To me, the blog concept is about three things: Frequency, Brevity, and Personality. This clarification has evolved over time, but I realized early on that what was significant about blogs was the format – not the content.'

 NICHOLSON STREET – *a global reading phenomenon* (1995)

In 1995, Jo Rowling finished her first novel, *Harry Potter and the Philosopher's Stone*. Much of it had been written on the first floor of Nicholson's Café in the shadow of

Marius Alexander

J.K. Rowling in Nicholson's Café where she wrote much of *Harry Potter and the Philosopher's Stone*

Edinburgh Castle. Eight publishers rejected her manuscript, but one, Bloomsbury in London, offered her a modest advance of £1,500 and agreed to publish it. Blooms-bury wanted her to have a more gender neutral name to appeal to boys, so she invented a middle initial and did not use her first name. She is therefore widely known as J.K. Rowling.

Neither Rowling nor Bloomsbury need have worried. Boys and girls alike loved *Harry Potter and the Philosopher's Stone.* Soon after its publication in 1997, it won the Smarties Children's Book prize, and word spread among children that this was the must-read of the year. In 2007, the seventh and final book in the series, *Harry Potter and the Deathly Hallows*, was published. It sold 11 million copies on the first day. In 2001, the film rights to the first two books were sold to Warner Brothers, and each book has now been made into a highly successful film. The films feed interest in the books, and as each new reader encounters the first book in the series, he or she wants to read the next one and the one after.

The Harry Potter stories are a global publishing phenomenon. The series has currently sold more than 400 million books and has been translated into sixty-five languages, making it the world's best-selling series. The Potter books are full of magical events and compelling ideas – an invisibility cloak, a Chamber of Secrets, a Whomping Willow, hippogriffs and boggarts, anti-cheating and bird-creating spells, Quidditch (seven-a-side aeriel hockey played on broomsticks). As well as the central trio of Harry Potter, Hermione Granger and Ron Weasley, there are other strongly drawn characters – Hagrid, Dumbledore, Mad-eye Moody and Draco Malfoy, for example. But it is the bond of friendship between Harry and his friends, and the tensions that this sets up with other children and with the adult world, that makes the stories so engaging.

Each book focuses on a year in Harry's life; we grow up with him and his friends, experiencing the highs and lows of teenage experiences. For young readers, this is a pleasurably empathic experience.

And the place – Hogwarts School of Witchcraft and Wizardry – is a delight, with its many unexpected magical features. Trains to Hogwarts depart from London's Kings Cross station from platform 9¾, reminding us that the fictional world is both close to and far from our real-world experiences.

THE POTTER EFFECT

The 11 million copies of the last book in the series were mostly bought by, or for, children. They simply could not wait, with many staying up to buy their copy then reading it solidly through the ensuing night and day. What more powerful indicator of the power of a story in English could there be?

At a time when computers, television and mobile telephony compete for our attention, Rowling proved that a good story can trump them all. In terms of the power of English, the Potter stories are part of a bigger phenomenon – books that appeal to boys *and* girls, children *and* adults.

A contemporary writer who has, in the view of some, bettered Rowling as a writer for children is Philip Pullman. His *Dark Materials* trilogy, which has had global sales and inspired a Hollywood film, tells the story of Lyra Belaqua's quest, with her friend, Will Parry, to the Northern Lights and beyond into strange and wonderful parallel universes. Inspired by Milton's *Paradise Lost*, Pullman tells a most skilful, clever, engaging story.

In the twenty-first century, both Rowling and Pullman serve as reminders of the power of English as a medium for story-telling.

94 WINDRUSH SQUARE – *multicultural London English* (1998)

In 1998, the area in front of the Tate Library in Brixton was renamed 'Windrush Square' to mark the 50th anniversary of the arrival in 1948 of the *Empire Windrush*, a ship that had landed 492 Jamaicans at the Port of London. The immigrants were given temporary housing in Clapham South, and they discovered that their nearest Labour Exchange was in Brixton. Those 492 were the founders of London's Afro-Caribbean community.

Getty Images

In 1948, the ship *Empire Windrush* landed 492 Jamaicans at the Port of London, heralding multicultural London English

Between 1948 and 1962 (when the Commonwealth Immigrants Bill became law), 125,000 West Indians came to Britain to find work. Their native language was English, and it had long been so for these men and women whose ancestors had come from Africa. The majority came from Jamaica, Trinidad and Barbados (see pages 79–81).

Immigrants commonly stick together, and that tendency was reinforced by the racial prejudice that West Indians encountered in Britain. They intermarried and, from whatever island they came, the dialectal variations of the Caribbean English of the immigrants blended into West-Indian English for their British-born children.

West Indian communities appeared in the major cities, but the largest communities formed in London, first in Brixton and, then, in Notting Hill. However, they were not the only non-white immigrants to Britain in the period between 1948 and 1962. There was major immigration from India and Pakistan, bringing peoples whose first language was not English. Asian communities appeared in all the major urban centres, with again large numbers in London.

THE BRITISH ASIAN VOICE

The British Asian dialects of London are themselves varied, and they are also highly influential on other London Englishes. 'Innit' as a sentence ending is an example. At the same time, among young people, London English is evolving rapidly, and language change is always greatest with young people. Estuarian, London Caribbean and London Asian are mixing and merging to produce something that some call Multicultural London English.

Multicultural London English is going to play out in surprising ways, we may be sure, in the next fifty years, and it may be that our grandchildren and our great-grandchildren will all be speaking it. It is quite possible that it will replace Cockney English, but another way of looking at that is to say that Cockney will survive by merging with Caribbean and Bangla.

95 SAN FRANCISCO - *Twitter English* (2006)

In San Francisco, on 21 March 2006, Jack Dorsey, 'Inventor, Founder, & Chairman', sent the first message on a new communication system. It said 'just setting up my twttr'. That message was perfect of its kind – immediate, intimate, inconsequential. A new way of life began, and today some 200 million do what Dorsey did. What he did, and what they are doing, is now calling tweeting. The messages themselves are called tweets.

There is a close link between texting (see pages 209–10) and tweeting, but the new communication system signalled its break from txt when 'twttr' expanded to Twitter. Txt became the old way, Twitter the new way – even though, at 140 characters a message, tweets have to be 20 characters shorter than the original txts.

Dorsey says that his invention was intended to do three things: 'minimize thinking around communication, expose trends in local and global circles, and spark interaction'. Since computers began communicating in the late 1950s, there has been a drive to 'minimize thinking around communication'. That amounts to a drive to make writing as easy as speaking. It is a drive to make writing natural. After the first clumsy exchange systems, came e-mail and then texting, and now Twitter.

What is special to Twitter is that you do not have to name anyone as the recipient of your messages. Dorsey's insight was to see, in 2006, how attractive it would be to fire off your thoughts as soon as they come to you. No thinking, no fuss, no delay. But you are not firing off into the blue like some blogger. No, you will have created your own world of followers, and you in turn will be in the worlds of those you are following. And people love to tweet. In 2011, Twitter was at 250 million tweets a day. A lot of those are sent by robots, but individuals sent hundreds a day to their followers.

With Twitter, followers can feel like leaders. Among the most followed people are CEOs and celebrities. If you sign up as their followers, you'll receive messages from them all day long. You not only know what they are doing hour by hour, but you feel as though they are talking to you personally.

Tweeting has now reached to the highest level of celebrity. On Ash Wednesday 2012, the Pope became a tweeter, and followers can get tweets from him every day through Lent. Monsignor Paul Tighe explains that 'many of the key Gospel ideas are readily rendered in 140 characters'. Rome has chosen to tweet because Twitter is liked by young people.

Twitter.com promises: 'Instant updates from your friends, industry experts, favorite celebrities, and what's happening around the world.' The immediacy and the intimacy of tweets have their obvious attractions, but their inconsequentiality contains a deep truth about language – a primary purpose of language is gossip.

Human apes are not only talking apes; they are also naked apes. When we lost our body fur, we lost an opportunity to group groom one another. Group grooming is the daily practice of the other great apes. It not only keeps everyone lice free; it also binds the groomers socially. Talk came to fill a gap, talk as a cheerful, quiet murmuring that keeps everyone onside.

Twitter is successful because with it text communication can be done with ease, and a great part of that ease comes from the fact that tweets have to be so short. The 140-character rule has not proved a hindrance; it has become a great strength. A tool created for gossip has become a powerful instrument in business and news. All those millions of messages coming from all over the world are telling us what is going on in the world minute by minute, second by second. CNN has one of the largest bands of followers. Food, wine and books are advertised by way of consumer and reader tweets. Politics, charities and events are all Twitter promoted.

'Twitter' was chosen by Jack Dorsey because it suggests that happy chatter of birds, but Twitter.com has as much to do with apes as birds. Group talk, perhaps the most important kind of talk, is also a despised kind. It is put down as gossip, but gossip is good for us, and Jack Dorsey in San Francisco in 2006 found a way to make gossip go global.

Twitter's logo

Twitter

96 BEVERLY HILLS – *Teen Speak* (2008)

The date of 2 September 2008 saw the premiere of a teen drama called *90210*. This number is the postal code of Beverly Hills, the Los Angeles suburb where Holly-wood's stars live. The drama is set in a fictional school called West Beverly Hills High; *90210* is a West Coast rival to the East Coast's *Gossip Girl*. The West Coast teenagers are shown to be more hip and more funky than the East Coasters: 'The girls of West Beverly High don't have to worry about drone-like school uniforms. The looks range from high-class prep Naomi to funkalicious Silver. Anna Lynne McCord, who plays Miss Popular Naomi Clark, says she knows who wins at least part of the fashion face-off: "We beat the makeup by far. I'll tell ya that"' (*Extra*).

Both teen dramas show themselves to be well versed in the language of teenagers, a form of the English language that is known in the United States as Teen Speak. Its most distinctive characteristic is the rapidity with which it changes. In that, it is like teen fashions. By adopting the latest clothes, hairstyle, music and language, teens say to their peer group, 'I am one of you; I am one of the group.'

Teen Speak is a language filled with exclamations. They punctuate, excite and electrify: Deezam!, Oh Snap!, Ooowee!, Ooowee Man!, Shut up!, That Bites!, Yo!, Who's Your Daddy!, OMG!, Boo-Yah! The phrase 'Shut up!' is not an insult, but an affirmation.

Much of the exclaiming is over sex, and the sexual act is well catered for: baggin, bangin, bonin, cuttin, ridin, smashin, spankin, tappin, hittin it, stickin it, pumpin it up, makin cookies, givin candi. It is a feature of Teen Speak (like other slangs and argots) that it multiplies words for certain things and activities. Why have one word, when you can have a hundred?

There several names for cocaine, ecstasy, heroin and methamphetamine: clucka, rock, crack, E, X, smack, dose, meth, tina. But the really big drug is marijuana. Its many names include: dope, chronic, hood scratch, code four-twenty, 420, dank, dime, dirty brown, dube, fatty, good, green, hydro, La La, leaf, lye, Mary, Mary Jane, nug, piff, purps, purple urple, reggin weed, shwagg, spliff, tree, zone.

Teen Speak uses the language of the ghetto freely. Bling, bling-bling, blang-blang, and blingin are 'da bomb' – a dated term that still means the best. Gangsta language provides terms like da hood, dis, gangsta (also G and O.G.), turf, smoking (shooting people), soldiers (pronounced sold-jas). The greeting 'Whasup G?' is one that you give to your best friend who is your B, Brah, Bro, Boo, Homie, Homeboy. In this language, women are hos, hoochies and bitches.

Teen Speak borrows words from other non-Standard Englishes so that many of its words are familiar forms from the older slangs of jazz and others: cool, two-cents (worth), bi, bird, bunk (useless), broad, cat, clock (hit), cop (acquire), fly, gat, head (as in oral sex), pad, pusher, raggedy, mug. Some of these words are close to Standard

English, and some are Standard English: bamboozled, clowning, gigolo, lame, poser, shabby. These borrowings seem to contradict the whole idea of a special Teen Speak, but they also suggest that Standard English is foreign to some teens, and so up for grabs.

We talk about Teen Speak as a different language, but the differences are almost exclusively related to vocabulary and, to some extent, accent. There are few differences in grammar. And within vocabulary, the changes are restricted essentially to the open class parts of speech: nouns, verbs, adjectives, adverbs and exclamations. Teenagers do not create new pronouns, prepositions, conjunctions or modals.

Most teenagers employ three distinct forms of the English language: the language of the home, the language of the school, and the language of the group. This is not just a teen thing, and most people will recognize that they vary their English between family, job and friends. Some parents find it difficult to grasp what is going on. As a result, they complain that while their child refuses to conform to family standards for dress, behaviour and speech, that same child is a complete conformist in relation to what friends wear, do and say. Since the 1960s, when many teens never switched to adult modes at the age of nineteen, genuine teens have had to work harder at making the difference. This may be a factor in the increasing speed with which Teen Speak changes, but websites and television shows also pump up the speed of change.

97 KIGALI – *English as an official language* (2008)

On Tuesday, 14 October 2008, the *Guardian* newspaper in London ran the headline: 'Rwanda to Switch from French to English in Schools'. That registered a stage in the campaign against the French language that has been conducted by the Rwandan Patriotic Front since it came to power in 1994. In 1996, having established itself in the capital city, Kigali, the new government made English an official language of the Republic of Rwanda.

That sudden promotion of the English language was a most unusual move because Rwanda is not an ex-British colony, it is an ex-Belgian colony. At its founding in 1962, the new republic designated two official languages, Kinyarwanda, spoken by the great majority of the population, and French, spoken by the administrative and trading classes. French was taught to children who stayed in education beyond primary school. In 1996, secondary-school children were given the option of studying either French or English. Today, French has disappeared from the Rwandan curriculum.

A Canadian online news report highlighted the blunt explanation for the abandonment of French given by Vincent Karega, Rwanda's Minister for Education, 'French is spoken only in France, some parts of west Africa, parts of Canada and

A suburb of Kigali in Rwanda, where English was declared the official language in 1996

Switzerland. English has emerged as a backbone for growth and development not only in the region but around the globe.' The linguistic picture and politics are a little more complicated than the minister admitted.

French is spoken in at least fifty-five countries, and it is notable that the minister omitted to mention Belgium as a francophone country. Hostility to the old colonial power remains, but the Rwandan Patriotic Front has an even greater hostility towards France because of the blame leading Rwandans put on France in the Rwandan Genocide. It was that event that brought the Patriotic Front to power.

Behind the politics of the new Rwanda language policy, there was (and is) considerable practicality. The Rwandan Patriotic Front leaders in exile had found themselves in English-speaking countries and had become familiar with the language. Once in power, they realized that their best way forward economically was to develop ties with bordering English-speaking countries. In 2007, Rwanda joined the East African Community created by Uganda, Kenya and Tanzania. Commerce as well as politics makes English a good bet as an official language.

Minster Vincent Karega may be wrong about the global spread of French, but he is quite right when he says that English is a language used 'round the globe'. There are major English-speech communities in over 100 countries, among them are Antigua and Barbuda, Australia, the Bahamas, Barbados, Beliza, Botswana, Brunei, Cameroon, Canada, Dominica, Ethiopia, Fiji, Gambia, Ghana, Grenada, Guyana, India, Ireland, Israel, Jamaica, Kenya, Kiribati, Lesotho, Liberia, Malawi, Malta, the Marshall Islands, Mauritius, Micronesia, Namibia, Nauru, New Zealand, Nigeria, Pakistan, Palau, Papua New Guinea, the Philippines, Rwanda, Saint Kitts and Nevis, Saint Lucia, Saint Vincent and the Grenadines, Samoa, Seychelles, Sierra Leone, Singapore, Solomon Islands, South Africa, Swaziland, Tanzania, Tonga, Trinidad and Tobago, Tuvalu, Uganda, United Kingdom, United States, Vanuatu, Zambia and Zimbabwe. The stories of English in a good number of those countries have been discussed in this book, but the story of English is different in all of them. Were there space enough and time, every one of those stories deserves to be told.

Rwanda is now one of the over seventy countries in the world to have English designated an official language; however, neither the United Kingdom nor the United States has designated English an official language. The reasons for that are no doubt linked to the reluctance of both countries to formalize matters of this kind; witness the refusal, in the eighteenth century, of both countries to establish an academy to monitor the national language.

None the less, there have been movements in the United States to make English the official language, and the campaign groups 'U.S. English' and 'English First' have had some success. English has been made the official language of thirty-one states. The majority have signed up to the Official English campaign in the last thirty years. Oklahoma did so in 2010. A driving force has been anxieties about growing numbers of Spanish-speaking migrants. Official English is a complex notion, and from Rwanda to the United States it can become as much a political as a linguistic issue.

98 NEWCASTLE – *the English language and contemporary regional accents* (2011)

In June 2011, *The Economist* reported that Newcastle upon Tyne's regional accent was alive and well. 'Geordie's still alreet', it said. This was good news for lovers of the countless accents that were once to be heard in the British Isles, but that many feared were dying out. The reasons given for that were the impact of radio, film and television on the one hand, and population change and movement on the other.

Are British accents under threat? Some experts say yes, and some say no. A main reason for this difference in opinion is what to make of language change. Has Latin died out, or is it living on as Italian? David Britain, a European dialectologist, says that if we compare a dialect survey made at the end of the nineteenth century with one made at the beginning of the twenty-first century, 'in most cases and in most places, dialect variation in England today seems radically less marked, less divergent and less locally orientated than that spoken just over one hundred years ago'.

None the less, David Britain argues that the British Isles are not becoming more homogenized. People are not all learning to talk BBC Posh (see pages 174–6) or Estuarian (see pages 187–9). Instead, British dialects have become highly mixed as a result of the movement of people about the country. Major change factors were the mixing of people in the services in the two world wars and National Service, immigration from the Caribbean and Asia, and economic migration mainly to the South. What we have now, says David Britain, are 'compromise' dialects, and dialect contact is leading 'to dialect death in England'.

On the other hand, *The Independent* reports Jonathan Robinson, Curator of Accents and Dialects at the British Library, as saying that 'it is a popular misconception that distinctive regional voices are disappearing'. Robinson argues that language is continuously changing and has been ever since English arrived in the British Isles 1,600 years ago, so that the 500 accents and dialects of the United Kingdom are in constant flux, creating words and forms at the same time as they are losing them. Robinson sees the greatest loss of variety through the development of suburbs. On the other hand, in southwest England, northern Scotland and Northern Ireland, accents and dialects have remained relatively unchanged.

The Economist bases its discussion of dialects on the work of a major study being conducted by Lancaster University. That study is drawing the conclusion that the major regional accents are expanding their areas at the expense of local dialects, but they are not giving up their regional distinctiveness. What the study calls the North-east dialect has pushed from its base across the country to the west coast. This is the speech popularly known as 'Geordie', the Newcastle dialect. It can now be heard in Cumbria. The old southwest dialect that in 1970 was restricted to the West Country is pushing east and is expected to retake west Hampshire – from where it originated long ago.

It is interesting to note that reports on American dialect studies may be showing a similar pattern of the loss of local dialects, but the expansion and the strengthening of regional dialects. In *American Voices*, Walt Wolfram cites the example of the long distinguished and admired dialect peculiar to the old port city of Charleston, South Carolina. It has now largely disappeared, but the South dialect which has absorbed it has lost none of its distinctiveness. The major dialectal differences are becoming more divergent so that, in the United States, there remain wide

The iconic Angel of the North statue which acts as an unofficial gateway to 'Geordie Land'

differences from North to South and from East to West.

The Lancaster University study offers an explanation that might apply as much to the United States as to the United Kingdom. The key to dialects, their expansion and their contraction, is the linguistic behaviour of children. They do not learn from parents, teachers, television or radio. They learn from other children. No more important lesson can be gleaned about the English language.

99 BEIJING – *English and Mandarin* (2012)

The population of China is over 1,100 million, and the word is that the twenty-first century will be the Chinese century and the twenty-first-century language will be Chinese. Time will tell. Chinese is undoubtedly a 'super-tongue', the only language to rival the English language in terms of numbers of speakers.

The English language is also a super-tongue despite the fact that there are only about 50 million English speakers in England. The crucial fact is that there are many more than a billion English speakers in the world. In 2001, *The New York Times Almanac* estimated that there were close to 2 billion English speakers worldwide. In 2003, David Crystal estimated that there were 1.5 billion. The real world number had not gone down; it is simply a matter of its being impossible to be accurate with such figures. But the import is clear.

English is the present-day global language, and it has a far greater number of speakers than does Chinese. Will that be true in 2050?

共和国万岁　世界人民大

The Forbidden City in Bejing with its traditional palatial architecture

The Chinese call their language Hanyu, Zhongwen, Zhongguohua, Huayu or Putonghua. In the West, it is called Mandarin. The multiple names for Chinese reflect the complexity of what it is that we call the Chinese language. While it is now common to talk about Englishes in the plural, it is not common to talk about Chineses, but it might be more reasonable to do so.

Despite the great range of world accents and dialects, all English speakers remain mutually intelligible. A Delhi businessman going to New York might have trouble understanding a Brooklyn cab driver, but they will make themselves understood. The traveller will get to his hotel and, within days, will be talking away to all and sundry.

Things are a little different with Chinese. For historical and political reasons, the Chinese insist that Chinese is one language, but, as a spoken language, that is not so. There are eight forms of Chinese, so different that some linguists are as reluctant to call them dialects as they are to call them language. Instead they call them 'regionalects'. The division into eight is contended; the number could be greater. The numbers speaking individual regionalects are impressive. Jiangsu-Zhejiang, spoken in the provinces of Jiangsu and Zhejiang, has 85 million speakers – enough to make it a major world language if it were counted as such. It is the Chinese spoken in Shanghai.

Of the eight Chineses, it is Putonghua that is the super-tongue rival to English. But here again, a qualification is needed. Putonghua is first of all the language spoken by the people of Beijing. Putonghua means 'Common Speech', and Putonghua also means what Westerners call Mandarin. Mandarin might be called formal Putonghua. It is said to be spoken by 715 million people in China, and many millions more in Taiwan, Hong Kong and Singapore.

Putonghua/Mandarin has a unique characteristic that raises its users to many millions more – its writing system. Its original pictograms evolved into symbols that likewise evolved into the modern characters that the Chinese call 'hanzi'. When Chinese children are taught to read, it is these hanzi that they learn, and it works for any regionalect. It means that even if the Shanghai traveller cannot understand his Beijing taxi driver's speech, both can understand a written note.

MANDARIN AS A GLOBAL LANGUAGE?

Wonderful as the hanzi are, they may be a barrier to Mandarin becoming a truly global language. It is notable that while English is found in many countries that have no native speakers, Mandarin is essentially restricted to China. It is spoken in Singapore, a state outside the traditional boundaries of the Middle Kingdom, but Singapore has a population of over 3 million people of Chinese origin (see pages 205–7).

Meanwhile, the Chinese government is keen for its people to learn English. In 2003, the Ministry of Education in Beijing reported that 'more than 239 million students' were being taught English. Such huge numbers of students require huge numbers of teachers, but there is some doubt about their quality. However, there is no doubt about Beijing's present commitment to the English language. If Beijing persists long enough, it will add another half a billion to the world's count of English speakers.

But the super-tongue battle is not over. Primary Mandarin, a website for teaching Chinese to children, reports a Singaporean businessman who believes that Mandarin will overtake English. 'The decline of the English language probably follows the decline of the US dollar,' he says. Who knows how the global languages will stand in 2050? Time will tell.

 VIENNA – *English as a global lingua franca* (2012)

If a Spanish pilot wants to speak to a Swedish air-traffic controller, he will use English. If a Russian scientist wants to compare notes with a Portuguese botanist, the chances are that they will speak in English. A Polish surgeon wanting to pick the brains of an Argentinean colleague will probably resort to English. Increasingly, there are universities and schools in non-English-speaking countries across the world where English is the medium of instruction. Whether we are considering business, scientific papers, 'snail mail' or e-mail, English is ubiquitous.

When English is used as a means of communication between speakers from different first-language backgrounds, it is called English-as-a-lingua franca (ELF). This phenomenon is currently being studied in many places, and not only at universities like Oxford. The University of Vienna is as active as Oxford in the field. In fact, Vienna and Oxford have collaborated to explore the ELF world.

VOICE, the Vienna-Oxford International Corpus of English, is the first computer-searchable, structured collection of ELF language data of its kind in the world. The collection currently has more than 1 million words of spoken ELF, recorded in different professional, educational and leisure contexts. This collection has been transcribed to create a searchable database called a 'corpus'. VOICE is a resource accessible by language scholars all over the world. ELF requires a new way of looking at English.

In 1985, Braj B. Kachru, an Indian-born linguist teaching in the United States, had an idea that provides a global context for ELF. Kachru proposed a graphic way of looking at the spread of the English language. It 'may be viewed,' he said, 'in terms of three concentric circles representing the types of spread, the patterns of acquisition and the functional domains in which English is used across cultures and languages.' Kachru identified an inner circle, an outer circle and an expanding circle. In the inner circle are those countries where English is the primary language, countries like England or the United States. In the outer circle are countries where English is a significant second language, countries like India or Singapore. In the expanding circle, Kachru put countries where English is widely taught as a foreign language, countries like China and Switzerland.

Kachru's circles have played an important part in subsequent thinking about the global development of English. His distinction between English as a second language (ESL) and English as a foreign language (EFL) is a keen one. It marks the difference in language acquisition between those people who pick up their English in a country where there are already many English speakers and those who learn their English in a country where English can only be heard in the classroom. Kachru's circles also point to the fact that there is as much history as geography in the spread of English.

Vienna is the hundredth place in *A History of the English Language in 100 Places*. The first place is Undley Common. Between the stories told about fifth-century Undley and twenty-first-century Vienna, there is a great gap in time. Between the stories told about Undley Common in England and Waitangi in New Zealand, there is a great gap in space. The dimensions are breathtaking.

10 AFTERWORD

A History of the English Language in 100 Places attempts to document the spread of English from a small island to right across the world. Stories from Australia to America, Singapore to Stockton-on-Tees, Chennai to Coupvray, Beijing to Baltimore, have indicated something of the extraordinary diversity of a language that Walt Whitman called 'the accretion and growth of every dialect, race, and range of time, and is both the free and compacted composition of all'.

One starting point for *A History of the English Language in 100 Places* was an assignment given to an English Project intern, Issy Millett of Wellington College. We asked her to list 100 language locations in England. Her list was quite a bit different from the list in this book, but remember the words of the Introduction:

> Readers will have their own lists of 100 places, and it would be a good thing to hear what those might be. If you have a place and topic that you think should be included, send it to the English Project at www.englishproject.org.

About the English Project

The English Project's mission is to explore and explain the English language in order to educate and entertain English speakers the world over.

If you enjoy books like this about the English language, then you might want to visit a centre that was solely devoted to telling the story of English, somewhere you could go to explore the English language in all its diversity, especially the spoken word. Through the power of interactive technology you could summon up sounds from the past and from across the world. You could hear, at first hand, how English has evolved across the centuries. You could see some of the documents referred to in this book.

At the present time, this centre does not exist.

But the goal of the English Project is to establish one in the next decade here in Winchester, Hampshire, in the United Kingdom. For here was the ancient capital of England and the place most associated with King Alfred the Great. Now that you have read our book you will appreciate that our imagined centre could, as well, be in 99 other places.

But we live in Winchester and are determined to make a start here.

We have already created English Language Day which happens on 13 October every year. On this date we can provide a focus for celebrating the diversity of the English language. (You can remind yourself why we selected this date by turning to the entry on Westminster on page xx.)

A History of the English Language in 100 Places is an early taste of what the English Project is producing. We very much hope you will tell us which other places you believe have had a significant role in shaping the English language by going to www.englishproject.org.

REFERENCES

A

ALDGATE – *the development of Middle English*
    Geoffrey Chaucer, *The Canterbury Tales*, p. 419;
    Derek Brewer, *The World of Chaucer*, p. 58;
    Harold Bloom, *Geoffrey Chaucer*, p. 407;
    Christopher Cannon, 'The Lives of Geoffrey Chaucer', p. 35;
    Edmund Spenser, *The Faerie Queen*, book 4, canto 2, stanza 32.
ARCHANGEL – *Business English*
    Alistair Simon Maeer, *The Cartography Of Commerce*, pp. 38–9;
    Mansel G. Blackford, *The Rise of Modern Business*, p. 19;
    Henryk Zins, *England and the Baltic in the Elizabethan Era*, pp. 35–7;
    John Micklethwait, *The Company*, p. 27;
    H.W. Hammond, *Style-Book of Business English*, p. 19;
    Andrea B. Geffner, *Business English*, p. 168.
ATLANTIC CITY – *Sexist English*
    Neil A. Hamilton, *American Social Leaders and Activists* p. 269;
    Lynn S. Chancer, *Reconcilable Differences*, pp. 157–8
    Albert Baugh, *A History of the English Language,* p. 238.
BALTIMORE – *the English language and the telegram*
    Michael B. Schiffer, *Power Struggles*, pp. 144, 222, 235;
    Mardy Grothe, *Viva La Repartee*, p. 124;
    Margot Peters, *The House of Barrymore*, p. 461;
    Piers Brendon, *The Dark Valley*, p. 99.

B

BEIJING – *English and Mandarin*
    George X. Zhang, *Chinese in Steps*, p. 7;
    John Wright, *The New York Times Almanac*, p. 492;
    David Crystal, *English as a Global Language*, p. 6;
    John DeFrancis, *The Chinese Language*, pp. 58–62, 240;
    George Braine, *Teaching English to the World*, p. xviii;
    Primary Mandarin, 'English or Mandarin', primarymandarin.com.
BELMOPAN – *the English language in Belize*
    Spanish SEO, 'Worldwide Spanish Speaking Population', www.spanishseo.org.
    European Union, *South America, Central America*, p. 98;
    Geneviève Escure, *Creole and Dialect Continua*, pp. 26–8;
    Silvana Woods, 'Say it like d' Belizean', www.belizeanjourneys.com.

BERDICHEV – *Exophonic English*
  Charles Arnold-Baker, The *Companion to British History*, p. 352; Harold Bloom,
    Joseph Conrad, pp. 1–2;
  'Conrad in East Anglia', *Journal of the Joseph Conrad Society*, 4.3:11–13;
  Joseph Conrad, *Almayer's Folly*, *passim*;
  New York Times, 'Joseph Conrad Dies' (4 August 1924), p. 1;
  Joseph Conrad, *A Personal Record*, p. 119.
BEVERLY HILLS – *Teen Speak*
  TV.Com, '90210.', www.tv.com/shows/90210;
  Extra, 'Fashion Face-Off', extratv.warnerbros.com;
  Fred Lynch, 'The Dictionary', www.thesource4ym.com/teenlingo;
  Pimpdaddy.com, www.pimpdaddy.com;
  Urban Dictionary, www.urbandictionary.com.
BLETCHLEY PARK – *English language and code*
  John Graham-Cumming, *The Geek Atlas*, p. 148;
  David Musgrove, *100 Places That Made Britain*, pp. 381–4;
  Martin Gardner, *Codes, Ciphers and Secret Writing*, pp. 35–6;
  Simon Singh, *The Code Book*, pp. 162, 243–4;
  John Howland Campbell, *Creative Evolution*, p. 80.
BOSTON – *The development of New England English*
  The Boston News-Letter (24 April 1704), p. 1;
  Abel Bowen, *The Boston News-Letter and City Record*, 1:66–7;
  Anthony R. Fellow, *American Media History*, pp. 21–3;
  Walt Wolfram, *American English: Dialects and Variation*, pp. 123–4;
  John Hurt Fisher, 'British and American', pp. 122–4;
  Thomas Chandler Haliburton, *The Clockmaker*, pp. 144–5.
BRUGES – *The English language and the printing press*
  Norman Francis Blake, *William Caxton*, pp. 2–3;
  George Duncan Painter, *William Caxton*, p. 173;
  Stephen Inwood, *A History of London*, p. 223.

C

CANONGATE – *British Sign Language*
  Jan Branson, *Damned for Their Difference*, pp. 100–101;
  Leila Frances Monaghan, 'A World's Eye View', pp. 2–4;
  Rachel Sutton-Spence, 'British Manual Alphabets', pp. 26–9;
  Nina Timmermans, *The Status of Sign Languages in Europe*, p. 115;
  Harriet Kaplan, *Speechreading*, pp. x–xi;
  Gallaudet University, *Mission and Goals*, www.gallaudet.edu.
CANTERBURY – *The adoption of the Roman alphabet*
  Carola Trips, *Lexical Semantics*, p. 63;
  Sue Carter, 'Oyez, Oyez', pp. 38–41.
CAPE TOWN – *The English language in South Africa*
  Olive Schreiner, *The Story of an African Farm*, *passim*;
  Encyclopedia Britannica, 'Schreiner, Olive', 20:102;
  Hildegard Schnell, *English in South Africa*, pp. 13–14;
  David Hopwood, *South African English Pronunciation*, pp. 1, 53;
  Oxford South African Concise Dictionary, www.oxford.co.za.

CARLETON – *The influence of Latin on the English language*
   Oxford Dictionary of National Biography, 'Sir Thomas Elyot', www.oxforddnb.com;
   Thomas Elyot, *The Boke Named the Governour, passim*;
   Robert Matz, *Defending Literature in Early Modern England*, p. 29;
   Steven M. Cerutti, *Cicero's Accretive Style*, p. 82;
   Oxford English Dictionary, www.oed.com;
   David Crystal, *The Stories of English*, pp. 154–5.
CERNE – *Classical Old English*
   University of Virginia, *Readings from Beowulf*, www.faculty.virginia.edu;
   Janet Bately, 'The Nature of Old English Prose', pp. 71–4;
   Aaron J. Kleist, 'The Aelfric of Eynsham Project', www.mun.ca;
   Aelfric, *Aelfric's Colloquy*, www.kentarchaeology.ac.
CHANCERY STREET – *Chancery English*
   David Crystal, *The Stories of English*, pp. 230–7;
   David Crystal, *Evolving English*, p. 27.
CHENNAI – *The English language in India*
   George Otto Trevelyan, *The Life and Letters of Lord Macaulay*, 1:261–2;
   Om Prakesh, 'The English East India Company and India', p. 1;
   Anthea Fraser Gupta, 'English and Empire', pp. 188–90;
   David Crystal, 'The Subcontinent Raises Its Voice', www.guardian.co.uk/education;
   Sourabh Jyoti Sharma, 'Debate', p. 733;
   R. Amritavalli, 'India', p. 58;
   Jason Baldridge, 'Linguistic and Social Characteristics', www.languageinindia.com;
   Braj B. Kachru, 'Models for Non-Native Englishes', pp. 67–8.
CHICHESTER – *English grammar*
   William Bullokar, *Pamphlet for Grammar, passim*;
   Oxford Dictionary of National Biography, 'Bullokar', www.oxforddnb.com;
   William Lily, *Institutio compendiaria totius grammaticae, passim*;
   Foster Watson, *The English Grammar School in 1660*, p. 260;
   William Cobbett, *Grammar of the English Language*, pp. 151–4;
   Samuel Johnson, *A Dictionary of the English Language,* pp. 17–35;
   Lindley Murray, *The English Grammar, passim*;
   Daniel Everett, *Don't Sleep, There are Snakes*, p. 198;
   David Crystal, *The Cambridge Encyclopedia*, p. 191.
CHRISTCHURCH COLLEGE – *English nonsense*
   Lewis Carroll, *Alice's Adventures in Wonderland*, p. 1;
   Lewis Carroll, *Through the Looking Glass*, pp. 8, 46–8;
   Edward Lear, *A Book of Nonsense: Twenty-Seventh Edition*, p. 123;
   G.K. Chesterton, *The Defendant*, pp. 29–30;
   Noam Chomsky, *Syntactic Structures*, p. 15.
COLOGNE – *The Bible in English*
   John D. Fudge, *Commerce and Print in the Early Reformation*, pp. 105–7.
   Christopher de Hamel, *The Book*, p. 175;
   Ian Robinson, *The Establishment of Modern English Prose*, pp. 74–6;
   David Norton, *A History of the English Bible as Literature,* p. 2;
   Eudora Welty, *One Writer's Beginnings,* p. 34.
COUPVRAY – *The English language in Braille*
   Freeman G. Henry, *Language, Culture, and Hegemony*, pp. 94–6;
   Frances A. Koestler, *The Unseen Minority*, pp. 102–5;
   David Salomon, *A Guide to Data Compression Methods*, p. x;
   Peter White, *See It My Way*, pp. 50–51.

D

DUBLIN – *Extreme English*
Richard Ellman, *James Joyce*, pp. 22–3;
James Joyce, *A Portrait of the Artist as a Young Man*, pp. 146, 3;
James Joyce, *Ulysses*, p. 32;
James Joyce, *Finnegans Wake*, pp. 3, 628.
DUNFERMLINE – *The English language in Scotland*
Christopher Harvie, *Scotland: A Short History*, p. 33;
Neil Wilson, *Edinburgh*, p. 52;
G.W.S. Barrow, *Kingship and Unity*, p. 177;
Peter Beauclerk Dewar, *Burke's Landed Gentry*, p. lxiv;
Paul Burns, *Favourite Patron Saints*, pp. 63–4;
Stephanie Hollis, *Anglo-Saxon Women*, pp. 218–19;
Pittin the Mither Tongue on the Wab, www.scots-online.org.

E

THE EMPIRE STATE BUILDING – *The language of advertising*
Geoffrey Leech, *English in Advertising*, p. 52;
Geoffrey K. Pullum, 'More than Words', p. 267;
Learn-English-Today, 'New Words', www.learn-english.
ETON – *The English of the English upper class*
Nancy Mitford (ed.) *Noblesse Oblige*, pp. 35–55;
Alan Ross, 'U and Non-U: An Essay in Sociological Linguistics', p. 2;
Damian Whitworth, 'Voice Coaching', women.timesonline.co.uk.
EXETER PLACE – *The English language and the telephone*
Robert V. Bruce, *Bell*, p. 180;
Catherine Mackenzie, *Alexander Graham Bell*, pp. 113–15;
World Bank, *Atlas of Global Development*, p. 45;
Harvey James Gonden, *Public Service Management*, p. 114;
Andrew Holmes, *Commoditization*, p. 27.

F

FLEET STREET – *Tabloid English*
Tony Harcup, *Newspaper Journalism*, p. 68;
Kevin Williams, *Read All About It!*, p. 84;
Kevin Glynn, *Tabloid Culture*, p. 115;
Guardian, 'Times Switches to Tabloid-Only', www.guardian.co.uk.

G

GENEVA – *The language of the World Wide Web*
Tim Berners-Lee, *Weaving the Web*, pp. 23, 89–90;
Mark Ward, 'How the Web Went World Wide', news.bbc.co.uk;
Internet World Stats, 'Usage', www.internetworldstats.com.
GISBORNE – *English slang*
Eric Partridge, *A Dictionary of Slang and Unconventional English*, *passim*;
Eric Partridge, *Slang Today and Yesterday*, *passim*;
Eric Partridge, *Eric Partridge in His Own Words*, pp. 109–10;
Bill Lucas and Edward Fennell, *Kitchen Table Lingo*, *passim*;
Urban Dictionary, www.urbandictionary.com;
John Ayto, *The Oxford Dictionary of Slang*.

GUERNSEY – *Modern English usage*
　　Henry Fowler, *The King's English*, passim;
　　Henry Fowler, *A Dictionary of Modern English Usage*, passim;
　　David Crystal, *The Stories of English*, pp. 474–5;
　　William F. Buckley, 'A Fowler's of Politics', www.nysun.com.

H

HAMILTON – *The English language in the West Indies*
　　David Watts, *The West Indies*, p. 173;
　　Michael J. Jarvis, *In the Eye of all Trade: Bermuda*, pp. 13, 457;
　　William Shakespeare, *The Tempest*, Act 1, Scene 2;
　　Renee Blake, 'Bajan Phonology', pp. 501–3;
　　Valerie Youssef, 'The Creoles of Trinidad and Tobago', p. 508;
　　Hubert Devonish, 'Jamaican Creole and Jamaican English', p. 450;
　　Louise Bennett, *Jamaica Labrish*, p. 69.
HAMMERWICH – *Mercian English, our ancestor dialect*
　　Paul Belford, *Archaeological Practice and Heritage*, p. 87;
　　Barbara Yorke, *Kings and Kingdoms of Early Anglo-Saxon England*, p. 100;
　　Daniel Donoghue, 'Early Old English', p. 161;
　　Robin Fleming, *Britain after Rome*, pp. 221–2;
　　Walter W. Skeat, *English Dialects from the Eighth* Century, pp. 79–81;
　　James Winny (ed.) *Sir Gawain and the Green Knight*, pp. 2–3.
HAMPTON COURT – *The English language and the King James Bible*
　　T.B. Howell, *A Complete Collection of State Trials* 4:407;
　　David Crystal, *The Stories of English*, pp. 271, 277–9, 317.
HANNIBAL – *English comic writing*
　　Mark Twain, *The Works of Mark Twain*, 1:61;
　　Mark Twain, *The Adventures of Huckleberry Finn*, passim;
　　William Hazlitt, *Lectures on the English Comic Writers*, p. 1;
　　Petroleum V. Nasby, *Divers Views, Opinions, and Prophecies*, p. 36;
　　Artemis Ward, *Artemus Ward, His Book*, p. 64.
HARTFORD – *Establishing an American standard for English*
　　Noah Webster, *A Compendious Dictionary of the English Language*, passim;
　　Noah Webster, *An American Dictionary of the English Language*, passim;
　　Noah Webster, *The American Spelling Book*, p. iii;
　　Appleton's Railway Guide, p. 358;
　　David Crystal, *The Stories of English*, p. 508;
　　Hermione Lee, *Edith Wharton*, p. 419.
HASTINGS – *The influence of French on the English language*
　　David Crystal, *The Stories of English*, p. 78;
　　Susan Irvine, 'The Benedictine Reform', pp. 49–50;
　　Christiane Dalton-Puffer, *The French Influence on Middle English*, p. 9;
　　Elly Van Gelderen, *A History of the English Language*, p. 101.
HAYMARKET – *Rude English*
　　George Bernard Shaw, *Pygmalion*, p. 72;
　　Jack W. Lynch, *The Lexicographer's Dilemma*, pp. 234, 242;
　　Oxford English Dictionary, www.oed.com;
　　Lawrence Sterne, *Tristram Shandy*, p. 357;
　　Laughing Policeman, 'The History of Swearing', www.laughingpoliceman.

HELSINKI – *The English language and texting*
Lon Safko, *The Social Media Bible*, pp. 399, 259;
Lingo2Word, 'Popular Texting TxT Lingo', www.lingo2word.com;
Urban Dictionary, www.urbandictionary.com.
Asa Briggs, *Social History of the Media*, p. 263;
Auslan Cramb, 'Girl writes English essay', www.telegraph.co.uk;
Crispin Thurlow, 'From Statistical Panic to Moral Panic', jcmc.indiana.edu;
Lynda Mugglestone, 'English in the Nineteenth Century', p. 276.

HOLBORN – *Making English the language of science*
Thomas Sprat, *The History of the Royal Society of London*, pp. 111–15;
Henry Lyons, *The Royal Society*, p. 20;
Charles Ferguson, 'Language Planning and Language Change', p. 59;
John Giba, *Preparing and Delivering Scientific Presentations*, p. 143;
Michael Faraday, *The Chemical History of a Candle*, p. 22.

HYDE PARK – *Industrialization and its impact on English*
Melvyn Bragg, *The Adventure of English*, pp. 238–9;
David Crystal, *The Stories of English*, p. 317;
Royal Commission, *Official Catalogue of the Great Exhibition, passim*.

I

ISLAMABAD – *The English language in Pakistan*
Christophe Jaffrelot, *A History of Pakistan*, pp. 9, 18–20, 44–5;
Tariq Rahman, 'The Role of English in Pakistan', p. 220;
Ahmar Mahboob, 'Pakistani English', pp. 1003–1004;
Mubina Talaat, 'The Form and Functions of English in Pakistan', eprints.hec.gov.pk.

ISLINGTON – *Plain English*
George Orwell, 'Politics and the English Language', pp. 223–26;
Ernest Gowers, *The Complete Plain Words, passim*;
*Plain English Campaign, www.*plainenglish.co.uk;
Plain Language, www.plainlanguage.gov.

J

JAMESTOWN – *The English language in the Americas*
Walt Wolfram, *American English: Dialects and Variation*, pp. 105–7;
Robert McCrum, *The Story of English*, p. 119;
David Hackett Fischer, *Albion's Seed*, pp. 226–8, 241–3.

K

KEW GARDENS – *Botanical English*
Kew, 'Francis Masson', www.kew.org;
Andrea Wulf, *The Brother Gardeners*, p. 235;
David C. Stuart, *The Plants That Shaped Our Gardens*, p. 74;
Liberty Hyde Bailey, *How Plants Get Their Names*, p. 4;
Gurcharan Singh, *Plant Systematics*, p. 16;
The Linnean Society, linnean.org;
John Ray, *Methodus Plantarum Nova, passim*;
Carl Linneus, *A System of Vegetables, passim*;
William Shakespeare, *Hamlet* Act 4, Scene 1.

KIGALI – *English as an official language*
    Guardian, 'Rwanda to Switch from French', www.guardian.co.uk;
    Gwynne Dyer, 'Rwanda Abandons French Language', www.straight.com;
    Samuel Gyasi Obeng, *Political Independence*, p. 89;
    David Crystal, *English as a Global Language*, pp. 4–5;
    Matt Rosenberg, 'English Speaking Countries', geography.about.com;
    Karen L. Adams, *Perspectives on Official English*, p. 18;
    U.S. English, 'U.S. States with Official English Laws', www.usenglish.org.
KILKENNY – *The English language in Ireland*
    Josef L. Althoz, *Selected Documents in Irish History*, pp. 19–21;
    Thomas Bartlett, *Ireland: A History*, p. 101;
    Jeffrey L. Kallen, 'English in Ireland', pp. 151–2, 180;
    Markku Filppula, *The Grammar of Irish English*, p. 211.
KOLKATA – *The birth of linguistics and the origins of English*
    William Jones, 'The Third Anniversary Discourse', p. 26;
    Benjamin W. Fortson, *Indo-European Language and Culture*, p. 46;
    Orrin W. Robinson, *Old English and Its Closest Relatives*, p. 248;
    Kalevi Wiik, 'The Uralic and Finno-Ugric Phonetic', pp. 262–3.

L

LICHFIELD – *Setting standards for the English language*
    James Boswell, *Life of Johnson*, 1:19–20, 286;
    David Crystal, *The Stories of English*, pp. 365, 379–81;
    Samuel Johnson, *A Dictionary of the English Language, passim*.
LIVERPOOL – *British urban English*
    Philip Larkin, 'Annus Mirabilis', *Collected Poems*, p. 167;
    D.H. Lawrence, *Lady Chatterley's Lover*, p. 177;
    Stephen Glynn, *A Hard Day's Night*, p. 22;
    L. Milroy, 'Urban Dialects in the British Isles', p. 200;
    Peter Trudgill, *The Dialects of England*, p. 72;
    The Beatles, *The Beatles Anthology*, pp. 17, 14.
LLANFAIRPWLLGWYNGYLL – *English place names*
    Mike Storry, *British Cultural Identities*, p. 222;
    Bill Bryson, *The Lost Continent*, p. 263;
    John Ayto, *Brewer's Britain & Ireland*, pp. 680–81, 11, 1209–10.
LOS ANGELES – *The language of e-mail*
    Katie Hafner, *Where Wizards Stay Up Late*, pp. 11, 187–92;
    Bernadette Hlubik Schell, *The Internet and Society*, p. 186;
    David Shipley, *Send, passim*;
    David Crystal, *Language and the Internet*, p. 133.

M

MANCHESTER – *The vocabulary of English and the thesaurus*
    Peter Mark Roget, *A Thesaurus of English Words, passim*;
    Oxford Dictionary of National Biography, 'Roget', www.oxforddnb.com.
MARYLEBONE – *The language of sport*
    Lord's, *The Code of Laws*, www.lords.org.
    David Underdown, *Start of Play*, p. 233;
    Baseball Farming, 'Baseball Lingo', www.baseballfarming.com;
    Online Etymological Dictionary, 'Sport', www.etymonline.com;
    Rice Cricket Club, 'Playing Cricket at Rice', www.ruf.rice.edu.

MONKWEARMOUTH – *Naming the English language*
James Campbell, 'Secular and Political Contexts', p. 28;
Lawrence T. Martin, 'Bede and Preaching', p. 156;
Robin Fleming, *Britain after Rome*, pp. 39–40, 61.

MONROVIA – *The English language in West Africa*
Tope Omoniyi, 'West African Englishes', pp. 174–75;
John Victor Singler, 'Optimality Theory', pp. 336–37, 348;
Allan E. Yarema, *American Colonization Society*, pp. 43–6;
Peter Bakker, 'Pidgins versus Creoles and Pidgincreoles', p. 139;
Godfrey Mwakikagile, *Ethnic Diversity and Integration*, p. 85;
P.M.K. Thomas, 'Krio', pp. 617–19.

MONTREAL – *The English language in Canada*
John Alexander Dickinson, *A Short History of Quebec*, pp. 53–4, 69;
Thomas Bender, 'Exit the King's Men', p. 16;
Charles Boberg, *The English Language in Canada*, pp. 111–14.

N

NEWCASTLE – *The English language and contemporary regional accents*
The Economist, 'England's Regional Accents', www.economist.com;
David Britain, 'The Dying Dialects of England', pp. 35–46;
Terry Kirby, 'The Big Question', www.independent.co.uk;
Walt Wolfram, *American Voices*, pp. 1, 33.

NEWGATE – *The English language and prison patter*
Peter Ackroyd, *London: A Biography*, pp. 247–50;
Vernon Tupper, *Anthology of Prison Slang in Australia*, csusap.csu.edu.au;
Oxford English Dictionary, www.oed.com;
Patrick Ellis, *The Prison-House and Language*, homes.chass.utoronto.ca;
Randy Kearse, *Street Talk*, p. iv;
Winchester Prison Patter, collected on an English Project visit.

NEW ORLEANS – *African American English*
Giles Oakley, *The Devil's Music*, pp. 33, 102;
Richard Wormser, 'Morton', p. 364;
Daniel Hardie, *The Ancestry of Jazz*, pp. 141–2;
David Hackett Fischer, *Albion's Seed*, pp. 263–4.
Walt Wolfram, *The Development of African American English*, pp. 12–14.

NEW YORK – *The language of crosswords*
New York World, 'Word-Cross Puzzle', 21 December 1913;
New York Times, 'Topics of the Times', 17 November 1924;
Nikki Katz, *Zen and The Art Of Crossword Puzzles*, p. 2;
Word Ways, www.wordways.com;
Dmitri Borgmann, *Language on Vacation*, p. 180.

NICHOLSON STREET – *A global reading phenomenon*
J.K. Rowling, *Harry Potter and the Philosopher's Stone*, passim;
Alan Murphy, *Edinburgh Handbook*, p. 247;
J.K. Rowling, *Harry Potter and the Deathly Hallows*, passim;
David Mehegan, 'In end, Potter magic extends only so far', www.boston.com;
Philip Pullman, *Dark Materials*, passim.

NÎMES – *Using place names to make up new words*
Lynn Downey, *A Short History of Denim*, www.levistrauss.com;
John Bemelmans Marciano, *Toponymity*, pp. 72–3.

NORTHOLT – *English spelling and the Great Vowel Shift*
John Hart, *The Opening, passim*;
Bror Danielsson, *John Hart's Works*, p. 115;
Pamela Gradon, Review of Bror Danielsson's *John Hart's Works*, p. 187;
Dennis Freeborn, *From Old English to Standard English*, pp. 293–7;
Marta Zapała-Kraj, *The Development of Early Modern English*, pp. 36–7;
Patricia M. Wolfe, *Linguistic Change and the Great Vowel Shift*, pp. 33–4;
Noah Webster, *American Dictionary of the English Language, passim*;
Jack W. Lynch, *The Lexicographer's Dilemma*, pp. 178–89.

O

OXFORD – *The Oxford English Dictionary*
Oxford English Dictionary, 12 vols, 1928;
Oxford English Dictionary, 20 vols, 1989;
Oxford English Dictionary at www.oed.com, 2000;
Richard Mulcaster, *Elementarie, passim*;
Robert Cawdrey, *A Table Alphabeticall, passim*;
Henry Cockeram, *An English Dictionarie, passim*;
Thomas Blount, *Glossographia, passim*;
Samuel Johnson, *A Dictionary of the English Language, passim*.

P

PARIS – *The beginnings of punctuation in the English language*
Urban Holmes, *A History of the French Language*, pp. 72–3;
Walter Martin Hill, *Early Printed Books*, p. 95;
William Shakespeare, *Love's Labours Lost* Act 4, Scene 2;
Malcolm B. Parkes, *Pause and Effects*, pp. 55–6;
David Crystal, *The Stories of English*, pp. 155–6;
Jennifer DeVere Brody, *Punctuation*, p. 8.
PEMBROKE – *The English language in Wales*
Marion Loffler, 'English in Wales', pp. 353–4;
Thomas Phillips, *Wales*, p. 14;
Martin John Ball, *The Celtic Languages*, p. 547;
John P.D. Cooper, *Propaganda and the Tudor State*, pp. 108–9;
Stanley Bertram Chrimes, *Henry VII*, p. 3;
Anthony Bradley, *Constitutional and Administrative Law*, pp. 36–7;
Braj B. Kachru, *The Handbook of World Englishes*, p. 36.
PETERBOROUGH – *The Anglo-Saxon Chronicle and the end of Old English*
The Anglo-Saxon Chronicle, pp. 5–6, 235;
John Blair, 'The Anglo-Saxon Period', pp. 112–13;
Elaine M. Treharne, *Old and Middle English*, pp. 20, 254.
PHILADELPHIA – *The development of Midland American English*
Barbara A. Somervill, *William Penn: Founder of Pennsylvania*, pp. 69–71;
David Hackett Fischer, *Albion's Seed*, pp. 470–75;
Albert C. Baugh, *A History of the English Language*, pp. 380–81;
Michael Montgomery, 'British and Irish Antecedents', pp. 111–15.

POLDHU – *The English language and the radio*
    Degna Marconi, *My Father, Marconi*, p. 122;
    Aaron A. Toscano, Marconi's *Wireless*, p. 60;
    Burton Paulu, *Television and Radio*, p. 6;
    Naomi S. Baron, *Alphabet to Email*, p. 113;
    Rick Thompson, *Writing for Broadcast Journalists*, p. 12;
    C. Sterling, 'BBC World Service', pp. 357–60;
    Tom Lewis, *Empire of the Air*, p. 231.
PORTLAND PLACE – *BBC English*
    Leonard W. Conolly, *Bernard Shaw and the BBC*, pp. 17–18;
    John Reith, *Broadcast over Britain*, p. 161;
    Arthur Lloyd James, *The Broadcast Word*, p. 39;
    Daniel Jones, *Outline of English Phonetics*, p. 139;
    Jürg Schwyter, 'The BBC Advisory Committee', p. 181.

R

READING – *The English language in popular song*
    Reginald Thorne Davies, *Medieval English Lyrics*, p. 52;
    Frank Llewellyn Harrison, *Music in Medieval Britain*, p. 135;
    Sigrid King, 'Sumer is icumen in', p. 447;
    Joseph Ritson, *A Select Collection of English Songs*, 2:1–5;
    Geoffrey Crossick, *The Petite Bourgeoisie in Europe*, pp. 207–8;
    William C. Banfield, *Cultural Codes*, p. 149;
    Ebony, 'Black Music History', pp. 140–43.

S

SALFORD – *Literacy and free libraries*
    Henry R. Tedder, *Transactions and Proceedings*, p. 117;
    Patrick Brantlinger, *The Reading Lesson*, pp. 2–3;
    Thomas Greenwood, *Public Libraries*, p. 35.
SALISBURY – *The English language and the language of the law*
    Samuel Pepys, *Diary*, 7:99;
    David Crystal, *The Stories of English*, pp. 154–5;
    Sue Carter, 'Oyez, Oyez', p. 38;
    Legal Latin Phrases, latin-phrases.co.uk;
    Her Majesty's Court Services, www.hmcourts-service.gov.uk.
SAN FRANCISCO – *Twitter English*
    Douglas W. Hubbard, *Pulse*, p. 107;
    Jack Dorsey, Foreword, p. xiv;
    Twitter, twitter.com;
    Alexia Tsotsis, 'Twitter Is at 250 Million', www.techcrunch.com;
    Social Barrel, 'Pope to Use Twitter', www.socialbarrel.com;
    Laura Fitton, *Twitter for Dummies*, pp. 266–8.
SAN JOSE – *The English language and text preservation*
    Hilary Poole, *The Internet*, pp. 127–8;
    Charles F. Goldfarb, *The SGML Handbook*, pp. xiv–xvi;
    TEI, *Text Encoding Initiative*, www.tei-c.org.
SEA OF TRANQUILLITY – *English on the moon*
    David Michael Harland, *First Men on the Moon*, p. 319;
    Jules Verne, *De la Terre à la Lune*, passim;
    H.G. Wells, *The First Men in the Moon*, passim.

St Martin-le-Grand – *The English language and the Uniform Penny Post*
    Bernhard Siegert, *Relays*, pp. 100–101;
    Horace Walpole, *Correspondence, passim*;
    Ted Hughes, *Letters, passim*.
St Mary-le-Bow – *Cockney English*
    Samuel Pegge, *Anecdotes of the English Language, passim*;
    Stephen Inwood, *A History of London*, p. 223;
    Julian Franklyn, *A Dictionary of Rhyming Slang*, pp. 3–4.
St Pancras – *The British Library*
    British Library, *Evolving English*, www.bl.uk/evolvingenglish;
    Jean Gottmann, *Megalopolis*, pp. 64–5;
    Library Journal, 'Google Book Search', www.libraryjournal.com;
    Google Books, google.com;
    Open Book Alliance, 'How Many More Books', www.openbookalliance.org.
St Paul's Churchyard – *The English language and the book trade*
    Ralph A. Griffiths, 'The Later Middle Ages', p. 246;
    Lister M. Matheson, *Death and Dissent*, p. 10.
Singapore – *English in Singapore*
    Anthea Fraser Gupta, *The Step-Tongue*, p. 146;
    Andy Kirkpatrick, *English as a Lingua Franca*, pp. 29–30;
    David Deterding, *Singapore English*, pp. 4, 10;
    Anthea Fraser Gupta, 'A Standard for Written Singapore English?', pp. 28–32.
Smock Alley – *English elocution*
    Thomas Sheridan, *A Course of Lectures on Elocution*, p. 19;
    Thomas Sheridan, *British Education*, p. i;
    James Boswell, *The Life of Samuel Johnson*, 2:161.
Stockton-on-Tees – *The English language and the steam engine*
    Anthony J. Bianculli, *Trains and Technology*, 1:33–4;
    Fanny Kemble, *Journal*, 1:169–70;
    Gideon M. Davison, *Traveller's Guide*, pp. 85, 93–95;
    Appletons' Illustrated Railway and Steam Navigation Guide, passim;
    H. Roger Grant, *Erie Lackawanna*, pp. 4–6;
    Edward Gibbon, *The Decline and Fall*, 6:389;
    Oxford English Dictionary, www.oed.com.
Stratford – *The development of Early Modern English*
    Marilyn Corrie, 'Middle English: Dialects and Diversity', pp. 86, 91–3;
    Appleton Morgan, *A Study in the Warwickshire Dialect*, pp. 15–18;
    Walter W. Skeat, *English Dialects*, pp. 65, 79–81;
    Paula Blank, 'The Babel of Renaissance English', p. 225.
Swarthmore – *The language of the blog*
    Justin Hall, *Justin's Links*, www.links.net;
    Jeffrey Rosen, 'Your Blog or Mine?', www.nytimes.com;
    Rebecca Blood, 'Weblogs: a history', www.rebeccablood.net;
    Samuel Pepys, *The Diary*, www.pepysdiary.com;
    Giles Turnbull, 'Interview with Evan Williams', writetheweb.com.

SYDNEY – *The English language in Australia*
  Stuart Macintyre, *A Concise History of Australia*, pp. 16–17;
  Samuel Pegge, *Anecdotes of the English Language,* pp. 22, 79–114;
  Desley Deacon, *Talking and Listening*, p. 101;
  Stephen Nicholas, *Convict Workers*, pp. 29–30;
  Göran Hammarström, *Australian English*, p. 4;
  Silke-Katrin Kunze, *A Survey*, pp. 4–6;
  Peter Collins, 'Prologue', p. 1;
  Keith Allan, 'Swearing', p. 361.

T

TEMPLE – *The idea of an English Language Academy*
  Jonathan Swift, *A Proposal*, p. 31;
  Oxford Dictionary of National Biography, 'Swift', www.oxforddnb.com;
  Robin Adamson, *The Defence of French*, pp. 121, 135;
  Germán Bleiberg, *Dictionary of the Literature of the Iberian Peninsula,* 1:8;
  James Crawford, *Language Loyalties*, p. 27.
THE BRONX – *The language of rap*
  Renford Reese, 'From the Fringe', www.csupomona.edu;
  Robert Hilburn, 'Year in Review', p. 6;
  Time, 'Hip Hop Nation', www.time.com.
  Rap Dictionary, 'Dictionary', www.rapdict.org;
  Tricia Rose, *Black Noise*, pp. 18, 124.
THE MERMAID TAVERN – *The refining of English punctuation*
  Ben Jonson, *The English Grammar, made by Ben Jonson, passim*;
  Sara van den Berg, 'Marking his Place', pp. 3–6;
  Malcolm B. Parkes, *Pause and Effect*, pp. 53, 302;
  Martin Davies, *Aldus Manutius, passim.*
THE STRAND – *English as a language of satire*
  Richard Price, *A History of Punch*, p. 354;
  Edmund Clarence Stedman, *A Victorian Anthology, passim*;
  George du Maurier, 'True Humility', *Punch Magazine*, 9 November 1895.
TIMES SQUARE – *The New York Times*
  Kevin Williams, *Read All About It!*, pp. 10, 84;
  Denis Thomas, *The Story of Newspapers*, p. 40;
  Allan M. Siegal, *The New York Times Manual of Style*, blurb.
TRINITY COLLEGE – *English proverbs*
  John Ray, *A Collection of English Proverbs, passim.*

V

VIENNA – *English as a global lingua franca*
  David Crystal, *The Cambridge Encyclopedia*, pp. 106–7;
  Barbara Seidlhofer, 'Closing A Conceptual Gap', p. 133;
  VOICE, 'Vienna-Oxford International Corpus', www.univie.ac;
  Anna Mauranen, *English as a Lingua Franca, passim*;
  Braj B. Kachru, 'Standards, Codification', p. 242;
  Walt Whitman, 'Slang in America', p. 445.

U

UNDLEY COMMON – *The earliest written English*
  R.I. Page, *An Introduction to English Runes*, pp. 183–4, 227;
  J.R.R. Tolkien, *The Lord of the Rings*, p. 1117;
  Ralph W.V. Elliott, *Runes: An Introduction*, p. 3.

W

WAITANGI – *The English language in New Zealand*
  Robert J. Miller, *Discovering Indigenous Lands*, p. 209;
  Jennifer Hay, *New Zealand English*, pp. 6, 84, 87, 92;
  Paul Warren, 'Intonation and Prosody in New Zealand English', p. 154;
  Harry Orsman, *Oxford Dictionary of New Zealand English, passim*;
  Pam Peters, *Australian and New Zealand English*, passim;
  Harry Orsman, *The Beaut Little Book of New Zealand Slang, passim*.
WESTMINSTER – *The recovery of the English language*
  Stephen Inwood, *A History of London*, p. 223;
  Peter Strevens, 'English as an International Language', p. 29;
  David Crystal, *The Stories of English*, p. 153.
WINCHESTER – *West Saxon English and King Alfred*
  David Crystal, *The Stories of English*, pp. 52–6;
  James Campbell, 'Secular and Political Contexts', p. 28.
WINDRUSH SQUARE – *Multicultural London English*
  Lambeth Council, 'A Short History of Brixton', www.lambeth.gov.uk;
  Janet Holmes, *An introduction to Sociolinguistics*, pp. 190–91;
  Chamberlain M. Staff, *Caribbean Migration*, pp. 213–14.

Y

YORK – *The Influence of Danish on the English language*
  Barbara A. Fennell, *A History of English*, pp. 91–2;
  James Graham-Campbell, *The Viking World*, p. 29;
  Edward C. Mackenzie Walcott, *The East Coast of England*, p. 124.

BIBLIOGRAPHY

A

Adams, Douglas, *The Hitchhiker's Guide to the Galaxy*, London: Pan Macmillan, 1979.

Adams, Karen L., and Daniel T. Brink, *Perspectives on Official English: The Campaign for English as the Official Language of the USA*, Berlin: Walter de Gruyter, 1990.

Adamson, Robin, *The Defence of French: A Language in Crisis?* Clevedon: Multilingual Matters, 2007.

Aelfric, *Aelfric's Colloquy*. Translated from the Latin by Ann E. Watkins.

Allan, Keith, and Kate Burridge, 'Swearing', *Comparative Studies in Australian and New Zealand English: Grammar and Beyond*. Ed. Pam Peters, Peter Collins, and Adam Smith, Amsterdam: John Benjamins Publishing Company, 2009, pp. 361–86.

Althoz, Josef L., *Selected Documents in Irish History*. Armonk: Sharpe, 2000.

Amritavalli, R., and K.A. Jayaseelan, 'India', *Language and National Identity in Asia*. Ed. Andrew Simpson, Oxford: Oxford University Press, 2007, pp. 55–83.

Anglo-Saxon Chronicle: According to the Several Original Authorities. 2 vols. Ed. and trans. Benjamin Thorpe, London: Longman, Green, Longman, and Roberts, 1861.

Appleton & Co., *Appletons' Illustrated Railway and Steam Navigation Guide: Contains the Time Tables, Stations, Distances, and Connections upon all the Railways throughout the United States and the Canadas*, New York: D. Appleton & Co., 1859.

Artemus Ward, *Artemus Ward: His Book*, London: J. C. Hotten, 1865.

Ayto, John, and Ian Crofton, *Brewer's Britain & Ireland: The History, Culture, Folklore and Etymology of 7500 Places in these Islands*, London: Weidenfeld & Nicolson, 2005.

Ayto, John, ed., *The Oxford Dictionary of Slang*, Oxford: Oxford University Press, 2003.

B

Bailey, Liberty Hyde, *How Plants Get Their Names*, New York: Dover, 1963.

Bakker, Peter. 'Pidgins versus Creoles and Pidgincreoles', *The Handbook of Pidgin and Creole Studies*. Ed. Silvia Kouwenberg, Oxford: John Wiley & Sons, 2008, pp. 130–57.

Baldridge, Jason, 'Linguistic and Social Characteristics of Indian English', *Language in India*. Ed. M.S. Thirumalai. www.languageinindia.com, 2002.

Ball, Martin John, and James Fife, *The Celtic Languages*, London: Routledge, 1993.

Banfield, William C., *Cultural Codes: Makings of a Black Music Philosophy: An Interpretive History from Spirituals to Hip Hop*, Lanham: Scarecrow Press, 2010.

Baron, Naomi S., *Alphabet to Email: How Written English Evolved and Where It's Heading*, London: Routledge, 2001.

Barrow, G.W.S., *Kingship and Unity: Scotland 1000–1306*. Edinburgh: Edinburgh University Press, 1989.

Bartlett, Thomas, *Ireland: A History*, Cambridge: Cambridge University Press, 2010.

Baseball Farming, 'Baseball Lingo.' www.baseballfarming.com/BaseballLingo-page5.html.

Bately, Janet, 'The Nature of Old English Prose', *The Cambridge Companion to Old English*, Cambridge: Cambridge University Press, 1986, pp. 71–87.

Baugh, Albert C., and Thomas Cable, *A History of the English Language*, London: Routledge, 1993.

Beatles, *The Beatles Anthology*, London: Cassell, 2000.

Belford, Paul, John Schofield, and John Carman, *Archaeological Practice and Heritage in Great Britain*, London: Springer, 2011.

Bender, Thomas, 'Exit the King's Men', *New York Times Sunday Book Review* (1 May 2011), p. 16.

Bennett, Louise, *Jamaica Labrish*, Kingston: Sangster's Book Stores, 1966.

Berg, Sara van den, 'Marking his Place: Ben Jonson's Punctuation', *Early Modern Literary Studies* 2 (1995), pp. 1–25.

Berners-Lee, Tim, *Weaving the Web: The Past, Present and Future of the World Wide Web by Its Inventor*. With Mark Fischetti. London: Orion, 1999.

Bianculli, Anthony J., *Trains and Technology: The American Railroad in the Nineteenth Century*, 4 vols, Cranbury: Associated University Presses, 2001.

Blackford, Mansel G., *The Rise of Modern Business: Great Britain, the United States, Germany, Japan and China*, Chapel Hill: University of North Carolina Press, 2008.

Blair, John, 'The Anglo-Saxon Period, *c.*440–1066', *The Oxford History of Britain*, Oxford: Oxford University Press, 2010, pp. 60–119.

Blake, Norman Francis, *William Caxton and English Literary Culture*, London: Hambledon Press, 1991.

Blake, Renee, 'Bajan Phonology', *A Handbook of Varieties of English: A Multimedia Reference Tool*. Ed. Bernd Kortmann and Edgar W. Schneider, Berlin: Mouton de Gruyter, 2004, pp. 501–7.

Blank, Paula, 'The Babel of Renaissance English', *The Oxford History of English*, Ed. Lynda Mugglestone, Oxford: Oxford University Press, 2006, pp. 212–39.

Bleiberg, Germán, *Dictionary of the Literature of the Iberian Peninsula*, Westport: Greenwood Publishing Group, 1993.

Blood, Rebecca, 'Weblogs: A History and Perspective', *Rebecca's Pocket* (7 September 2000), www.rebeccablood.net.

Bloom, Harold, ed., *Joseph Conrad*, New York: Infobase, 2010.

Bloom, Harold, *Geoffrey Chaucer*, New York: Infobase Publishing, 2007.

Boberg, Charles, *The English Language in Canada: Status, History and Comparative Analysis*, Cambridge: Cambridge University Press, 2010.

Borgmann, Dmitri, *Language on Vacation*, New York: Scribner, 1965.

Boswell, James, *Boswell's Life of Johnson*, 2 vols, Boston: Carter, Hendee and Co., 1832.

Bowen, Abel, *The Boston News-Letter and City Record*, Boston: Abel Bowen, 1826.

Bradley, Anthony Wilfred, and Keith D. Ewing, *Constitutional and Administrative Law*, Harlow: Pearson Education, 2007.

Bragg, Melvyn, *The Adventure of English: The Biography of a Language*. London: Hodder & Stoughton, 2003.

Braine, George, *Teaching English to the World: History, Curriculum, and Practice*, Mahwah: Routledge, 2005.

Branson, Jan, and Don Miller, *Damned for Their Difference: The Cultural Construction of Deaf People as 'Disabled': A Sociological History*, Washington: Gallaudet University Press, 2002.

Brantlinger, Patrick, *The Reading Lesson: The Threat of Mass Literacy in Nineteenth-Century British fiction*, Bloomington: Indiana University Press, 1998.

Brendon, Piers, *The Dark Valley: A Panorama of the 1930s*, New York: A.A. Knopf, 2000.

Brewer, Derek, *The World of Chaucer*, Woodbridge: Boydell & Brewer, 2000.

Briggs, Asa, and Peter Burke, *Social History of the Media: From Gutenberg to the Internet*, Cambridge: Polity Press, 2009.

Britain, David, 'The Dying Dialects of England?' *Historical Linguistic Studies of Spoken English*. Ed. Antonio Bertacca, Pisa: Edizioni Plus, 2005, pp. 35–46.

British Library, *Evolving English*, www.bl.uk/evolving english.

Brody, Jennifer DeVere, *Punctuation: Art, Politics, and Play*, Durham: Duke University Press, 2008.

Bruce, Robert V., *Bell: Alexander Graham Bell and the Conquest of Solitude*, Ithaca: Cornell University Press, 1990.

Bryson, Bill, *Mother Tongue: The English Language*, London: Penguin Books, 1990.

Bryson, Bill, *The Lost Continent: Travels in Small-Town America*. 1989, New York: HarperCollins, 2001.

Buckley, William F., 'A Fowler's of Politics', *New York Sun* (4 February 2008), www.nysun.com/opinion/fowlers-of-politics.

Bullokar, William, *William Bullokarz pamphlet for grammar: Or rather too be saied hiz abbreuiation of hiz grammar for English, extracted out-of hiz grammar at-larg*, London: Edmund Bollifant, 1586.

Burns, Paul. *Favourite Patron Saints*. London: Continuum International Publishing Group, 2005.

C

Campbell, James, 'Secular and Political Contexts', *The Cambridge Companion to Bede*. Ed. Scott DeGregorio, Cambridge: Cambridge University Press, 2010, pp. 25–39.

Campbell, John Howland, and J. William Schopf, *Creative Evolution*, Boston: Jones & Bartlett Learning, 1994.

Cannon, Christopher, 'The Lives of Geoffrey Chaucer', *The Yale Companion to Chaucer*. Ed. Seth Lerer, New Haven: Yale University Press, 2006, pp. 31–86.

Cannon, Garland Hampton, *The Life and Mind of Oriental Jones: Sir William Jones, the Father of Modern Linguistics*, Cambridge: Cambridge University Press, 1990.

Carter, Sue, '"Oyez, Oyez': American Legal Language and the Influence of the French", *Michigan Bar Journal* (October 2004), pp. 38–41.

Cerutti, Steven M., *Cicero's Accretive Style: Rhetorical Strategies in the Exordia of the Judicial Speeches*. Boston: University Press of America, 1996.

Chancer, Lynn S., *Reconcilable Differences: Confronting Beauty, Pornography, and the Future of Feminism*, Berkeley: University of California Press, 1998.

Chaucer, Geoffrey, *The Complete Works of Geoffrey Chaucer*. Ed. Walter W. Skeat, Oxford: Oxford University Press, 1951.

Chesterton, G. K., *The Defendant*, London: J. M. Dent, 1901.

Chomsky, Noam, *Syntactic Structures*, Berlin: Walter de Gruyter, 2002.

Chrimes, Stanley Bertram, *Henry VII*, Berkeley: University of California Press, 1972.

Clemens, Samuel, 'A Gallant Fireman', *Hannibal Western Union* (16 January 1851), p. 3.

Cobbett, William, *A Grammar of the English Language, in a Series of Letters. Intended for the Use of Schools and of Young Persons in General; But, More Especially for the Use of Soldiers, Sailors, Apprentices, and Plough-Boys*, London: Thomas Dolby, 1819.

Collins, Peter, 'Prologue', *Comparative Studies in Australian and New Zealand English: Grammar and Beyond*. Ed. Pam Peters, Peter Collins, and Adam Smith, Amsterdam: John Benjamins Publishing Company, 2009, pp. 1–9.

Conolly, Leonard W., *Bernard Shaw and the BBC*, Toronto: University of Toronto Press, 2009.

Conrad, Joseph, *Almayer's Folly: A Story of an Eastern River*, Cambridge: Cambridge University Press, 1994.

Cooper, John P.D., *Propaganda and the Tudor State: Political Culture in the Westcountry*, Oxford: Oxford University Press, 2003.

Corrie, Marilyn, 'Middle English: Dialects and Diversity', *The Oxford History of English*. Ed. Lynda Mugglestone, Oxford: Oxford University Press, 2006, pp. 86–119.

Cramb, Auslan, 'Girl Writes English Essay in Phone Text Shorthand', *The Telegraph* (3 March 2003), www.telegraph.co.uk/news/uknews.

Crawford, James, *Language Loyalties: A Source Book on the Official English Controversy*, Chicago: University of Chicago Press, 1992.

Crossick, Geoffrey, and Heinz-Gerhard Haupt, *The Petite Bourgeoisie in Europe 1780–1914: Enterprise, Family and Independence*, London: Routledge, 1997.

Crystal, David, 'How Many Millions?', *English Today*, 1, 1985, pp. 7–9.

Crystal, David, 'The Scope of Internet Linguistics', *Paper presented at the American Association for the Advancement of Science Meeting*, 2005.

Crystal, David, 'The Subcontinent Raises Its Voice', *The Guardian* (19 November 2004), http://education.guardian.co.uk.

Crystal, David, *English as a Global Language*, Cambridge: Cambridge University Press, 2003.

Crystal, David, *Evolving English, One Language, Many Voices*, London, British Library, 2010.

Crystal, David, *Internet Linguistics: A Student Guide*, New York: Routledge, 2011.

Crystal, David, *Language and the Internet*. Cambridge: Cambridge University Press, 2001.

Crystal, David, *The Cambridge Encyclopedia of the English Language*, Cambridge: Cambridge University Press, 1995.

Crystal, David, *The Stories of English*, London, Penguin Books, 2005.

Crystal, David, *The Story of English in 100 Words*, London: Profile Books, 2011.

D

Dalton-Puffer, Christiane, *The French Influence on Middle English Morphology: A Corpus-Based Study of Derivation*, New York: Mouton de Gruyter, 1996.

Daniell, David, *The Bible in English: Its History and Influence*, New Haven: Yale University Press, 2003.

Danielsson, Bror, *John Hart's Works on English Orthography and Pronunciation*, 2 vols, Stockholm: Almqvist & Wikseli, 1955.

Davies, Martin, *Aldus Manutius: Printer and Publisher of Renaissance Venice*, London: British Library, 1995.

Davison, Gideon M., *The Traveller's Guide through the Middle and Northern States, and the Provinces of Canada*, Saratoga Springs: G. M. Davison, 1833.

De Hamel, Christopher, *The Book: A History of the Bible.* London: Phaidon, 2001.

Deacon, Desley, *Talking and Listening in the Age of Modernity: Essays on the History of Sound*, Canberra: Australian National University Press, 2007.

DeFrancis, John, *The Chinese Language: Fact and Fantasy*, Honolulu: University of Hawaii Press, 1984.

DeGregorio, Scott, ed., *The Cambridge Companion to Bede*, Cambridge: Cambridge University Press, 2010.

Deterding, David, *Singapore English*, Edinburgh: Edinburgh University Press, 2007.

Devonish, Hubert, and Otelemate G. Harry, 'Jamaican Creole and Jamaican English', *A Handbook of Varieties of English: A Multimedia Reference Tool*. Ed. Bernd Kortmann and Edgar W. Schneider, Berlin: Mouton de Gruyter, 2004, pp. 450–80.

Dewar, Peter Beauclerk, *Burke's Landed Gentry of Great Britain*, Wilmington: Burke's Peerage, 2001.

Dickinson, John Alexander, and Brian J. Young, *A Short History of Quebec*. Kingston: McGill-Queen's University Press, 2003.

Donoghue, Daniel, 'Early Old English', *A Companion to the History of the English Language*. Ed. Haruko Momma and Michael Matto, Oxford: Wiley-Blackwell, 2008, pp. 156–64.

Dorsey, Jack, Foreword, *Twitter For Dummies*. Ed Laura Fitton, Michael Gruen, and Leslie Poston, Hoboken: John Wiley, 2010.

Downey, Lynn, *A Short History of Denim*, www.levistrauss.com.

Dyer, Gwynne, 'Rwanda Abandons French Language', *Straight.com*. www.straight.com.

E

Ebony, 'The 25 Most Important Events in Black Music History', *Ebony* (June 2000), pp. 140–6.

Economist, 'England's Regional Accents: Geordie's Still Alreet', *The Economist* (2 June 2011): www.economist.com.

Elliott, Ralph W. V., *Runes: An Introduction*, Manchester: Manchester University Press, 1980.

Ellis, Patrick, *The Prison-House and Language*, http://homes.chass.utoronto.ca.

Ellman, Richard, *James Joyce*, New York: Oxford University Press, 1959.

Elyot, Thomas, *The Boke Named the Governour*, London: Thomas Berthelet, 1531.

Encyclopedia Britannica, Chicago: Encyclopedia Britannica, 1964.

Escure, Geneviève, *Creole and Dialect Continua: Standard Acquisition Processes in Belize and China*, Philadelphia: John Benjamins Publishing, 1997.

European Union, Publications, *South America, Central America and the Caribbean 1991*, Luxembourg: Europa Publications, 1990.

Everett, Daniel, *Don't Sleep, There are Snakes: Life and Language in the Amazonian Jungle*, London: Profile Books, 2008.

Extra. 'Fashion Face-Off.' http://extratv.warnerbros.com/2008/09/fashion_fa ceoff_gossip_girl_v.php.

F

Faraday, Michael, *The Chemical History of a Candle*. 1860-61, Mineola: Dover, 2002.

Fellow, Anthony R., *American Media History*, Boston: Cengage Learning, 2009.

Fennell, Barbara A., *A History of English: A Sociolinguistic Approach*, Oxford: Wiley-Blackwell, 2001.

Ferguson, Charles, 'Language Planning and Language Change', *Progress in Language Planning: International Perspectives*. Ed. Juan Cobarrubias and Joshua A. Fishman, Tubingen: Walter de Gruyter, 1983, pp. 29–86.

Filppula, Markku, *The Grammar of Irish English*, London: Routledge, 1999.

Fischer, David Hackett, *Albion's Seed: Four British Folkways in America*, New York: Oxford University Press, 1989.

Fisher, John Hurt, 'British and American, Continuity and Divergence', *The Cambridge History of the English Language: Volume VI. English in North America*. Ed. John Algeo, Cambridge: Cambridge University Press, 2001, pp. 59–85.

Fitton, Laura, Michael Gruen, and Leslie Poston, eds, *Twitter for Dummies*. Hoboken: John Wiley, 2010.

Fleming, Robin, *Britain after Rome: The Fall and Rise 400 to 1070*, London: Penguin Books, 2011.

Fortson, Benjamin W., *Indo-European Language and Culture: An Introduction*. John Wiley & Sons, 2009.

Fowler, Henry, *A Dictionary of Modern English Usage*, Oxford: Clarendon Press, 1926.

Fowler, Henry, *A Dictionary of Modern English Usage: The Classic First Edition*, with introduction by David Crystal, Oxford: Oxford University Press, 2008.

Fowler, Henry, and F.G. Fowler, *The King's English*, Oxford: Clarendon Press, 1906.

Franklyn, Julian, *A Dictionary of Rhyming Slang*, London: Routledge, 1992.

Freeborn, Dennis, *From Old English to Standard English*, London: Palgrave, 2006.

Fudge, John D., *Commerce and Print in the Early Reformation*, Leiden: BRILL, 2007.

G

Gallaudet University, *Mission and Goals*, www.gallaudet.edu.

Geffner, Andrea B., *Business English: A Complete Guide to Developing an Effective Business Writing Style*, Hauppauge: Barron's Educational Series, 2004.

Gelderen, Elly van, *A History of the English Language*, Philadelphia: John Benjamins Publishing Company, 2006.

Giba, John, and Ramón Ribes, *Preparing and Delivering Scientific Presentations*, Heidelberg: Springer, 2011.

Gibbon, Edward, *The History of the Decline and Fall of the Roman Empire*. Ed. J.B. Bury, 7 vols, London: Methuen, 1912.

Glynn, Kevin, *Tabloid Culture: Trash Taste, Popular Power, and the Transformation of American Television*, Durham: Duke University Press, 2000.

Glynn, Stephen, *A Hard Day's Night*, London: Tauris, 2005.

Goldfarb, Charles. F., *The SGML Handbook*, Oxford: Clarendon Press, 1992.

Gonden, Harvey James, Arthur W. Park, and James Blythe Wootan, *Public Service Management*, Chicago: Utilities Publication Company, 1921.

Google Books, http://books.google.com/googlebooks.

Gottmann, Jean, *Megalopolis: The Urbanized Northeastern Seaboard of the United States*. 1961, Cambridge: MIT Press, 1973.

Gowers, Ernest, *The Complete Plain Words,* London: Her Majesty's Stationery Office, 1954.

Gradol, David, and others, eds, *Changing English*, Abingdon: Routledge, 2007.

Gradon, Pamela, Review. *John Hart's Works on English Orthography and Pronunciation*, Stockholm: Almqvist & Wikseli, 1955, p. 338.

Graham-Campbell, James, *The Viking World*, London: Frances Lincoln, 2001.

Graham-Cumming, John, *The Geek Atlas: 128 Places Where Science and Technology Come Alive*, Sebastopol: O'Reilly Media, 2009.

Grant, H. Roger, *Erie Lackawanna: The Death of a Railroad*, Palo Alto: Stanford University Press, 1994.

Greenwood, Thomas, *Public Libraries: A History of the Movement and a Manual for the Organization and Management of Rate-Supported Libraries*, London: 1894.

Griffiths, Ralph A., 'The Later Middle Ages', *The Oxford History of Britain*. Ed. Kenneth O. Morgan, Oxford: Oxford University Press, 2010, pp. 192–256.

Grothe, Mardy, *Viva La Repartee: Clever Comebacks and Witty Retorts from History's Great Wits and Wordsmiths*, New York: HarperCollins, 2005.

Guardian, 'Rwanda to Switch from French to English in Schools', *Guardian* (14 October 2008), www.guardian.co.uk.

Guardian, 'Times Switches to Tabloid-Only Saturday', *Guardian* (29 October 2004), www.guardian.co.uk/media.

Gupta, Anthea Fraser, 'A Standard for Written Singapore English?', *New Englishes: The Case of Singapore*. Ed. Joseph Foley, Singapore: Singapore University Press, 1988, pp. 27–50.

Gupta, Anthea Fraser, 'English and Empire: Teaching English in Nineteenth-Century India', *Learning English: Development and Diversity*. Ed. Neil Mercer and others, London: Routledge, 1996, pp. 188–94.

Gupta, Anthea Fraser, *The Step-Tongue: Children's English in Singapore*, Adelaide: Multilingual Matters, 1994.

H

Hale, Constance, and Jessie Scanlon, *Wired Style: Principles of English Usage in the Digital Age*, New York: Broadway Books, 1999.

Haliburton, Thomas Chandler, *The Clockmaker, or, The Sayings of Samuel Slick*, London: Richard Bentley, 1840.

Hall, Justin, *Justin's Links*, www.links.net.

Hamilton, Neil A., *American Social Leaders and Activists*, New York: Facts on File, 2002.

Hammarström, Göran, *Australian English: Its Origin and Status*, Hamburg: Buske Verlag, 1980.

Hammond, H.W., *Style-Book Of Business English, Designed for Use in Business Courses*, New York: Isaac Pitman & Sons, 1911.

Harcup, Tony, and Peter Cole, *Newspaper Journalism*, London: SAGE Publications, 2009.

Hardie, Daniel, *The Ancestry of Jazz: A Musical Family History*, Lincoln: iUniverse, 2004.

Harrison, Frank Llewellyn, *Music in Medieval Britain*, London: Routledge & Kegan Paul, 1963.

Hart, John, *The Opening of the Unreasonable Writing of Our Inglish Toung*. See Bror Danielsson's *John Hart's Works on English Orthography and Pronunciation*. Part 1. Stockholm: Almqvist & Wikseli, 1955, pp. 115–17.

Harvie, Christopher, *Scotland: A Short History*, Oxford: Oxford University Press, 2002.

Hay, Jennifer, Margaret Maclagan, and Elizabeth Gordon, *New Zealand English*, Edinburgh: Edinburgh University Press, 2008.

Hazlitt, William, *Lectures on the English Comic Writers*, London: Taylor and Hessey, 1819.

Henry, Freeman G., *Language, Culture, and Hegemony in Modern France: 1539 to the Millennium*, Vestavia: Summa Publications, Inc., 2008.

Her Majesty's Courts Services, www.hmcourts-service.gov.uk.

Hilburn, Robert, 'Year in Review/Pop Music; In the Shadow of Hip-Hop; Rap is Where the Action is, and its Popularity Still Hasn't Peaked. Could Rock 'n' Roll Be Finally Dead?', *The Los Angeles Times* (27 December 1998), p. 6.

Hill, Walter Martin, *Early Printed Books*, Chicago: W.M. Hill, 1921.

Hollis, Stephanie, *Anglo-Saxon Women and the Church: Sharing a Common Fate*, Woodbridge: Boydell & Brewer, 1992.

Holmes, Andrew, *Commoditization and the Strategic Response*, Aldershot: Gower Publishing, 2008.

Holmes, Janet, *An Introduction to Sociolinguistics*, Harlow: Pearson Education, 2008.

Holmes, Urban, and Alexander H. Schutz, *A History of the French Language*, New York: Farrar & Rinehart, 1938.

Hopwood, David, *South African English Pronunciation*, Cape Town: Juta & Company, 1929.

Howell, T.B., *A Complete Collection of State Trials and Proceedings*, London: Longman, Hurst, Rees, Orme and Brown, 1816.

http://faculty.virginia.edu/OldEnglish/Beowulf

Hubbard, Douglas W., *Pulse: The New Science of Harnessing Internet Buzz to Track Threats and Opportunities*, Hoboken: John Wiley & Sons, 2011.

Hughes, Ted, *Letters of Ted Hughes*. Ed. Christopher Reid, London: Faber & Faber, 2009.

I

Internet World Stats, 'Usage', ww.internetworldstats.com.

Inwood, Stephen, *A History of London*, London: Macmillan, 1998.

Irvine, Susan, 'The Benedictine Reform and the Regularizing of Old English', *The Oxford History of English*. Ed. Lynda Mugglestone, Oxford: Oxford University Press, 2006, pp. 32–60.

J

Jaffrelot, Christophe, ed., *A History of Pakistan and its Origins*, London: Anthem Press, 2004.

James, Arthur Lloyd, *The Broadcast Word*, London: K. Paul, Trench, Trubner, 1935.

Jarvis, Michael J., *In the Eye of all Trade: Bermuda, Bermudians, and the Maritime Atlantic*, Chapel Hill: University of North Carolina Press, 2010.

Johnson, Samuel, *Dictionary of the English language: in which the words are deduced from their originals, and illustrated in their different significations by examples from the best writers To which are prefixed, a history of the language, and an English grammar*, 2 vols, London: J. and P. Knapton, 1755.

Jones, Daniel, *An Outline of English Phonetics*, London: E.P. Dutton, 1940.

Jones, William, 'The Third Anniversary Discourse', *The Works*, 6 vols, London: G.G. and J. Robinson, 1799, 1, pp. 19–34.

Jonson, Ben, *The English Grammar, Made by Ben Jonson, for the Benefit of All Strangers, Out of the Observation of the English Language, Now Spoken and in Use*. Ed. Strickland Gibson, London: Lanston Monotype Corp., 1928.

Joseph Conrad, *A Personal Record*, New York: Doubleday, 1912.

Journal of the Joseph Conrad Society. 'Conrad in East Anglia', *Journal of the Joseph Conrad Society*, 4.3 (February 1979), pp. 11–13.

Joyce, James, *A Portrait of the Artist as a Young Man*, London: Wordsworth Editions, 1992.

Joyce, James, *Finnegans Wake*, London: Faber & Faber, 1939.

Joyce, James, *Ulysses*, London: Echo Library, 2009.

K

Kachru, Braj B., 'Models for Non-Native Englishes', in *The Other Tongue: English Across Cultures*. Ed. Braj B Kachru, Urbana: University of Illinois Press, 1992, pp. 48–74.

Kachru, Braj B., 'Standards, Codification and Sociolinguistic Realism: The English Language in the Outer Circle', *World Englishes*. Ed. Kingsley Bolton and Braj B. Kachru, Abingdon: Routledge, 2006, pp. 241–69.

Kachru, Braj B., Yamuna Kachru, and Cecil L. Nelson, *The Handbook of World Englishes*, Oxford: Wiley-Blackwell, 2006.

Kallen, Jeffrey L., 'English in Ireland', *The Cambridge History of the English Language: English in Britain and overseas*. Ed. R.W. Burchfield and Roger Lass, Cambridge: Cambridge University Press, 1994, pp. 148–96.

Kaplan, Harriet, Scott J. Bally, and Carol Garretson, eds, *Speechreading: A Way to Improve Understanding*, Washington: Gallaudet University Press, 1995.

Katz, Nikki, *Zen and the Art of Crossword Puzzles: A Journey Down and Across*, Avon: Adams Media, 2006.

Kearse, Randy, *Street Talk: Da Official Guide to Hip-Hop & Urban Slanguage*, Fort Lee: Barricade Books, 2006.

Kemble, Fanny, *Journal*, 2 vols, London: John Murray, 1835.

Kenyon, Frederic G., 'English Versions', *Dictionary of the Bible*, Ed. James Hastings, New York: Charles Scribner's Sons, 1909.

Kew History and Heritage, 'Francis Masson', www.kew.org.

King, Sigrid, 'Sumer is icumen in', *Encyclopedia of Medieval Literature*. Ed. Robert T. Lambdin and Laura C. Lambdin, Westport: Greenwood Publishing Group, 2000, p. 447.

Kirby, Terry, 'The Big Question: Are Regional Dialects Dying Out, And Should We Care If They Are?', *The Independent* (28 March 2007), www.independent.co.uk.

Kirkpatrick, Andy, *English as a Lingua Franca in ASEAN: A Multilingual Model*, Hong Kong: Hong Kong University Press, 2010.

Kleist, Aaron J., 'The Aelfric of Eynsham Project: An Introduction', *The Heroic Age: A Journal of Early Medieval Northwestern Europe*, 11, May 2008.

Koestler, Frances A., *The Unseen Minority: A Social History of Blindness in the United States*, New York: American Foundation for the Blind, 2004.

Kunze, Silke-Katrin, *A Survey of the Pronunciation of Australian English*, Munich: GRIN Verlag, 1998.

L

Lambeth Council, 'A Short History of Brixton', *Local History*, www.lambeth.gov.uk.

Larkin, Philip, *Collected Poems*. Ed. Anthony Thwaite, London: Faber & Faber, 1988.

Laughing Policeman, 'The History of Swearing', www.laughingpoliceman.com/swear.htm.

Lawrence, D.H., *Lady Chatterley's Lover*. Ed. Michael Squires, Cambridge: Cambridge University Press, 2002.

Lear, Edward, *A Book of Nonsense: Twenty-Seventh Edition*.

Learn-English-Today, 'New Words', www.learn-english-today.com

Leech, Geoffrey, *English in Advertising: A Linguistic Study of Advertising in Great Britain*, London: Longman, 1966.

Legal Latin Phrases, http://latin-phrases.co.uk/quotes/legal.

Lewis Carroll, *Alice's Adventures in Wonderland*, London: Macmillan, 1865.

Lewis Carroll, *Through the Looking Glass and What Alice Found There*, London: Macmillan, 1871.

Lewis, Tom, *Empire of the Air: The Men Who Made Radio*, New York: HarperPerennial, 1993.

Library Journal, 'Google Book Search by the Numbers', *Library Journal* (4 May 2012), www.libraryjournal.com.

Lily, William, *Institutio compendiaria totius grammaticae*, London: Thomas Berthelet, 1540.

Lingo2Word, 'Popular Texting TxT Lingo', www.lingo2word.com/lists/txtmsg_listA.html.

Linnean Society of London, *A Forum for Natural History*, http://linnean.org.

Linneus, Carl, *A System of Vegetables, According to their Classes, Orders, Genera, Species: With their Characters and Differences*, Lichfield: Leigh and Sotheby, 1783.

Loffler, Marion, 'English in Wales', *A Companion to the History of the English Language*. Ed. Haruko Momma and Michael Matto, Oxford: Wiley-Blackwell, 2008, pp. 350–57.

Lord's, The Code of Laws, www.lords.org/laws-and-spirit/laws-of-cricket.

Lucas, Bill, and Fennell, Edward, *Kitchen Table Lingo*, London: Virgin Books, 2008.

Lynch, Fred, ed., 'The Dictionary',*The Source for Youth Ministry*, www.thesource4ym.com/teenlingo/index.asp.

Lynch, Jack W., and John T. Lynch, *The Lexicographer's Dilemma: The Evolution Of 'Proper' English, from Shakespeare to South Park*, New York: Bloomsbury Publishing, 2009.

Lyons, Henry, *The Royal Society*, London: The Royal Society, 1944.

M

Macintyre, Stuart, *A Concise History of Australia*, Cambridge: Cambridge University Press, 2009.

Mackenzie, Catherine, *Alexander Graham Bell*, Boston: Houghton Mifflin Company, 1928.

Mackenzie, Edward C. Walcott, *The East Coast of England, from the Thames to the Tweed*, Edward Stanford, 1861.

Maeer, Alistair Simon, *The Cartography Of Commerce: The Thames School of Nautical Cartography and England's Seventeenth Century Overseas Expansion*, Ann Arbor: ProQuest, 2006.

Mahboob, Ahmar, and Nadra Huma Ahmar, 'Pakistani English: Phonology', *A Handbook of Varieties of English*. Ed. Bernd Kortmann and Edgar W. Schneider, Tubingen: Walter de Gruyter, 2004.

Malcolm, Noel, *The Origins of English Nonsense*, HarperCollins, 1997.

Marciano, John Bemelmans, *Toponymity: An Atlas of Words*, London: Bloomsbury, 2010.

Marconi, Degna, *My Father, Marconi*, Toronto: Guernica, 2001.

Mark Twain, *Early Tales and Sketches, 1851–1864, The Works of Mark Twain*. Volume 1. Ed. Edgar Marquess Branch and Robert H. Hirst, Berkeley: University of California Press, 1973.

Mark Twain, *The Adventures of Huckleberry Finn*, New York: Charles L. Webster & Co., 1885.

Martin, Lawrence T., 'Bede and Preaching', *The Cambridge Companion to Bede*. Ed. Scott DeGregorio, Cambridge: Cambridge University Press, 2010, pp. 156–69.

Matheson, Lister M., *Death and Dissent: Two Fifteenth-Century Chronicles*, Woodbridge: Boydell & Brewer, 1999.

Matz, Robert, *Defending Literature in Early Modern England: Renaissance Literary Theory in Social Context*, Cambridge: Cambridge University Press, 2000.

Mauranen, Anna and Elina Ranta, eds, *English as a Lingua Franca: Studies and Findings*, Cambridge: Cambridge Scholars Publishing, 2009.

McCrum, Robert, William Cran, and Robert McNeil, *The Story of English*, London: Faber& Faber, 1992.

McWhorter, John H., ed., *Language Change and Language Contact in Pidgins and Creoles*, Philadelphia: John Benjamins Publishing Company, 2000.

Mehegan, David, 'In End, Potter Magic Extends Only So Far', *The Boston Globe* (9 July 2007), www.boston.com.

Micklethwait, John, and Adrian Wooldridge, *The Company: A Short History of a Revolutionary Idea*, London: Phoenix, 2005.

Miller, Robert J., Larissa Behrendt, and Tracey Lindberg, *Discovering Indigenous Lands: The Doctrine of Discovery in the English Colonies*, Oxford: Oxford University Press, 2010.

Mills, Sara, *Language and Sexism*, Cambridge: Cambridge University Press, 2008.

Milroy, L., 'Urban Dialects in the British Isles', *Language in the British Isles*. Ed. Peter Trudgill, Cambridge: Cambridge University Press, 1984, pp. 199–218.

Mitford, Nancy, ed., *Noblesse Oblige*, London: Penguin Books, 1956.

Monaghan, Leila Frances, 'A World's Eye View: Deaf Cultures in Global Perspective', *Many Ways To Be Deaf: International Variation in Deaf Communities*. Ed. Leila Frances Monaghan, Washington: Gallaudet University Press, 2003, pp. 1–24.

Montgomery, Michael, 'British and Irish Antecedents', *The Cambridge History of the English Language: Volume VI. English in North America*. Ed. John Algeo, Cambridge: Cambridge University Press, 2001, pp. 86–153.

Morgan, Appleton, *A Study in the Warwickshire Dialect*, London: Kegan Paul, Trench, Trubner, 1899.

Mortensen, Torill, and Jill Walker, 'Blogging Thoughts: Personal Publication as an Online Research Tool', *Researching ICTs in Context*. Ed. Andrew Morrison, Oslo: Intermedia, 2002, p. 25.

Mugglestone, Lynda, 'English in the Nineteenth Century', *The Oxford History of English*, Oxford: Oxford University Press, 2008, pp. 274–304.

Mugglestone, Lynda, ed., *The Oxford History of English*, Oxford: Oxford University Press, 2006.

Murray, Lindley, *The English Grammar Adapted to the Different Classes of Learners. With an Appendix, Containing Rules and Observations, for Assisting the More Advanced Students to Write with Perspicuity and Accuracy*, York: Wilson, Spence, and Mawman, 1795.

Musgrove, David, *100 Places that made Britain*, London: BBC Books, 2011.

Mwakikagile, Godfrey, *Ethnic Diversity and Integration in the Gambia,* Dar es Salaam: Continental Press, 2010.

N

Nasby, Petroleum V., *Divers Views, Opinions, and Prophecies*: *Of Yoors Trooly*. Cincinnati: R.W. Carroll, 1866.

New York Times, 'Joseph Conrad Dies, Writer of the Sea', *New York Times* (4 August, 1924), p. 1.

New York Times, 'Topics of the Times' (17 November 1924), p. 18.

Nicholas, Stephen, *Convict Workers: Reinterpreting Australia's Past*, Cambridge: Cambridge University Press, 1988.

Norton, David, *A History of the English Bible as Literature*, Cambridge: Cambridge University Press, 2000.

O

Oakley, Giles, *The Devil's Music: A History of the Blues*, London: BBC, 1983.

Obeng, Samuel Gyasi, and Beverly Hartford, *Political Independence With Linguistic Servitude*, Hauppauge: Nova Publishers, 2002.

Omoniyi, Tope, 'West African Englishes', *The Handbook of World Englishes*. Ed. Braj B. Kachru, Yamuna Kachru, and Cecil L. Nelson, Oxford: Wiley-Blackwell, 2006, pp. 172–87.

Online Etymological Dictionary, 'Sport', www.etymonline.com.

Open Book Alliance, 'How Many More Books-Has Google Scanned Today', www.openbookalliance.org/2010/02.

Orsman, Harry, and Des Hurley, *The Beaut Little Book of New Zealand Slang*, Auckland: Reed Publishing, 1994.

Orsman, Harry, *Oxford Dictionary of New Zealand English: A Dictionary of New Zealandisms on Historical Principles*, Auckland: Oxford University Press, 1997.

Orwell, George, 'Politics and the English Language', *The English Language Volume 2*. Ed. W.F. Bolton and David Crystal, Cambridge: Cambridge University Press, 1969, pp. 217–28.

Oxford Dictionary of National Biography, www.oxforddnb.com.

Oxford English Dictionary, www.oed.com.

Oxford South African Concise Dictionary, www.oxford.co.za/page/about-us.

P

Page, R.I., *An Introduction to English Runes*, Woodbridge: Boydell Press, 2006.

Painter, George Duncan, *William Caxton: A Biography*, London: Putnam, 1977.

Parkes, Malcolm B., *Pause and Effects: An Introduction to the History of Punctuation in the West*, Berkeley: University of California, 1993.

Partridge, Eric, *Eric Partridge in His Own Words*. Ed.David Crystal, London: A. Deutsch, 1980.

Partridge, Eric, *Slang Today and Yesterday*, London, Routledge & Kegan Paul, 1933.

Partridge, Eric, *A Dictionary of Slang and Unconventional English*. 1st edition: London, Routledge & Kegan Paul, 1937.

Paulu, Burton, *Television and Radio in the United Kingdom*, Minneapolis: University of Minnesota Press, 1981.

Pearson's Magazine (February 1922).

Pegge, Samuel, *Anecdotes of the English Language: Chiefly Regarding the Local Dialect of London and its Environs*, London: F. and C. Rivington, T. Payne, and J. White, 1803.

Pepys, Samuel, *The Diary of Samuel Pepys*. 7 vols. Ed. Henry B. Wheatley, New York: C.T. Brainard, 1985.

Pepys, Samuel, *The Diary of Samuel Pepys*, www.pepysdiary.com

Peters, Margot, *The House of Barrymore*, New York: A.A. Knopf, 1990.

Peters, Pam, and Peter Collins, Adam Smith, eds, *Comparative Studies in Australian and New Zealand English: Grammar and Beyond*, Philadelphia: John Benjamins, 2009.

Phillips, Thomas, *Wales: The Language, Social Condition, Moral Character, and Religious*, London: J. W. Parker, 1849.

Pimpdaddy.com, www.pimpdaddy.com.

Pittin the Mither Tongue on the Wab, www.scots-online.org.

Plain English Campaign, www.plainenglish.co.uk.

Plain Language.gov., www.plainlanguage.gov.

Poole, Hilary, ed., *The Internet: A Historical Encyclopedia*, New York: MTM Publishing, 2005.

Prakesh, Om, 'The English East India Company and India', *The Worlds of the East India Company*. Ed. H. V. Bowen, Margarette Lincoln, Nigel Rigby, London: Woodbridge: Boydell Press, pp. 1–18.

Pratt, Fletcher. *Secret and Urgent: the Story of Codes and Ciphers*. Garden City: Blue Ribbon Books, 1939.

Price, Richard, *A History of Punch*, London: Collins, 1957.

Primary Mandarin, 'Is English or Mandarin the language of the future?', 22 February 2012, primarymandarin.com.

Pullum, Geoffrey K., and Barbara C. Scholz, 'More than Words', *Nature*, 413 (27 September 2001), p. 367.

R

Rahman, Tariq, 'The Role of English in Pakistan with Special Reference to Tolerance and Militancy', *Language Policy, Culture, and Identity in Asian Contexts*. Ed. Amy Tsui and James W. Tollefson, Mahwah: Routledge, 2007, pp. 219–40.

Rap Dictionary, 'Dictionary', www.rapdict.org.

Ray, John, *A Collection of English Proverbs: With a Collection of English Words not Generally Used*, London: W. Otridge, 1768.

Ray, John, *Methodus Plantarum Nova*, London: S. Smith & B. Walford, 1703.

Reese, Renford, 'From the Fringe: The Hip Hop Culture and Ethnic Relations', *Popular Culture Review*, 9.2 (Summer 2000), www.csupomona.edu.

Reginald Thorne Davies, *Medieval English Lyrics: A Critical Anthology*, Ayer Publishing, 1972.

Reith, John, *Broadcast over Britain*, London: Hodder & Stoughton, 1924.

Rice Cricket Club, 'Playing Cricket at Rice', www.ruf.rice.edu/~rcc/fun/fun.html.

Ritson, Joseph, *A Select Collection of English Songs, With Their Original Airs: And a Historical Essay on the Origin and Progress of National Song, by the Late Joseph Ritson, Esq*. Additions and Notes by Thomas Park, 3 vols, London: Rivington, 1813.

Robinson, Ian, *The Establishment of Modern English Prose in the Reformation and the Enlightenment*, Cambridge: Cambridge University Press, 1998.

Robinson, Orrin W., *Old English and Its Closest Relatives: A Survey of the Earliest Germanic Languages*, Palo Alto: Stanford University Press, 1993.

Roget, Peter Mark, *A Thesaurus of English Words and Phrases Classified and Arranged so as to Facilitate the Expression of Ideas and Assist in Literary Composition*, London: Longman, Brown, Green, and Longmans, 1852.

Rose, Tricia, *Black Noise: Rap Music and Black Culture in Contemporary America*, Middletown: Wesleyan University Press, 1994.

Rosen, Jeffrey, 'Your Blog or Mine?', *New York Times Magazine* (14 December 2004), www.nytimes.com.

Rosenberg, Matt, 'English Speaking Countries', *About.comGeography*, geography.about.com.

Ross, Alan S.C., 'U and Non-U: An Essay in Sociological Linguistics' 1954, *Noblesse Oblige*. Ed. Nancy Mitford, London: Penguin Books, 1965, pp. 9–32.

Rowling, J.K., *Harry Potter and the Deathly Hallows*, London: Bloomsbury, 2007.

Rowling, J.K., *Harry Potter and the Philosopher's Stone*, London: Bloomsbury, 1997.

Royal Commission, *Official Catalogue of the Great Exhibition of the Works of Industry of All Nations, 1851*, London: Spicer Brothers, 1851.

Rushdie, Salman, *Imaginary Homelands*, London: Granta Books, 1992.

S

Safko, Lon, *The Social Media Bible: Tactics, Tools, and Strategies for Business Success*, Hoboken: John Wiley, 2010.

Salomon, David, *A Guide to Data Compression Methods*, New York: Springer, 2002.

Schiffer, Michael B., *Power Struggles: Scientific Authority and the Creation of* Practical, Cambridge: MIT Press, 2008.

Schnell, Hildegard, *English in South Africa: Focusing on Linguistic Features of Black South African English*, Munich: Grin Press, 2010.

Schreiner, Olive, *The Story of an African Farm*, London: Chapman and Hall, 1883.

Schwyter, Jürg, 'The BBC Advisory Committee on Spoken English or How (not) to construct a "standard" pronunciation', *Standards and Norms in the English Language*, edited by Miriam A. Locher, Jürg Strässler, Berlin: Walter de Gruyter, 2008, pp. 175–94.

Seidlhofer, Barbara, 'Closing a Conceptual Gap: The Case for a Description of English as a Lingua Franca', *International Journal of Applied Linguistics* 11 (2001), pp. 133–58.

Sellar, W. and Yeatman, R., *1066 and All That: A Memorable History of England, comprising all the parts you can remember, including 103 Good Things, 5 Bad Kings and 2 Genuine Dates*, London: Methuen and Co Ltd, 1930.

Sennett, Richard, *The Fall of Public Man*, New York: Knoppf, 1977.

Shakespeare, William, *The Tragedy of Hamlet: Prince of Denmark*, New Haven: Yale University Press, 1963.

Sharma, Sourabh Jyoti, 'Debate', *Pratiyogita Darpan* (October 2009), pp. 732–4.

Shaw, George Bernard, *Pygmalion*, Charleston: Forgotten Books, 2008.

Sheridan, Thomas, *A Course of Lectures on Elocution: Together with two Dissertations on Language; and Some Other Tracts Relative to those Subjects*, London: W. Strahan, 1762.

Sheridan, Thomas, *British Education*, Dublin: George Faulkner, 1756.

Siegal, Allan M., and William G. Connolly, eds, *The New York Times Manual of Style and Usage*, New York: Times Books, 1999.

Siegert, Bernhard, *Relays: Literature as an Epoch of the Postal System*, Stanford: Stanford University Press, 1999.

Silva, Penny, ed., *Oxford Dictionary of the English of South Africa on Historical Principles*, New York: Oxford University Press, 1996.

Singh, Gurcharan, *Plant Systematics: An Integrated Approach*, Enfield: Science Publishers, 2004.

Singh, Simon, *The Code Book: The Science of Secrecy from Ancient Egypt to Quantum Cryptography*, New York: Anchor Books, 2000.

Singler, John Victor, 'Optimality Theory, the Minimal-Word Constraint, and the Historical Sequencing of Substrate Influence in Pidgin/Creole Genesis', *Language Change and Language Contact in Pidgins and Creoles*. Ed. John H. McWhorter, Philadelphia: John Benjamins, 2000, pp. 336–51.

Skeat, Walter W., *English Dialects from the Eighth Century to the Present Day*, Cambridge: Cambridge University Press, 1911.

Social Barrel, 'Pope to Use Twitter to Stoke Interest in Lent', socialbarrel.com.

Somervill, Barbara A., *William Penn: Founder of Pennsylvania*, Deerfield: Deerfield Compass Point Books, 2006.

Spanish SEO, 'Worldwide Spanish Speaking Population', www.spanishseo.org.

Spenser, Edmund, *The Works:* 5 vols. London: Bell and Daldy, 1866.

Sprat, Thomas, *The History of the Royal Society of London, for the Improving of Natural Knowledge*, London: J. Martyn, 1667.

Staff, Chamberlain M., *Caribbean Migration: Globalized Identities*, London: Routledge, 2002.

Stedman, Edmund Clarence, ed., *A Victorian Anthology, 1837–1895*.

Sterling, C., 'BBC World Service', *Encyclopedia of Radio*, New York: Fitzroy Dearborn, 2003, pp. 357–65.

Sterne, Laurence, *The Life and Opinions of Tristram Shandy, Gentleman*. Ware: Wordsworth Editions, 1996.

Storry, Mike, *British Cultural Identities*, London: Routledge, 2007.

Strevens, Peter, 'English as an International Language', *The Other Tongue: English Across Cultures*. Ed. Braj B. Kachru, Urbana: University of Illinois Press, 1992, pp. 27–47.

Stuart, David C., *The Plants that Shaped Our Gardens*, London: Frances Lincoln, 2008.

Sutton-Spence, Rachel, 'British Manual Alphabets in the Education of Deaf People since the 17th Century', *Many Ways to Be Deaf: International Variation in Deaf Communities*. Ed. Leila Frances Monaghan, Washington: Gallaudet University Press, 2003, pp. 25–48.

Swift, Jonathan, *A Proposal for Correcting, Improving and Ascertaining the English Tongue: In a Letter to the Most Honourable Robert, Earl of Oxford and Mortimer, Lord High Treasurer of Great Britain*, London: Benjamin Tooke, 1712.

T

Talaat, Mubina, 'The Form and Functions of English in Pakistan', *Pakistan Research Repository*, Higher Education Commission Pakistan, http://eprints.hec.gov.pk/1631/1/1191.HTM.

Tedder, Henry R., and Ernest C. Thomas, *Transactions and Proceedings of the Second Annual Meeting of the Library Association of the United Kingdom*, London: Chiswick Press, 1880.

TEI, *Text Encoding Initiative*, ww.tei-c.org/About/faq.xml#body.1_div.1_div.1.

Thomas, Denis, *The Story of Newspapers*, London: Methuen, 1965.

Thompson, Rick, *Writing for Broadcast Journalists*, Abingdon: Routledge, 2010.

Thurlow, Crispin, 'From Statistical Panic to Moral Panic: The Metadiscursive Construction and Popular Exaggeration of New Media Language in the Print Media', *Journal of Computer-Mediated Communication*, 11.3 (2006), http://jcmc.indiana.edu/vol11/issue3/thurlow.html.

Time, 'Hip Hop Nation: After 20 Years How It's Changed America' (5 February 1999), www.time.com.

Timmermans, Nina, *The Status of Sign Languages in Europe*, Strasbourg: Council of Europe, 2005.

Tolkien, J.R.R., *The Lord of the Rings*, New York: Houghton Mifflin, 2004.

Toscano, Aaron A., *Marconi's Wireless and the Rhetoric of a New Technology*, New York: Springer, 2012.

Treharne, Elaine M., *Old and Middle English c.890–c.1400: An Anthology*, Oxford: Wiley-Blackwell, 2004.

Trevelyan, George Otto, *The Life and Letters of Lord Macaulay*, 2 vols, London: Routledge, 1959.

Trimble, John F., *5,000 Adult Sex Words & Phrases*, North Hollywood: Brandon House, 1966.

Trips, Carola, *Lexical Semantics and Diachronic Morphology*, Tubingen: Walter de Gruyter, 2009.

Trudgill, Peter, *The Dialects of England*, Oxford: Wiley-Blackwell, 1999.

Tsotsis, Alexia, 'Twitter Is At 250 Million Per Day', *TechCrunch*, techcrunch.com.

Turnbull, Giles, 'The State of the Blog', *Writing the Web*, 28 February 2001, http://kwalla200.blogspot.co.uk/2012/01/week-2-blogging.html.

TV.Com, '90210', www.tv.com/shows/90210.

Twitter, twitter.com.

U

U.S. English, 'U.S. States with Official English Laws', www.us-english.org.

Underdown, David, *Start of Play: Cricket and Culture in Eighteenth-Century England*, London: Allen Lane, 2000.

University of Virginia, *Readings from Beowulf*, http://faculty.virginia.edu/OldEnglish/Beowulf.Readings/Beowulf.Readings.html.

Urban Dictionary, www.urbandictionary.com.

V

Verne, Jules, *De la Terre à la Lune*, 1865.

VOICE, 'Vienna-Oxford International Corpus', www.univie.ac.at/voice.

W

Walpole, Horace, *The Yale Edition of Horace Walpole's Correspondence*. Ed. W. S. Lewis, 34 vols, New Haven: Yale University Press, 1937–71.

Ward, Mark, 'How the Web Went World Wide', BBC News, 2010, www.bbc.co.uk.

Warren, Paul, 'Intonation and Prosody in New Zealand English', *New Zealand English*. Ed. Allan Bell, Wellington: Victoria University Press, 2000, pp. 146–72.

Watson, Foster, *The English Grammar School in 1660*, London: Routledge, 1968.

Watts, David, *The West Indies: Patterns of Development, Culture, and Environmental Change since 1492*, Cambridge: Cambridge University Press, 1990.

Webster, Noah, *American Dictionary of the English Language*, 2 vols, New York: S. Converse, 1828.

Wells, H.G., *The First Men in the Moon*, London: George Newnes, 1901.

Welty, Eudora, *One Writer's Beginnings*, Cambridge: Harvard University Press, 1995.

White, Peter, *See It My Way*, London: Little, Brown, 1999.

Whitman, Walt, 'Slang in America', *Complete Prose Works*, Whitefish: Kessinger Publishing, 2004, pp. 445–8.

Whitworth, Damian, 'Voice Coaching: A Cure for Irritable Vowel Syndrome', *The Times* (18 November 2008), http://women.timesonline.co.uk, 2008.

Wiik, Kalevi, 'The Uralic and Finno-Ugric Phonetic Substratum in Proto-Germanic', *Linguistica Uralica*, 33.4 (1997), pp. 258–80.

Williams, Kevin, *Read All About It!: A History of the British Newspaper*, Abingdon: Routledge, 2010.

Wilson, Neil, *Edinburgh*, Oakland: Lonely Planet, 2004.

Winny, James, ed., *Sir Gawain and the Green Knight: Middle English Text with Facing Translation*, Peterborough: Broadview Press, 1992.

Wolfe, Patricia M., *Linguistic Change and the Great Vowel Shift*, Berkeley: University of California Press, 1972.

Wolfram, Walt, *American Voices: How Dialects Differ from Coast to Coast*, Oxford: Wiley-Blackwell, 2006.

Wolfram, Walt, and Erik R. Thomas, *The Development of African American English*, Oxford: Wiley-Blackwell, 2002.

Wolfram, Walt, and Natalie Schilling-Estes, *American English: Dialects and Variation*, Oxford: Wiley-Blackwell, 2006.

Woods, Silvana, 'Say it like d' Belizean', *Belizean Journeys*, www.belizeanjourneys.com/features/kriol.

Word Ways: The Journal of Recreational Linguistics, www.wordways.com.

World Bank, *Atlas of Global Development*, Washington: World Bank Publications, 2009.

Wormser, Richard, 'Morton', *Harlem Renaissance Lives from the African American National Biography*. Ed. Henry Louis Gates and Evelyn Brooks Higginbotham, New York: Oxford University Press, 2009, pp. 362–4.

Wright, John. *The New York Times Almanac 2002*. New York: Penguin Books, 2001.

Wulf, Andrea, *The Brother Gardeners: Botany, Empire and the Birth of an Obsession*, London: Windmill Books, 2009.

Y

Yarema, Allan E., *American Colonization Society*, Lanham: University Press of America, 2006.

Yorke, Barbara, *Kings and Kingdoms of Early Anglo-Saxon England*, London: Seaby, 1990.

Youssef, Valerie, and Winford James, 'The Creoles of Trinidad and Tobago', *A Handbook of Varieties of English: A Multimedia Reference Tool*. Ed. Bernd Kortmann and Edgar W. Schneider, Berlin: Mouton de Gruyter, 2004, pp. 508–24.

Z

Zapała-Kraj, Marta, *The Development of Early Modern English*, Munich: GRIN Press, 2010.

Zhang, George X., Linda M. Li, and Lik Suen, *Chinese in Steps*, London: Cypress Book Company, 2006.

Zins, Henryk, *England and the Baltic in the Elizabethan Era*, Manchester: Manchester University Press, 1972.